P9-DNS-331

Weekend Navigator

By the Same Author

At Home in Deep Waters

Bruce Fraser

Weekend Navigator

JOHN de GRAFF, INC.

© Bruce Fraser, 1981
ISBN 8286 0090 2

John de Graff, Inc.
Clinton Corners, N.Y. 12514

Printed and bound in U.S.A.

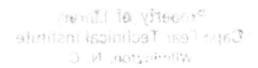

To Gerhard Kremer (1512–94),
better known as Mercator,
the Flemish mathematician and geographer
who made life a lot easier
for simple sailors.

Acknowledgements

Figures 2.1, 2.2, 3.2, 3.3, 6.1, 6.4, 7.15, 8.2, 8.4, 8.9, 8.13, 8.14, 11.4, 11.5, 11.12, 11.13 and the extract from British Admiralty Chart No 2675 shown on the jacket of this book, are here produced with the sanction of the Controller, HM Stationery Office and of the Hydrographer of the Navy.

Figures 2.3, 2.4 and the extract from US Chart No 25600 shown on the jacket, are reproduced by kind permission of the Defense Mapping Agency Hydrographic/Topographic Center, Washington DC.

Figures 11.21, 11.22 and 11.23 are reproduced by kind permission of the Director, National Ocean Survey, National Oceanic and Atmospheric Administration, United States Department of Commerce.

Figures 11.6, 11.7, 11.8, 11.10, 11.11, 11.13, 11.15, 11.17, 11.19 and 11.20 are reproduced by kind permission of Thomas Reed Publications, from their Nautical Almanacs.

Contents

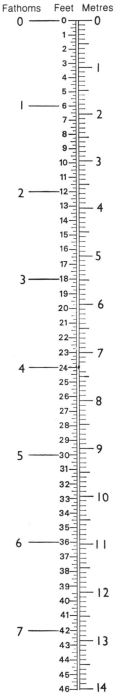

Fig. 1.1　Conversion scale.

1
Acquiring confidence

Learning to navigate a small boat so you can voyage out of sight of land is a major step in any sailing man or woman's career, as big as graduating from sailing dinghies to keelboats. Yet it is often learned on an oddly parochial basis, even though there is a boom in the bareboat charter business, in which you take your sailing clothes by plane to the other side of the world, to cruise in a fully-equipped boat waiting there for your enjoyment. The sort of navigation that considers only your local conditions of tides, charts and soundings is going to be a great limitation if you hope to advance one day to sailing in far-off waters, even though lack of time may mean that you must fly there to meet your charter boat.

So this is a primer of coastal navigation — for both shores of the North Atlantic, and the seas connected to it. It is laid out in step by step fashion, so that the total beginner can learn without burdening himself at the start with technical detail better left until later, but everything the weekend and holiday cruising man will need is covered. Even the quite experienced navigator under sail or power may find it useful.

Now that increasing numbers of charts are falling into line with the international metric system, it is important for every international seaman to become used to metric soundings and heights. So here I introduce foot-and-fathom-bound Americans (as well as metric-resistant Britons, of whom there are a lot) to metres, which are the depth measure for much of the world. Throughout, metres and feet are mixed up together, to remind those who have come to think normally in metres, what a large part of the world is still best served by British or American charts scaled in feet and fathoms. So that you can switch easily from one to the other, there is a conversion scale on page (ix).

Most of all, this weekend navigator's handbook underlines the key differences likely to be met with when sailing in strange waters, and the British, American and European way of doing things are compared where they differ.

I navigated not unsuccessfully for years before I discovered that the American system of buoyage was exactly the opposite to that used by most of the rest of the maritime nations. An American or Canadian sailor, brought up

1

on 'red right returning' (red buoys to starboard entering with the flood) could be distinctly embarrassed if he chartered a boat in England, and set out without knowing that a red mark is left to port when going with the flood tide. There is a glossary on page 6 for those cases where words have a different meaning on either side of the Atlantic.

Nearly all my examples are based on the most difficult situation — a slow-moving sailboat working in strong tidal streams and areas of large rise and fall. It will do even the powerboat man, used to surging about at over 20 knots, nothing but good to study navigation this way — some day he may be limping home at five knots with one engine dead and the other screw damaged. Since one of the most navigationally difficult, yet at the same time most rewarding, areas in which to navigate is that part of the English Channel which washes the coasts of Normandy, the Channel Islands (not the ones off Santa Barbara, but those which the French call the Iles Normandes) and Brittany, I have taken many of my examples from this area. Americans used to the generally meeker tides of their coasts should not be intimidated, and they will find a number of examples from more familiar waters.

Any navigation manual has to refer to tide tables, which may be obtained from many sources. The main tables used here are from *Reed's Nautical Almanac,* which is available in two editions, one for Western Europe and another for the east coast of North America. They contain not only tide tables but a vast amount of additional information of value to yachtsmen, including lists of lights. Slightly greater accuracy can be obtained by using British Admiralty Tide Tables or the United States National Ocean Survey Tide Tables, which are both similar in principle. Tides, however, are subject to considerable variation from strong winds, and this extra accuracy is seldom if ever needed even with the strongest tides.

Most people who start to study coastal navigation have some experience of small boats, sailing dinghies perhaps, or powered runabouts. They start on the road to becoming real seamen when they begin thinking about the problems of going out of sight of land. Electronics, with their tendency to fail under the influence of sea air just when they are most needed, are only a small part of the answer. You need to know how to use the old-fashioned mariner's basic tools, the magnetic compass and the chart.

If you are tied by circumstances to learning about the business from books, you come up here against a sinister conspiracy of the sea. With honourable exceptions, few books on navigation are for people who know nothing yet want to learn. They are for pundits who already know all about it and are being press-ganged by the author to admire the system he has evolved of making a basically simple subject more difficult to grasp. These readers are expected to have picked up trigonometry with their nursery toys, and to be able to put themselves to sleep counting secants jumping over haversines.

People of this sort can put my book down at once. It is intended for simple souls like me and you who can, if pressed, add, subtract, multiply, divide, measure the length of a line with a ruler or dividers, draw a circle or a part of one with a pair of compasses, measure or draw an angle with a protractor, and look up a figure in simple tables. That is the total mathematical knowledge required.

Except that it provides a brief introduction to the use of electronic pocket calculators in navigation, there is nothing new or original in this book — most of what it explains can be found in the standard serious tomes. But I hope everything here will be *easier to understand*.

If you really try, you can make navigation very difficult. And I have often felt that those who teach it really do put as much effort into complicating it as to making it clear. There are not many books on navigation that do not:

(a) assume that the would-be navigator has a chart table eight feet across which never moves, a shipload of scientific devices any one of which would cost more than his boat, a staff of trained assistants to run about at his behest and, above all, a cast-iron stomach that *never* complains when the sea gives a bit of the old heave-ho;

(b) start with one of those discouraging drawings like a slashed watermelon, and pack the first three pages with words no ordinary man has ever heard of.

This can be disheartening for a seaman who only wants to get his 25-footer across to another shore not so many miles out of sight without hitting a rock or a sandbank, and also without spending most of his time, in a spanking day for a sail, with his head down in discomfort over a chart or a book.

STEP BY STEP

Finding your way around on the sea is, like many things, best learned step by step. I have tried to arrange things here to make the subject specially simple and free of discouragement for the beginner, without losing what is useful for the more experienced man. When a dinghy sailor, whose experience is perhaps confined to inland waters or his local estuaries, buys a cruiser he is not going to wait on his moorings or marina berth until he has learned every finer detail of accurate navigation — on a fine day he is going to dash off for a sail. And these people often get into navigational trouble, as you can see almost any weekend in summer when people run themselves aground on well-known and well-marked dangers.

The early chapters are therefore devoted to inshore pilotage, treated in the most elementary way, and with only an introduction to the compass. This use of short-cut methods may upset those who believe in *always* doing it the hard way. But I think it is better for someone to say to himself on the basis of a quick check 'I can't get over the bar of that river between 4 o'clock and 6 o'clock because there isn't enough water for this deep keel boat', than to fail to check because working out tides exactly is such a bore. Using Tide Tables he might have been able to say 'There's enough water for us except between 1621 and 1713'. This is really wasted effort, however, since an ample margin must be left. Even so, too many people make the approach just looking at an echo sounder without any reference at all to tables, and the result may be an undignified bump.

Finer detail of all aspects of coastal navigation is reached later, not skimped. My experience has been that those who first learn to work by rule of thumb take easily to the full way when it is necessary, whereas many beginners are put off right at the start by being thrown into the deep end, so to speak, of things like tide tables.

MENTAL SHORTHAND

If you have ever done any seagoing with an experienced skipper you may have thought, or even said, in a baffled way: 'Well, he never actually seems to *do* any navigation when it's fine, he just looks at the chart now and then and says "Steer about such and such a course and, in a couple of hours, you should be able to see a light flashing twice every five seconds on your starboard bow". Then he goes below, has a Scotch and rolls into his bunk . . . and he's usually right too.'

This is not witchcraft, it is familiarity with the navigator's art until it can be done by a kind of mental shorthand, in just the same way that you can drive to the railway station to go to the office, without thinking about which way to go. You will find that these apparently casual navigators have in fact kept a careful record of courses steered and speeds through the water, so that if visibility closes down a proper plot can immediately be drawn. In the early stages of becoming a navigator, which may be in your own boat, never try to imitate the casual air of the experienced man without being absolutely sure that you have done it all (if your family are with you, they will never let you get away with it anyway). It is important to check and recheck to make sure there are no important gaps in your knowledge.

I once did a little light navigation to get a boat across the English Channel that had been bought by a young and very skilful dinghy sailor, whose sailing had mostly been done on rivers and reservoirs. On the way home, when visibility was remarkable and after dark we could see the loom of Alderney, Portland, Cap de la Hague and St Catherine's Point lights on either side of the 60 mile crossing simultaneously, I casually showed him how the direction finding radio worked, and how to plot the not very precise fixes you get from it. The following weekend he loaded the boat with friends, announced 'Bruce taught me how to navigate last weekend' and set off on a Channel crossing himself bound for Guernsey. All went well until they reached Alderney Race, the stretch of water between Alderney and the Cherbourg Peninsula, where the tide often runs at over seven knots. Here the boat mysteriously ceased to make progress over the ground, although she was visibly churning through the water at her maximum speed under full sail. After some six hours of this they were starting to make progress, but a lengthy conference of all aboard had decided that only mugs tried to go southwest through the Race and, taking advantage of the commanding northwesterly, they eventually turned round and headed more or less northeast, with the restaurants of Cherbourg in mind. They were considerably puzzled by the fact that soon the boat, while creaming through the water, was still getting nowhere while pointing this way too. No, they're not still there, the penny eventually dropped, but it does emphasize that it's a subject you have to get a rounded picture of before regarding it as your own.

THE HARDEST PART

It is widely agreed that the hardest part of coastal navigation is recognising landfalls on a coast with which you are unfamiliar. The rest is a matter of learning a simple technique so that you do not make silly mistakes — in other words plenty of practice, which can often be done at home rather than at sea.

GLOSSARY

Some navigational terms differ between American practice and British, and indeed whether navigation has been learned from a Navy, a Merchant Navy or a Flying School. American usages are coming into wider acceptance since a specific vocabulary has been laid down, but few American sailors of my acquaintance seem to adhere to it. Most people are very casual, and I would like to keep it that way, but with people knowing what is meant.

So here are some terms that may be confusing, and the one that comes first is the one I prefer. I have used other phrases ocassionally where they may help American readers.

British		**American or alternative**
Transit	Line given by two identifiable objects on chart	Range
Track	Line over the ground followed by a boat subject to tidal streams or current	Course made good, course angle or sometimes course over ground, or just course
Course	Direction relative to 360° or N (usually True)	Heading or course, sometimes course line
Heading	Direction a boat points at any given moment	See above
Course after leeway, or Wake course	The boat's course, to which leeway correction has been applied	Wake course. This is the most valuable of the many and confusing American terms incorporating the word 'course'
DR position	Position derived from True course and distance travelled through the water	Variously used to mean either as here, or as estimated position
Estimated position	DR position corrected to allow for current or tidal stream	See above
Position line (PL)	Line from bearing, transit (range), sextant angle or d/f radio bearing that can contribute to a fix. May also be derived from an astro sight	Line of position (LOP)
Set and Drift	These are very loosely used in British navigation, though they refer to the effect of tidal streams or currents. In America they have a precise meaning. Set is the *direction* in which the water moves; drift is its *speed* of movement in knots	Set and Drift

2
Elementary pilotage — Charts

You are beginning to apply the art of pilotage the moment you get your boat under way. Much of it is common sense — even an absolute landlubber, seeing a big red post sticking out of the river will think that it probably marks shallow water. He then looks around and sees a black or green post on the other side and realises that the deep channel runs in between.

But there is one bit of common sense that is surprisingly often neglected: never put to sea in waters with which you are not familiar without looking at, and preferably keeping beside you, a proper chart. By proper chart, I mean a fully corrected nautical chart giving the depths of water. Don't imitate the man I once met setting out with a newly bought boat from Cowes to Chichester Harbour, which he had never entered, planning to navigate his 15 mile trip on one-inch to the mile survey maps. The reason I met him was that, in casting off his mooring under power, he had tangled the buoy line with his propeller, so he was knitted to the ground by his stern, which perhaps saved him getting into greater trouble. After we had helped him get free, the epic of the maps emerged, and I was able to lend him a chart which, since it was eventually returned, I presume enabled him to get there safely.

The reason a chart is so much more important to the seaman than a road map to the motorist is that a driver, though he may bump into a lamp post or other cars, does not have to cope with *invisible* dangers on a fine, clear day. What may look a nice, safe stretch of open water can have unmarked rocks close under the surface, which may not reveal themselves even to the experienced. The only certain way of knowing about them is to examine the chart. Even an echo sounder can only tell you if the water is getting shallower — it cannot say 'You are going to hit a vertical-sided rock in five seconds'.

Although pilotage is basically short-range work, checking your way along the chart from buoy to buoy, sometimes even from post to post at the entrance to a river, it also brings in many aspects of the art used in deepwater seagoing, and is the best practical introduction to it. Most people find pilotage in tricky waters, with strong tidal streams setting you across the line you are trying to

7

maintain, the most fascinating and satisfying part of navigation, and the better you are at pilotage, the better seaman you are. It is worth remembering that many maritime disasters have occurred in broad daylight and fine, clear weather, with land and prominent landmarks in sight, purely because ordinary aids to pilotage and common sense were neglected. Most readers will be able to recall the stranding of various giant oil tankers, despite the availability of every modern aid to navigation.

CHART CHARACTERISTICS

The chart is a map of the sea which not only shows land masses in their proper relationship to each other (so it can be used for **plotting**) but it also tells you the depth of water by **soundings**—these are the figures all over the water areas. It marks all dangers, such as rocks close under the surface, or those which are sometimes above and sometimes below the surface, according to the state of the tide, and shows landmarks likely to be of use in checking your position, as well as all seamarks like buoys, lighthouses and beacons.

Here it becomes important to define the type of chart you are going to use. There are simplified charts for pleasure craft, and sketch charts to show details of anchorages, all of which have some virtues. But nearly all are based on surveys done by the national hydrographic authority for the area, or perhaps a survey done by one of two bodies — the Royal Navy or the United States Navy, whose work is published in charts printed by the Admiralty Hydrographic Department, or the United States National Ocean Survey. Although other national authorities, including other American authorities, also do their own surveys and publish charts, few except the Scandinavian ones are drawn and engraved as well as the British and American productions, and English-speaking people will probably meet language difficulties. Would you understand 'Danger — submarine exercise area' if it were written in Greek?

So at this early stage of your pilotage career, I would urge you for the moment to concentrate on making yourself familiar with the standard chart rather than a simplified one, even though you may think it shows detail unnecessarily complicated for the owner of a 25-footer. I shall deal mainly with the British Admiralty chart, because American inland and inshore waters are covered by a variety of hydrographic authorities; British and American charts have many of their symbols in common. Their chief difference is that the **datum**, the level from which depths are measured, is higher on East Coast American charts.

British Admiralty charts are in the process of changing over from soundings in fathoms and feet to metres, and charts of British waters are at present being redrawn in the metric system. While the change, which will take some years, is being made the opportunity is being seized to use more colour, and other improvements are also being introduced which will work towards the aim of an international standard chart. Meanwhile the majority of symbols are the same for both ordinary and metric charts. The aim is to fall into line with standard international practice, a step in the right direction.

Those who fuss about understanding metres are akin to those who fuss over a change to decimal coinage. Except that a large number of keel boats draw about six feet of water, there is nothing particularly natural about the six feet of a fathom, and in any case the difference between a fathom and two metres can be measured between most people's first finger and thumb. So learn to think in metres, and life will become simpler at once. A few people may find the soundings under 20 metres, given as metres and decimetres (tenths of a metre) a little bit confusing, but if you think of a decimetre as four inches, you will be pretty close. For those wedded irretrievably to feet and fathoms, each metric chart has a conversion scale.

Some people complain of drawbacks in metric charts. The two main ones are:

1. In reducing the number of soundings to make for clarity, a lot of shoal soundings and drying heights of particular value to yachtsmen have been omitted.

2. The authority seems to assume a bottomless pocket and inexhaustible chart stowage space for the user, neither of them notable characteristics of the ordinary sailing man. Some charts leave quite large spaces blank and refer to a larger scale chart or harbour plan.

The first of these objections has a bit of truth in it — you may find that drying heights in particular are too meagre. This has always been a complaint of small boat men. But soundings are adequately replaced by much more effective and visible contour lines. The two metre contour, in combination with the dotted line enclosing groups of dangers, is most valuable to the small boat man and, when skirting the shallows to avoid an adverse tide, these are much more quickly picked out than the old system of easily confused contour lines and innumerable soundings.

The second objection, which I have heard voiced by a number of people, just does not in my opinion stand up to inspection. The metric charts are often more generous with inset plans than the old ones.

CHART SYMBOLS

The meanings of the symbols on charts, metric or old-style, are given on special key charts, US Chart No 1 or British Admiralty Chart 5011, which are in fact

Dangers

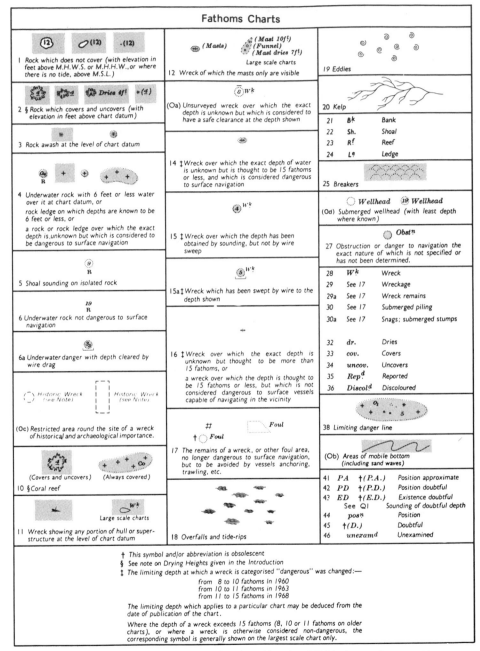

Fig. 2.1   This page from British Admiralty chart Number 5011 shows dangers as printed on fathom charts.

Dangers

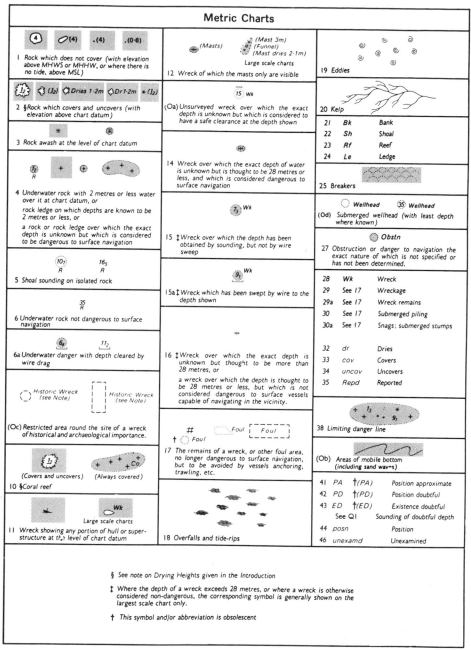

Fig. 2.2   Here are approximately the same dangers as shown on international metric charts.

booklets. These should be looked at in conjunction with *Figs. 2.1–2.4*, which show the points other than soundings where metric charts differ from the old style. There are not many, and they have mostly been done for clarity. Both should be carefully studied, with a chart of your local waters in front of you. Most people who have sailed around in dinghies with only a casual glance at a chart now and then, find their first look at a chart symbol key is as dazzlingly illuminating as the lights going on after a power cut.

FOLD, DON'T ROLL

Your charts will probably be delivered to you rolled up, and at this stage you must apply the first lesson about charts: unroll them, and never roll them again. Charts are designed to be kept flat, folded if necessary. A chart that is constantly trying to roll itself up as you look at it or plot on it is a curse. They are rolled because, in small quantities, this is the only really practical way of sending them through the post.

Study any chart you are going to work with very carefully in conjunction with *Figs. 2.1–2.4*. It would not be unreasonable to spend at least half an hour on each chart, or longer if you were about to make a passage through the waters concerned. A frantic discovery of a danger as you narrowly miss it is not navigation — it is luck. You should have found out about the danger beforehand and taken avoiding action.

THE CHART TO CHOOSE

For accurate pilotage, *always use the largest scale chart available*. It is astonishing how a piece of water which looks quite daunting on a small or medium scale chart becomes simple when you have the proper large scale one. Judicious choice of charts can save you money, but economising by buying a single chart on a smaller scale, when what you really need are two of a larger scale, is as foolish as skimping on some vital feature of your boat, like the keel bolts.

Scale

The title of the chart will state its scale, which is not given like a road map in miles to the inch, but in a proportional figure such as, for a chart on a large scale, 1:12,500. This means that one inch or centimetre on the chart is equal to 12,500 inches or centimetres on the land — just over 347 yards to the inch, or 125 metres to the centimetre, or 1 km to eight centimetres.

Small scale charts for passage making may often be on a scale of 1:500,000, sometimes expressed as $\frac{1}{500,000}$. There may be an even greater figure for ocean charts, but we need not concern ourselves with the actual figure, which is only an aid to selecting a chart from a list. The best way to make your choice is to use a chart agent's catalogue which illustrates the area covered, so that the right one can easily be picked.

THE GREAT CIRCLE

If you were to stretch a string on a globe and draw a line on the surface along the string, you would have drawn a **great circle** – the shortest distance between two points on the earth, and a useful thing if you are planning a long voyage across an ocean. The distance saved is only appreciable where the overall journey is measured in thousands rather than hundreds of miles and, because the course changes with a great circle as the distance is covered, its use for navigation is restricted to deep water sailing. Almost all the benefit can, however, be more simply obtained by drawing the great circle on one of the charts with special projection for the purpose, called gnomonic charts, and then transferring a number of points at, perhaps, 500 mile or other convenient intervals along the line of the great circle onto a standard Mercator chart. These points are then joined by rhumb lines (explained below) and the individual courses are steered one after the other. A completed great circle always slices a globe through its centre.

POSITION BY LATITUDE AND LONGITUDE

Positions can be defined on any chart or land map carrying a graticule of latitude and longitude. By convention latitude is always given first, either north or south of the equator, and longitude is given second, either east or west of the meridian passing through Greenwich. Each degree — which is an angular measurement at the centre of the earth — is subdivided into 60 minutes, and each minute further subdivided into 60 seconds; each angle of one minute of latitude is (very closely) one nautical mile at the surface, which is why the nautical mile persists in these days of metrication (metric charts use metres only for heights and depths). In *Fig. 7.15* the position of the Roches Douvres light can quickly be found, by laying a straight-edge across the chart parallel to the latitude and longitude lines, to be N49° 06′ 20″ W2° 48′ 09″. The seconds, in fact, are usually omitted or expressed in decimals of minutes, unless a very exact position is being plotted on a large scale chart. On such charts, subdivisions of a minute are normally made in tenths of a minute, each tenth

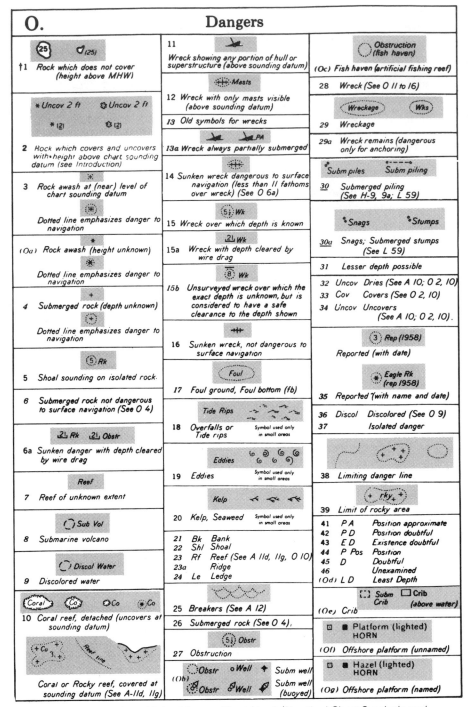

O. Dangers

†1 Rock which does not cover (height above MHW)

2 Rock which covers and uncovers with • height above chart sounding datum (see Introduction)

3 Rock awash at (near) level of chart sounding datum

Dotted line emphasizes danger to navigation

(Oa) Rock awash (height unknown)

Dotted line emphasizes danger to navigation

4 Submerged rock (depth unknown)

Dotted line emphasizes danger to navigation

5 Shoal sounding on isolated rock.

6 Submerged rock not dangerous to surface navigation (See O 4)

6a Sunken danger with depth cleared by wire drag

7 Reef of unknown extent

8 Submarine volcano

9 Discolored water

10 Coral reef, detached (uncovers at sounding datum)

Coral or Rocky reef, covered at sounding datum (See A-11d, 11g)

11 Wreck showing any portion of hull or superstructure (above sounding datum)

12 Wreck with only masts visible (above sounding datum)

13 Old symbols for wrecks

13a Wreck always partially submerged

14 Sunken wreck dangerous to surface navigation (less than 11 fathoms over wreck) (See O 6a)

15 Wreck over which depth is known

15a Wreck with depth cleared by wire drag

15b Unsurveyed wreck over which the exact depth is unknown, but is considered to have a safe clearance to the depth shown

16 Sunken wreck, not dangerous to surface navigation

17 Foul ground, Foul bottom (fb)

18 Overfalls or Tide rips   Symbol used only in small areas

19 Eddies   Symbol used only in small areas

20 Kelp, Seaweed   Symbol used only in small areas

21 Bk   Bank
22 Shl Shoal
23 Rf   Reef (See A 11d, 11g, O 10)
23a   Ridge
24 Le   Ledge

25 Breakers (See A 12)

26 Submerged rock (See O 4),

27 Obstruction

(Ob)   Obstr Well Subm well
          Obstr Well Subm well (buoyed)

Obstruction (fish haven)

(Oc) Fish haven (artificial fishing reef)

28 Wreck (See O 11 to 16)

29 Wreckage

29a Wreck remains (dangerous only for anchoring)

30 Submerged piling (See H-9, 9a; L 59)

30a Snags; Submerged stumps (See L 59)

31 Lesser depth possible

32 Uncov Dries (See A 10; O 2, 10)
33 Cov   Covers (See O 2, 10)
34 Uncov Uncovers (See A 10; O 2, 10).

Reported (with date)

35 Reported (with name and date)

36 Discol Discolored (See O 9)
37   Isolated danger

38 Limiting danger line

39 Limit of rocky area

41 P A   Position approximate
42 P D   Position doubtful
43 E D   Existence doubtful
44 P Pos Position
45 D   Doubtful
46   Unexamined
(Od) L D Least Depth

(Oe) Crib

(Of) Offshore platform (unnamed)

(Og) Offshore platform (named)

Fig. 2.3   This page from United States Chart No. 1 (Nautical Chart Symbols and Abbreviations) shows dangers as printed on American charts and how very similar they are to British charts.

†P. Various Limits, etc.

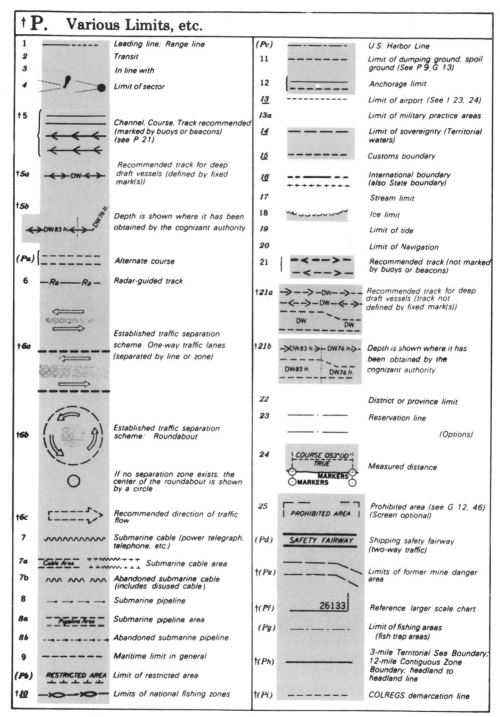

1	Leading line; Range line
2	Transit
3	In line with
4	Limit of sector
†5	Channel, Course, Track recommended (marked by buoys or beacons) (see P 21)
†5a	Recommended track for deep draft vessels (defined by fixed mark(s))
†5b	Depth is shown where it has been obtained by the cognizant authority
(Pa)	Alternate course
6	Radar-guided track
†6a	Established traffic separation scheme. One-way traffic lanes (separated by line or zone)
†6b	Established traffic separation scheme: Roundabout
	If no separation zone exists, the center of the roundabout is shown by a circle
†6c	Recommended direction of traffic flow
7	Submarine cable (power telegraph, telephone, etc.)
7a	Submarine cable area
7b	Abandoned submarine cable (includes disused cable)
8	Submarine pipeline
8a	Submarine pipeline area
8b	Abandoned submarine pipeline
9	Maritime limit in general
(Pb)	Limit of restricted area
†10	Limits of national fishing zones

(Pc)	U.S. Harbor Line
11	Limit of dumping ground, spoil ground (See P 9; G 13)
12	Anchorage limit
13	Limit of airport (See I 23, 24)
13a	Limit of military practice areas
14	Limit of sovereignty (Territorial waters)
15	Customs boundary
16	International boundary (also State boundary)
17	Stream limit
18	Ice limit
19	Limit of tide
20	Limit of Navigation
21	Recommended track (not marked by buoys or beacons)
†21a	Recommended track for deep draft vessels (track not defined by fixed mark(s))
†21b	Depth is shown where it has been obtained by the cognizant authority
22	District or province limit
23	Reservation line
	(Options)
24	COURSE 053°00' TRUE MARKERS Measured distance
25	PROHIBITED AREA Prohibited area (see G 12, 46) (Screen optional)
(Pd)	SAFETY FAIRWAY Shipping safety fairway (two-way traffic)
†(Pe)	Limits of former mine danger area
†(Pf)	26133 Reference larger scale chart.
(Pg)	Limit of fishing areas (fish trap areas)
†(Ph)	3-mile Territorial Sea Boundary; 12-mile Contiguous Zone Boundary; headland to headland line
†(Pi)	COLREGS demarcation line

Fig. 2.4   Another page from American Chart No. 1 showing various limits and markings which might be considered as dangers.

being a **cable**, which is considered to be 200 yards. The angular measure of one minute varies where it arrives at the earth's surface because the earth is not an exact sphere so, by international agreement, an average value for the nautical mile has recently been set at 1852 metres or 6076·115 feet, which is a slight reduction from the figure of 6080 feet hitherto generally used by navigators; the change has no practical effect for small boats.

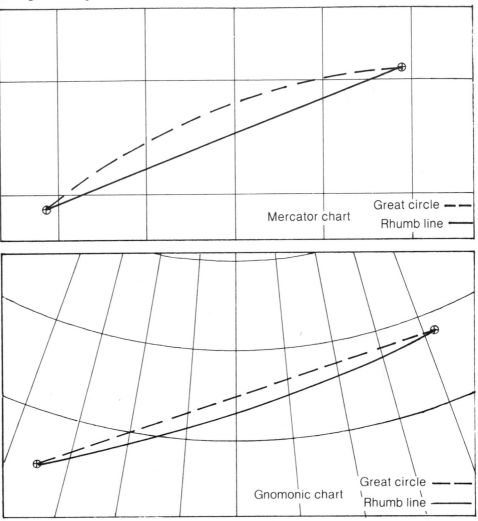

Fig. 2.5   Characteristics of a Mercator chart are the parallel meridians and straight lines of latitude. A rhumb line is a straight line crossing all the meridians at the same angle. A great circle, the shortest distance between two points on a globe, is a curve on a Mercator chart. On a gnomonic chart the meridians come together towards the north or south, parallels of latitude are curved and a great circle course is a straight line. A rhumb line is a curve.

PROJECTION

The projection of a chart is the system used in reducing to a flat piece of paper the curvature of a sphere, the earth. The majority of sea charts are drawn on Mercator's projection, a system devised in the sixteenth century by the noted Flemish mathematician and chart maker, Gerhard Kremer, who also used the name Mercator.

All such alteration from curved to flat representation must introduce some form of distortion, and this must always be borne in mind when working with charts. Mercator's idea was to draw all the vertical meridians of longitude parallel to one another and at right angles to the (horizontal) parallels of latitude. This, of course, is not the case in reality, because longitude meridians converge north and south of the equator until they meet at the poles, but it makes for ease of measuring compass courses, and the distortion is small enough to be ignored over short trips — except in the case of measurement of distance, of which more later.

Many characteristics of a Mercator chart are visible on simple maps of the

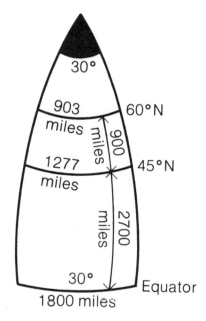

Fig. 2.6   Because on the globe the meridians come together at the Poles, the actual length of a given number of degrees of longitude varies, being longest at the equator and decreasing towards the poles. Thus you must always use the latitude scale at the side of the chart, not the scale at top or bottom, for measuring distance, and on a Mercator chart you must use it at the latitude at which you are working. The length in nautical miles of 30 degrees of longitude at different latitudes is shown here. When an angular measurement of longitude is converted to miles like this it is called departure.

world like those hung on schoolroom walls. They include:

1. Parallels of latitude gradually increase their distance from each other as they get further away from the equator.

2. The meridians, or lines of longitude, have been distorted so that they are parallel, instead of converging as they do on a globe.

If your map or chart shows the meridians curved or converging, it is not on Mercator's projection. Obviously a Mercator chart will distort areas a long way from the equator enormously, making Greenland appear a vast continent instead of its real size. But this does not matter much in the more temperate latitudes nearer the equator which we are considering; even at high latitudes this distortion can be allowed for if distances are measured *using the scale at the side, never the top or bottom, opposite the latitude at which you are working*. You will notice that on a Mercator chart a minute of longitude is usually quite different from a minute of latitude; the former bears no constant relation to distance (though it does to time), and it is only latitude which is a unit of measurement.

RHUMB LINE

The special advantage to the navigator of a Mercator chart is that any straight line drawn on it crosses all meridians at the same angle; this is known as a **rhumb line**. If sailing friends try to confuse you by brightly saying that a rum line is really the line of empty bottles marking the wake of indulgent boats, baffle them right back by saying 'I mean the loxodrome', which is the word for an extended rhumb line. If you transfer to a globe points on a long rhumb line they will lie on a spiral which, if extended, would end at one of the poles. Note that *on the globe* it does not cross all the meridians at the same angle.

The Mercator chart's properties make it specially easy to plot lines showing direction. As I have already said, it is always drawn so that meridians run vertically north and south, and of course the parallels of latitude run east and west. On any chart there will always be a few of the meridians and parallels shown, and you can find the direction of any line you draw to represent a track you intend to follow on the chart, by simply laying a protractor against it where it crosses a meridian or a parallel.

POSITION BY BEARING AND DISTANCE

There will be many times in a small boat, probably because you are having to work with a folded chart, when a position by latitude and longitude is most inconvenient to plot; it is a system whose main advantages are when far from land. In coastal waters, where there is usually a charted landmark nearby like a lighthouse, a position can be defined just as well by its direction and distance from the landmark, which is known as a **position by bearing and distance,** although it is not necessarily a bearing by compass (which is described later), it is a direction plotted with a sighting device and a protractor on the chart. Commonly a port authority which has set up a new navigational beacon will define its position by calling it 'Bloody Point Light, 168°T 2·9 miles'. Most people would interpret this as meaning that you find the new beacon's position by drawing with a protractor a line on 168° relative to a meridian of longitude, starting at Bloody Point Light, and then measuring off 2·9 miles to the scale of the chart.

There is, however, a possibility of confusion here. Some authorities define a direction *from* a landmark, and some by giving the bearing from seaward as is normally done when describing the arc of visibility of a light (see Chapter 4). Careful study will usually make it clear immediately which system is being used — if the position of a buoy is being described, you have obviously got it wrong if you end up with it two miles inland.

You may one day be using this system, perhaps by radio to a rescue service. If there is a prominent lighthouse within five miles, you could define your position as being, say 'Such-and-such Light bears 280° True five miles', which means that you are roughly five miles just south of east of the light. If you wanted to define to a coastguard service where you had seen a boat in distress, you could equally define the same position as being 'from such-and-such Light, 100° True five miles'. Note the use of the word *from*, and keep the difference clear in your mind.

MEASURING DISTANCE

We have seen that one minute of latitude is equal to one nautical mile at the earth's surface. Mercator's projection not only spreads the meridians of longitude as they go north and south, it also introduces an enlargement in the latitude scale in order to expand the contours evenly and maintain a fair outline of the land and sea. The length of one minute of latitude on a Mercator chart is therefore slightly longer at the top than the bottom of a chart showing any part of the northern hemisphere, and vice versa south of the equator.

So distance on a Mercator chart is measured in nautical miles only by reference to the scale of latitude at the side of the chart close to where you are working (one minute equals one mile). Remember that it is the distortion in a Mercator projection, that makes it important to use that part of the scale at the same latitude to the distance being measured (so that the same expansion shall

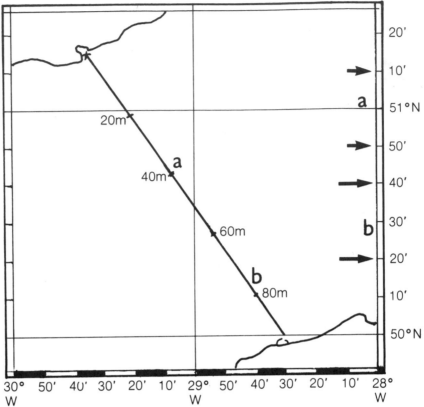

Fig. 2.7　On this chartlet of a passage, distances from departure point to **a** should be measured in the region of the short arrows on the right; those between **a** and **b** should be taken where the longer arrows lie.

be used for the scale and the contours). Don't worry what figures are written on the scale, these refer to degrees and minutes north or south of the equator; spread your dividers over one, two, five or any convenient number of *minutes* and tenths of a minute and walk them along the distance to be measured.

THE USELESS ROSE

British Admiralty charts, American charts and some others carry a *compass rose* or kind of printed protractor, which shows the direction of true north (the northern end of the axis round which the earth rotates), and another rose showing **magnetic north** (the direction of the point in Canada some hundreds of miles from the true pole to which a magnetic compass north-seeking needle points). The angle between the two is the **variation,** which is a kind of built-in permanent error which alters annually and depending on your location, and has to be carefully allowed for. It will be covered when discussing the use of the compass and, except for being the only place on some charts where the extent of variation is given, the compass rose is a useless thing in small boats, and not much more use in large ones. It is devised so that a traditional, and in small boats impractical, navigational status-symbol, the parallel rule, can be used.

Never waste money on buying, or stowage space carrying, a 'stepping' parallel rule in a small boat. Those who advocate their use have never tried to step one across a chart in a small sailing boat beating to windward in force 7 and a brisk sea. It is another aspect of navigation that has been thrust down the necks of small boat sailors by people used to working on a totally stationary chart table about six feet (sorry, two metres) square. I have even seen their use advocated in dinghy cruising! Everything a parallel rule can do can be done much better by a protractor, preferably a large square one, or best of all by one of the several makes of 'plotter', which is basically a protractor with an arm pivoted at the centre. There is more about them when plotting instruments are discussed in Chapter 12.

SOUNDINGS

The first thing to do when consulting any chart is to check the units in which the soundings, the figures showing the depth of water, are given, which may be feet, fathoms (one fathom equals six feet), fathoms and feet, or metres; this is usually given in the title of the chart. British metric charts say *Depth in Metres* in large letters in several places as well as in the title, but the older style charts give depth units only in the title.

Since the older charts sometimes give soundings in feet and sometimes in fathoms (usually with feet as well, in depths of under 11 fathoms) it is important to be quite sure. A particular point to watch for is inset chartlets in a larger chart. The chartlets will often have soundings in feet, where the main body of the chart is in fathoms. When a chart uses both fathoms and feet, the fathoms are in a larger figure, with the feet below, similar to a chemical formula, like this 5_2. This is five fathoms and two feet, a total of 32 feet. Metric charts do the same with metres and decimetres.

Drying Heights

It is important to note as you plan a passage any area in which soundings are underlined — this is a drying height, which at low water stands above the surface by the amount given. In a place where the rise of tide is 6·2 metres, a

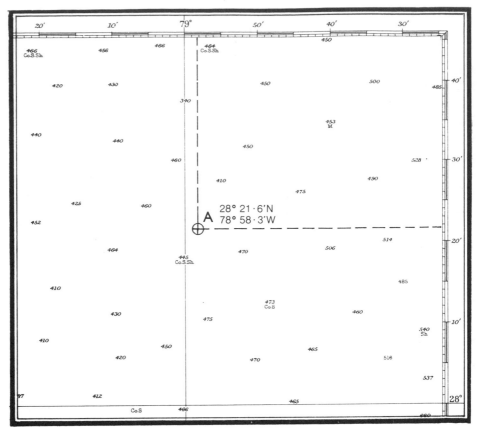

Fig. 2.8   Position in open water out of sight of land is best defined as a latitude and longitude, with latitude always given first. Such a position can be plotted on either a Mercator or a gnomonic chart, or transferred from one to the other. Position A here, in the Atlantic north of the Bahamas, is 28° 21·6′ North, 78° 58·3′ West. The final figure can be given in seconds, but on small scale charts like this is usually given as a decimal of a minute.

rock that dries 5·1 metres is going to be just over a metre below the surface at high water, and it is then much more of a danger than at low water when it is there for all to see. On a large flat drying area like a sandbank, the drying height given is normally the highest point, and not nearly as many drying heights will be given as soundings in deep water. This is often tricky when, towards high water, you are safely sailing over a mudbank that dries at low water, and you want to know where the hummocks are.

As an additional warning, drying areas are tinted green on metric charts, and on older black and white charts are cross-hatched or shaded.

Chart Datum

All depths on any chart are stated in relation to a level described as chart datum. This is close to, but not always exactly at, the lowest water likely to occur, which may only happen once in a year. British and most other metric charts are always drawn to a datum of the lowest possible level to which the tide can be predicted to fall, known as **Lowest Astronomical Tide** (LAT). With the older style of British chart, however, datum was usually, though not always, **Mean Low Water Spring Tide** (MLWS), quite appreciably above LAT; American charts have an even higher datum, which can make them dangerously optimistic. This irritating inconsistency, which can only be detected by checking the small print on the chart, is more fully explained later,

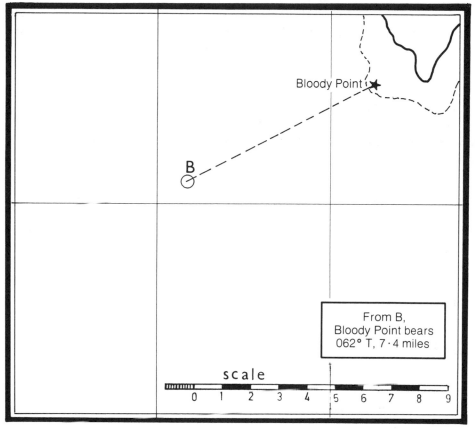

Fig. 2.9   In small boats, where the edge of the chart may be folded away for lack of space, the handiest way of defining position when a landmark is in sight, is by a bearing and distance. The bearing should always be corrected to True. Here Position B can be defined in two ways: 1. Bloody Point light bears 062° T, 7·4 miles. 2. Bloody Point, 242° T 7·4 miles. Care should be taken to make it clear which is being used.

and for the moment we will take chart datum as being near lowest low water. Just bear in mind that you are likely, even at a low spring tide, to have a little more water under you than is shown on a metric chart, and with an old-style British chart you may sometimes have a little less; with an American chart you may have quite a lot less.

Better Than it Seems

Consideration of chart datum makes it clear that a chart is a pessimist — it has to be. It shows you everything in the worst possible light, with the least amount of water over shallows, because that *might* just be the time when you are there. But in any tidal waters, and most of the waters of the world are tidal, there will be, in addition to the depth given on the chart, extra water caused by the amount that the tide has risen. If you live in an area of large tides, where many places are shown on your local chart as drying, you have probably happily sailed across them at high water with many feet of good wet stuff between you and that rock or mudbank. Obviously being able to work out how much water there is at any given point in addition to the charted depth will be immensely useful, and can sometimes be essential, as for instance when you want to enter an anchorage that has a shallow bar which you can only cross by taking advantage of the rise of tide.

SHORE HEIGHTS

The heights of prominent objects which are always high above water and which may be useful landmarks are usually given on charts. These are measured not from chart datum but above the level of High Water Spring tides. Their main purpose is as general aids to navigation, but the heights of lighthouses and other lofty marks have a particular use for fixing position, as will be shown later.

BUOYS AND BEACONS

Charts show the positions of beacons which are fixed to rocks and headlands exactly, but buoys can only be marked in their theoretical positions; they move around their moorings with the ebb and flow of the water, so they may be as much as one hundred yards from their charted spot; they have also been known to drag right out of position.

Buoys which mark the edge of a danger are laid far enough from it for a vessel passing close to the buoy on its proper side to be quite safe, and with most standard buoys this allows for a large ship. In other words, a small pleasure boat usually has a good margin of safety, even when very close to the buoy. This is not likely to be equally true for a beacon, which often stands right on its particular rock or danger.

Charts show shape, colour, light if any, and topmark of all important navigational buoys. There are, however, many uncharted buoys such as racing marks, fisherman's buoys and privately-laid buoys, most of which are unlit. European countries have recently standardised their coastal marks to System A of the International Association of Lighthouse Authorities. American waters continue to have several systems, which all differ from IALA System A; they will eventually standardise on a System B, but meanwhile the mariner is confronted with some interesting variations.

For those able to switch rapidly from Europe to America and back, the principal difference to remember is that, when going with the flood tide, the Old World keeps red buoys to port (red navigation light side), whereas the New World keeps them to starboard (green navigation light). With such a confusing contrast, you may be surprised to learn that anybody is so sensible as to use green buoys and to keep them to the same side as their green navigation light. But that is precisely what is done under the IALA System A in Europe. The American IALA System B, still some way off, will apparently perpetuate the anachronism of red buoys to starboard. These are points to watch for, particularly in Caribbean waters where you can switch quickly from American to British and then to French systems.

This book is not an exhaustive study of these various buoyage schemes, but a brief summary may prove helpful.

IALA System A

This contains two basic methods of buoyage: lateral marks showing main channels, and cardinal marks showing individual hazards. Both are illustrated in the endpapers of this book.

LATERAL MARKS. As already stated, channel marks are red (with even numbers) and green (with odd numbers), both in colour by day and in lights by night; these are left red to port and green to starboard when going in the conventional direction of buoyage. This direction is basically with the flood tide, or in the general direction of approach to port from seaward (the idea being that tides usually flow towards a port, so you need to have the buoyage geared to your entry to a strange destination; once arrived, you may be presumed to know a bit more about the local waters, so should be able to reverse the procedure coming out i.e. leave red to green at the exit). Some tides are not always clearly towards a port, or may give rise to local variation; in such cases the convention is to consider that they flow clockwise round land masses and the direction is arbitrarily fixed in this fashion. Note that numbering of buoys follows the custom of holding the starboard hand as the senior side, so that starboard buoys start from one, and numbering then proceeds alternately port and starboard, giving odd numbers to starboard and even numbers to port.

CARDINAL MARKS. These individual hazard buoys are used in conjunction with the compass, and they obey the general principle of guarding the four quadrants. They are always pillar or spar buoys, coloured black and yellow, and their principal distinguishing qualities are two triangular topmarks by day (taking care not to confuse a topmark with a radar reflector, you can tell where safe water lies by the direction in which the triangles are pointing) and quick flashing or very quick flashing white lights at night — characteristics which are unique to this type of mark.

ADDITIONAL MARKS. There are, of course, additional marks. These denote isolated dangers (red and black buoys), safe water (red and white buoys) and special marks to denote spoil ground, water ski areas, military exercise areas, or traffic separation zones (yellow buoys). Finally there is a whole range of smaller marks, usually laid by yacht clubs or fishermen, to denote their own private positions; they are often inflated marks in bright dayglow orange, or else small round objects with flags on them.

US Lateral System

This is used in American and Canadian waters, but is by no means general even in those areas. Be prepared to leave buoys to port or starboard according to shape or colour much as elsewhere.

MAIN CHANNEL. Black lattice can-shaped odd numbered buoys or pillars with green or white lights are left to port from seaward. Red lattice nun-shaped (cut off cone) or conical-shaped even numbered buoys with red or white lights are left to starboard from seaward.

MIDDLE GROUND. These are red and black horizontal striped buoys, and denote the preferred channel by having the top band and the colour of light to conform with Main Channel marks above.

MID CHANNEL.   Black and white vertical striped can or conical buoys with short-long flashing lights are left either side.

SPECIAL BUOYS.   As with other systems, a variety of other buoys may be used to mark quarantine areas, dredging, fishing etc. These are usually can buoys, and often incorporate white in the colouring.

Other US Systems

There are various other systems in use in US waters, and the mariner would do well to seek more specialist information than I can give here.

INTRACOASTAL WATERWAY.   These buoys are generally similar to those of the US lateral system, but they include a narrow border or band of yellow.

WESTERN RIVERS.   This buoyage also bears a similarity to the lateral pattern, but variations occur, particularly in the lights.

CARDINAL.   Some areas have no designed channel. Various white buoys denote the safe passage north, south, east or west (black is north or east, red south or west).

DAY MARKERS.   Many areas have triangular, square or octagonal boards or shapes on posts, with coloured borders or bands. These often bear a relationship to the cardinal buoys, but this is by no means reliable.

Sound Signals on Buoys

Many buoys of all systems carry whistles, bells or horns to help location in poor visibility. But fog does odd things to sound, so that they are often of little help in these conditions, apart from identification. Under sail, where there are no thundering horses drowning all other sound, a powerful whistle is sometimes the first thing to draw your attention to a buoy which you have not previously sighted, even in good visibility.

Lights on Buoys

To make it easier in the dark to follow a channel or to avoid an isolated danger such as a sunken wreck or rock, many buoys are lit. Each light sends out a particular signal known as a characteristic, to enable it to be identified.

Basically lights either **flash** or they **occult**. A flashing light is one which is illumined for a shorter time than it is covered or switched off; an occulting light is on for a longer period than it is off. The variations are many, from single flashes to morse coding, from group flashes to quick flashes, and now new characteristics called **very quick** (more than 100 flashes per minute, or double the rate of normal **quick flashing**) and **ultra quick** (160–300 flashes per minute). A light which is on and off for an equal time is an **Isophase**. On American charts they are marked **E int,** for equal interval.

Shapes of Buoys

Besides their characteristic topmarks, buoys vary in shape from system to system and according to their function. Broadly speaking, channel marks which are square or flat topped should be left to port going with the flood, and those which are curved, conical or nun shaped should be left to starboard; their topmarks conform broadly with this generalisation (square to port, triangular to starboard). Many modern marks are, however, pillar buoys, and you should always look first at the topmark (remember to differentiate between topmark and radar reflector) and then at the colour.

BEACONS.   Beacons and pylons may also mark channels. They may be anything from an iron stake with a topmark, to a stone tower painted almost any colour (there is a depressing tendency to use black, with or without contrasting white or red — not unnatural, perhaps, where the danger is called Black Rock or Devil's Outcrop, as so many of them are). They are almost always mounted on rocks which are washed by the tide, or else on headlands to mark bends in a channel, perhaps forming part of a transit or range to form leading marks.

STAKES.   Stakes are also stuck into the ground, i.e. like beacons and pylons they do not float. They may vary from stout wooden poles erected with lights and topmarks by the authorities, to small branches stuck by local boatmen into the edge of a channel used only by small boats. In Germany and Scandinavia quite complicated top marks are put on stakes.

SPAR BUOYS.   Spar buoys are tall thin pillars, floating like vertical spars as their name would suggest. They will usually be painted to conform to the system of buoyage in the area, and may have standard topmarks and lighting.

Buoy Hopping

If you have studied your chart properly and made yourself familiar with the buoyage systems, you should have no difficulty now in finding your way in daylight and good visibility in and out of a well-marked estuary, even if you are not familiar with it. Lines of buoys are usually carefully laid, so the next one can be seen well before the last drops out of sight, and sometimes they crowd together so thickly that it is hard to tell one from the other. But a check on colour and topmarks, using binoculars, will quickly tell you which is which.

Lighthouses, which have light characteristics in the same way as buoys, are sufficiently important to have a whole chapter to themselves. But before turning to them we need to study the changing level of the water — tides.

EXERCISES

2.1.   You have been at sea for 36 hours in thick weather, and are short of fuel for the motor. You signal a passing ship by lamp and ask your position (I hope that after reading this book, this will be the last time you will ever need to do such a thing!); he gives you 49°28′N 03°12′W. Referring to *Fig. 7.15*, define this position as a (True) bearing and distance from the nearest prominent lighthouse.

2.2.   Again using *Fig. 7.15*, give the latitude and longitude of the buoy at the western end of Plateau de Barnouic (a). And (b) what is its bearing (True) and distance in nautical miles from La Corbière light on the south west coast of Jersey?

2.3.   Referring to *Fig. 8.13*, what are (a) the true course and (b) the distance in nautical miles from Fowey Rocks light south of Miami to Great Isaac light north of Bimini?

Answers are in the Appendix, page 298.

3
Elementary pilotage — Tides

The first time you sail on any tidal water (and this covers most waters of the world except some large inland seas such as the Mediterranean or the Baltic), you become aware as you pass any buoy or beacon that the body of the water is moving laterally, as well as having waves on its surface. Sometimes the horizontal movement is very fast indeed, perhaps faster than your boat can sail, where a large quantity of water has to get through a narrow channel in a relatively short time, like the Race east of Long Island Sound, or the Needles Channel at the west end of the Solent.

You will also have observed that the level of the water rises and falls, and that the time of high water is not the same each day, being later by some fifty minutes, nor is the height variation the same. Obviously the rise and fall of level, 'the tide', is associated with the tidal streams, even though in many areas the direction of tidal stream seems quite irrational in relation to the rise and fall of water level. But tides all over the world have been studied for many centuries, and most of their vagaries and rhythms have been plotted and can be predicted with fair accuracy.

Tidal levels with their timings are predicted in tide tables, and tidal streams are given in tidal atlases or by tables on charts; the position, direction and speed for each hour relative to some major port's time of high water is shown by arrows or in words. In north west Europe and most of the Atlantic coast of America there are usually two high tides in 24 hours (Semidiurnal tides), but some parts of the world such as part of the Gulf of Mexico and the Caribbean have only one (Diurnal tides); there are also waters which have some of the characteristics of both patterns (Mixed tides). Unusual patterns are quite common, but are all documented if you locate the correct publication for your area.

TIDE TABLES

Far the most convenient source of tidal information for English speaking yachtsmen in the northern hemisphere is *Reed's Nautical Almanac*. The

European edition covers an area extending from Gibraltar to Denmark, and the American edition runs from Nova Scotia to Galveston, Texas, and includes some of the Caribbean.

All national navigation authorities put out tidal information and, if your sailing area is limited, the local tide table is often the best. With the increase in book production costs, *Reed's* has become quite a big item in the small boat navigator's budget so, if a simpler set of tables is available more cheaply, do not scorn them. The western end of the English Channel is well covered by a yachting almanac called *Channel West and Solent*. A number of people, myself included, have cruised the tide-scoured waters of North Brittany, with its 40 foot plus rise and fall, using only a yachtsman's diary for the time of HW Dover, and obtaining local constants from charts or various pilot books. This is not a counsel of perfection, or even to be advised, in areas of powerful tidal streams, though it would be quite adequate for many of the modest tides of the eastern seaboard of the USA.

Whatever tide tables you decide to obtain, make sure that they give more than just the time of high water. You need to know the height of high and, if possible, low water, so that you have the necessary information to work out the level of tide at any intermediate moment. Many of the tide tables in *Reed's* give only the height of high water, but the necessary level of low water can be derived from the mean level given on a different page.

Need for a Margin

Before finding out how to work out tide levels, it is important to realise that tidal predictions can be thrown out completely by freak, or even just unusual, weather, particularly if such conditions are prolonged. So, although tide tables enable you to work out levels to an exactitude of a few inches or centimetres, you must *never* apply these in practice without a wide safety margin. If your calculations say that at 1621 hrs there will be *exactly* enough water for you to sail over a certain shoal, and you arrive there at 1622 hrs, you may be in for a nasty shock, even if there are no waves to make your boat rise and fall above her normal average level of flotation. To cross a rock it would be wise to allow a *minimum* extra depth of one metre, more in areas of large rise and fall or if it is rough. If you have already observed that the time of high water does not coincide with the prediction in your tables, you should be prepared to allow a bigger margin.

In the English Channel, for instance, there are sometimes prolonged periods of east winds during the spring and early summer, which hold back the flood tide coming up-Channel, and help it coming south and east into the North Sea.

The result is that, all along Britain's south and east coasts, predicted times of high water and levels are thrown completely out. At Yarmouth, Isle of Wight, I once observed a level only two feet above lowest low level only half an hour before predicted high water. Actual high water arrived over three hours late, and was much lower than the predicted level. These fluctuations are cumulative, and become more marked the longer the freak conditions persist. In the English Channel or Long Island Sound five days of easterly winds would only just be beginning to have any effect on predicted tides, unless they were very strong, but quite a light similar wind going on for three weeks could be expected to have a considerable effect. In the North Sea prolonged northerly winds give similar freak tides. The effects on the strength and direction of tidal streams can be just as dramatic as on the levels.

ORIGIN OF TIDES

It is not necessary at this stage to know full details of how tides originate. They are looked at in greater detail in Chapter 11. Here I will just mention that they are caused by the gravitational attraction of the Moon, and to a lesser extent the Sun. The effect is that in most sea areas of the world connected fairly directly to large oceans there are two daily peaks of high water, and two moments when the level is low. These peaks and troughs succeed each other in a regular daily rhythm, getting later each day by approximately fifty minutes.

Because the tide-generating forces of the Moon and Sun work sometimes together and sometimes in opposition, the levels of high and low water change in a fortnightly cycle. When the Sun and Moon are working together, they produce a very high tide known as a **spring tide**, and the matching low tide will also be very low. In the following days the Sun and Moon gradually work less and less together until, at the end of seven days, they are in opposition and the tide rises and falls only moderately; this is known as a **neap tide**. The word 'spring' in spring tides has nothing to do with the season, it derives from an old Norse word meaning 'swelling'.

The tidal levels for most areas change in a fairly regular progression between spring tides, usually contracted to springs and neaps. But the level at one spring tide is almost never the same as at the following springs — it will vary according to astronomical factors. This is why tidal observations lasting less than a year are almost useless, and for reasonable accuracy have to be made over several years. As a very rough guide, in a month the level will work up to one pretty high spring tide and one moderate one just after full and new moons, with neap tides following a similar pattern.

A look at *Fig. 3.1* will explain tidal definitions more clearly than any number

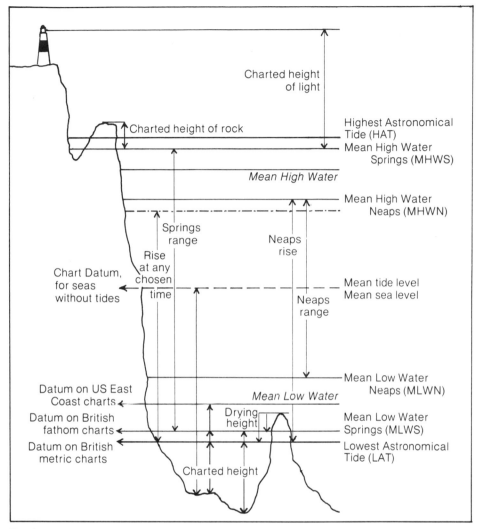

Fig. 3.1 This tidal diagram explains the meaning of all the tidal definitions you will need. Notice that, although on modern charts soundings are measured from lowest astronomical tide (LAT), heights are measured above Mean High Water Spring Tides (MHWS).

of words. There are a few points that may cause puzzlement, particularly if you have already met the letters MHWS or MLWS, which would seem much clearer if just expressed as HW or LW, perhaps with S or N added to define whether it is springs or neaps.

Mean High Water Spring tides describes water level at an average high spring tide, and is a height above which a tide will seldom rise except in exceptional circumstances. It is the height above which landmark heights on charts are measured, and you can see it on most steep coasts such as rocks or cliffs as a visible line. This is basically where saltwater life stops — even that which doesn't need to be continuously wet, but cannot exist on a surface wetted only rarely.

Mean Low Water Spring tides denotes the level of an average low spring tide. It is chart datum on the old British charts, but not on the new metric charts, and is a level below which a tide seldom falls, perhaps eight or nine times a year. When this happens, a tide table working to a datum of MLWS would give a negative height such as '−0·8 feet'; when using a chart working to this datum you would have to subtract this amount from any sounding given. You would only need to do this for the short period of about an hour each side of low water if making a passage, but it must be remembered if leaving a boat in an anchorage where the depths are minimal for your draft.

Lowest Astronomical Tide is much more important, even though one may occur only once a year, and some years not at all. It is the lowest level to which the tide can be predicted to fall — in other words, only freak conditions will ever cause the tide to fall below it. It is the **datum** for British and international metric charts.

American charts complicate life by varying their datum. Those for the Atlantic coast use **Mean Low Water,** which is an average of all low tides, and well above MLWS. On the Pacific a datum of **Mean Lower Low Water** is used, which is an average of the lower of the two daily low tides, a little above MLWS. One can only hope that American charts will fall into line with most of the rest of the world soon and use LAT, which is already surreptitiously in use on some American charts based on foreign information.

Mean High Water Neaps and **Mean Low Water Neaps** are self-explanatory, but I must emphasize again that **Mean High Water** and **Mean Low Water** must be carefully distinguished from MHWS and MLWS — they are an *average* of all high tides and all low tides, so Mean High Water is lower than MHWS, and Mean Low Water is higher than MLWS. Most people in British waters, if they have occasion to refer to it, will probably mean MLWS when they say Mean Low Water, but to an American it would have a specific meaning, the datum of his chart.

RISE OF TIDE

It is important to distinguish between **Range** of tide and **Rise** of tide. The first, the difference between high and low water levels on any particular day, is what you need to know when working out if it safe to stay at an anchor in a given spot over more than one low tide; the second, the present height above chart datum, is what you need to know when, say, passing over a drying height.

Rise of tide is the safety margin you have above the various nasty things shown on the chart, your height above chart datum; it is the mariner's friend. Sometimes, if you know it, you can even obtain a fix or position line by taking a sounding and subtracting the rise from it; on a conspicuously contoured shore, the depth you have left can be picked out on the chart. The range for the day is usually needed to work out the rise.

Working Out the Rise

To know what the rise is at any given moment, you need a tide table that tells you the time of the last high water or next high water and, if there is much irregularity, the times of the relevant low waters, and the depth of high and low water, which gives you the range. By working out how much the tide has risen or fallen from the last point given in the table, you then add or subtract as appropriate to give you the rise at the moment.

There is a great variety of ways of working out the rise of tide. The most complicated method is not always the best, though it may be the safest. Critically-exact navigators, working in large ships, normally use British Admiralty or United States National Ocean Survey tables, and volumes covering all the world's seas and oceans are available. Instruction on using these is given in Chapter 11.

But many people in small craft find this an unnecessarily complicated, cumbersome and expensive way of checking depths and, since a safe margin must be allowed, a less exact method will usually suffice, certainly in waters where the rise and fall is less than five metres (16 feet). For these waters a satisfactory rule of thumb method, working only on the basis of local time of high water and low water and range of tide for the day, will be enough. Intermediate in accuracy between this system and the Admiralty Tide Tables is the system used in *Reed's Almanac,* which is also covered in Chapter 11.

Rule of Thumb

This system works on the basis that an average tide, in an ordinary area with two high tides each day, rises one twelfth in the first hour, two twelfths in the second hour, three twelfths in the third and fourth hours, two twelfths in the fifth hour, and one twelfth again in the sixth and final hour. It is assumed to fall again the same way, like this: 1 : 2 : 3 : 3 : 2 : 1 — all in twelfths of the total range of tide.

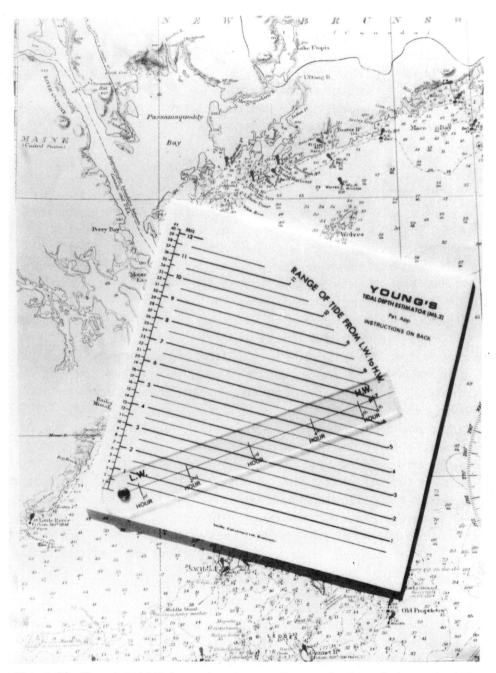

Plate 1. The Young's Tidal Estimator is a cheap, easily stowed and practical way of quickly resolving straightforward tidal problems. It can be used only in places where the graph of the tide is a simple curve, and is no use for places like the Solent, which have more complex tidal patterns.

EXAMPLE 1.   You are close to a port on a day when the range of tide there is 4·8 metres (16 ft). The time is two hours before high water. You obtain a depth on your echo sounder of 6·2 metres (20 ft). How much water will there be at the next low water?

Two hours to high water, will give you that it rises two twelfths plus one twelfth of the range:

So $\frac{4\cdot8 \times 3}{12}$ is the amount it will rise in the next two hours = 1.2 metres

Then depth at high water will be 6·2 metres + 1·2   = 7.4 metres

Depth at low water will be 7·4 metres minus 4·8 (range) = 2.6 metres

If you are in a boat drawing 1·5 metres, you will have over one metre below your keel at low water; the same mathematics are used for measurements in feet.

This method of working in twelfths was evolved for working in feet and inches so, although it works quite well in metres, it may be slightly easier to work a percentage system for metric depths.

A convenient system to adopt is that the tide will rise or fall 10 per cent, 15 per cent, 25 per cent, 25 per cent, 15 per cent and finally 10 per cent for each hour of the average six-hour tide cycle. Mathematically inclined readers will notice that this does not agree exactly with the twelfths method, but it is close enough.

EXAMPLE 2.   You are at anchor on a day when the range derived from tables is 3·9 metres. It is one hour after low water. You see a rocky ledge just awash. How long before it will be safe for you to sail over it in a boat drawing 1·5 metres?

1. You reckon you want 1·5 metres safety margin, so what you need to know is when the level will have risen three metres.

2. In the next hour it is going to rise 15 per cent of 3·9 metres.

3. In the following two hours it is going to rise twice 25 = 50 per cent of 3·9 metres, and in the next hour another 15 per cent.

4. Adding these figures up, you can see that in the next four hours it is going to rise 80 per cent of 3·9 metres.

$$80 \text{ per cent of } 3\cdot9 \text{ metres} = \frac{3\cdot9}{1} \times \frac{80}{100} = 3\cdot12$$

So in four hours you will have more than your desired safety margin. If you want to be more exact you work out the rise for *three* hours and interpolate by eye. In three hours the tide will have risen 65 per cent of 3·9 metres =

$$\frac{3\cdot9}{1} \times \frac{65}{100} = 2\cdot53$$

This is definitely not enough. During this hour the tide will of course, as it does over the whole six hours, be rising at an uneven rate. But you will not be much out if for this limited period, *but only for this limited period*, you take it as rising at a steady rate of $3 \cdot 12 - 2 \cdot 53 = \cdot 59$ metres during the hour. The distance you want it to rise is 3 metres, less the 2.53 it will have reached after three hours $= \cdot 47$ metres. Just by eye you can see this is pretty well five-sixths of the total for the hour. So the level will be what you want at three hours and five sixths of an hour $= 3$ hours 50 minutes.

In practice the whole of this last section is academic — you would have said four hours straight away and stopped fiddling about with tiny percentages of a metre.

Simplified Tables

At this stage you may be saying to yourself a shade peevishly: 'This chap is getting too complicated — I haven't *got* any tables which tell me what the range is for the day. All I have is a table which tells me that the next high water where I am today is at 1702 hrs, and the height then is 16 ft 4 ins (you have got hold of an old-fashioned, but still much-used, table given away each year by a local boatyard) and all I want to know is, what is the situation on the shallow bar right now, at 1145 hrs, and is it safe for me to go out in my boat drawing 5 ft? Have I got justification for spending an hour and a half over a drink and a bite of lunch before I catch the tide?'

Applying Rule of Thumb

Not to worry, the rule of thumb is made for chaps like us: all you need to swing it into action is a chart and, if you have not got one of those for where you are lying, you are not a genuine seaman, you are a pedestrian or a motorist. I will assume you have the latest metric chart which gives low water depth over the bar as $1 \cdot 2$ metres — quick reference to the conversion table makes this just under four feet and, since it is less than an hour from low water at the moment, you can start right now working out which hostelry you are going to favour with your custom. You reckon you need at least eight feet of water over the bar to go out with comfort since there is a bit of swell running. As your chart is metric, let's go all metric and decide you want the tide to rise $1 \cdot 3$ metres, so you will have a depth of $2 \cdot 5$ metres (a shade over 8 feet) as you go out.

To work everything in metres you must convert your level of high water to metres — 16 ft 4 ins $= 5$ metres almost exactly. Now the advantages of working in metres become apparent, because all the rest of the working is done in the decimal system, which makes everything much easier.

In the corner of the chart, as with all proper charts, is a small panel headed 'Tidal levels referred to datum of soundings'. This tells you that MHWS is 5·3 metres and MHWN is 4·1 metres, i.e. the difference in level is 1·2 metres. The level which your table when converted to metres gives for today is 5·0 metres, so you are $\frac{9}{12}$ of the way from MHWN to MHWS. This can be expressed as $\frac{3}{4}$ or 75 per cent, whichever comes more easily for you.

You can now apply this correction to LW and you will have low water level for today, and thus the range.

The same panel on the chart tells you that MLWN is 2·1 metres and MLWS is 0·7 metres, a difference of 1·4 metres. It is rather easier to arrive at your result by adding a quarter of 1.4 metres to MLWS than subtracting three quarters from MLWN, but it does not matter which way you do it. The answer is that low water level today is 1·05 metres. Since the ·05 is about the width of two fingers, you can ignore it and say that low water level is 1 metre.

This figure of one metre, added to the charted depth of 1·2 metres means that at low water, which you work out would have been at 1102 hrs, the depth was 2·2 metres, and you only need 2·3 metres.

My God, what are we doing wasting time drinking!

Luckily your crew is a man of calmness and resource, with a gift for getting his priorities right. He points out that he has not finished his lunch or his Scotch, nor have you. To drive it home he orders a couple more, meanwhile reminding you that you still have hours of tide to get round the headland and, within reason, leaving it for another hour and half will mean that you will travel faster. A crew to treasure.

Just as a matter of interest, let us work out the time you could have gone. The tide only has to rise 0·1 metre to give you the level you have decided on. The range you have found for today is 4 metres, and we have already seen that in the first hour it would rise 10 per cent of this = 0·4 metres.

You could in fact have gone a quarter of an hour after low water. Since under the influence of lunch and liquor you too have become a mellow, calm, unworried yachtsman, you actually reach the bar (of the estuary) at two o'clock, and by this time the tide has risen 50 per cent of 4 metres, so you have oceans below your keel. Your only worry is whether the light wind will die and you will miss the tide. But all is well, as it usually is for mellow yachtsmen, provided they do their figuring right.

SPECIAL TIDES

The most important thing to remember is that the rule of thumb system can only be applied to areas where the tide rises and falls steadily with two peaks in

SWANAGE TO NAB TOWER

(To be used for finding intermediate heights in metres for places named)

Place	Height of H.W. at Portsmouth m.	\n3b	\n2b	\n1b	HIGH WATER AT PORTSMOUTH\nH.W.	\n1a	\n2a	\n3a	\n2b	\n1b	LOW WATER AT PORTSMOUTH\nL.W.	\n1a	\n2a	\n3a	Height of L.W. at Portsmouth m.
SWANAGE	4·7	1·6	1·5	1·2	1·0	1·1	0·9	0·5	0·3	0·0	0·5	1·0	1·4	1·5	0·6
	4·3	1·3	1·3	1·2	1·2	0·9	1·1	0·8	0·6	0·5	0·7	1·0	1·2	1·3	1·2
	3·8	1·2	1·2	1·2	1·2	1·3	1·2	1·0	0·9	0·8	0·9	1·0	1·1	1·1	1·8
POOLE ENTRANCE	4·7	1·7	1·6	1·3	1·1	1·2	1·1	0·6	0·4	0·0	0·5	1·0	1·3	1·6	0·6
	4·3	1·3	1·3	1·2	1·2	1·2	1·2	0·8	0·7	0·5	0·6	0·9	1·2	1·3	1·2
	3·8	1·1	1·2	1·2	1·2	1·3	1·2	1·0	0·9	0·8	0·8	0·9	1·0	1·1	1·8
POOLE BRIDGE	4·7	1·9	1·9	1·6	1·3	1·3	1·4	1·0	0·9	0·4	0·3	0·8	1·3	1·6	0·6
	4·3	1·5	1·4	1·3	1·4	1·5	1·5	1·2	1·1	0·7	0·5	0·8	1·*	1·4	1·2
	3·8	1·2	1·2	1·3	1·4	1·5	1·5	1·2	1·2	1·0	0·9	1·0	1·2	1·2	1·8
BOURNE-OUTH	4·7	1·8	1·7	1·4	1·2	1·2	1·2	0·6	0·4	0·0	0·3	0·9	1·4	1·6	0·6
	4·3	1·3	1·4	1·3	1·3	1·3	1·2	0·9	0·7	0·5	0·5	0·9	1·1	1·2	1·2
	3·8	1·2	1·2	1·2	1·2	1·3	1·2	1·1	1·0	0·8	0·8	0·9	1·0	1·1	1·8
CHRIST- † CHURCH HARBOUR	4·7	1·8	1·8	1·5	1·3	1·5	1·1	0·7	0·7	0·5	0·4	0·9	1·3	1·6	0·6
	4·3	1·5	1·5	1·4	1·5	1·5	1·2	0·9	0·8	0·6	0·6	0·9	1·2	1·4	1·2
	3·8	1·2	1·2	1·3	1·4	1·4	1·1	0·9	0·8	0·6	0·7	0·9	1·0	1·1	1·8
FRESHWATER BAY	4·7	2·4	2·5	2·4	2·2	2·2	1·9	1·1	0·9	0·5	0·8	1·5	2·0	2·2	0·6
	4·3	2·2	2·3	2·2	2·2	2·2	1·9	1·4	1·2	0·9	1·1	1·5	1·8	2·0	1·2
	3·8	1·9	2·0	2·2	2·2	2·2	2·0	1·6	1·6	1·3	1·3	1·6	1·7	1·8	1·8
TOTLAND BAY	4·7	2·3	2·5	2·4	2·3	2·3	2·1	1·4	1·1	0·5	0·8	1·4	1·8	2·1	0·6
	4·3	2·1	2·3	2·3	2·3	2·2	2·1	1·6	1·4	0·9	1·1	1·4	1·7	1·9	1·2
	3·8	2·0	2·1	2·3	2·3	2·2	2·1	1·8	1·7	1·4	1·4	1·6	1·8	1·8	1·8
HURST-POINT	4·7	2·3	2·6	2·7	2·5	2·5	2·3	1·6	1·2	0·5	0·7	1·3	1·7	2·0	0·6
	4·3	2·0	2·3	2·5	2·5	2·4	2·3	1·7	1·5	1·1	1·0	1·4	1·7	1·9	1·2
	3·8	1·9	2·1	2·3	2·3	2·3	2·2	1·8	1·7	1·4	1·3	1·5	1·7	1·9	1·8
YARMOUTH I.O.W.	4·7	2·4	2·8	3·0	2·8	2·8	2·7	1·8	1·5	0·7	0·8	1·4	1·8	1·8	0·6
	4·3	2·2	2·5	2·7	2·7	2·7	2·6	1·9	1·6	1·1	1·2	1·6	1·8	2·0	1·2
	3·8	2·0	2·3	2·5	2·7	2·5	2·3	1·9	1·7	1·5	1·5	1·6	1·7	1·8	1·8
LYMINGTON	4·7	2·2	2·6	3·0	2·8	2·9	2·8	2·1	1·7	0·7	0·5	1·1	1·6	1·9	0·6
	4·3	2·0	2·3	2·7	2·7	2·7	2·6	2·1	1·8	1·1	1·0	1·3	1·5	1·7	1·2
	3·8	1·9	2·2	2·4	2·5	2·5	2·4	2·0	1·8	1·5	1·4	1·5	1·6	1·7	1·8
SOLENT BANKS	4·7	2·4	2·9	3·4	3·3	3·2	3·0	2·2	1·8	0·7	0·6	1·2	1·8	2·0	0·6
	4·3	2·2	2·6	3·0	3·1	3·0	2·9	2·2	1·9	1·2	1·1	1·4	1·6	1·9	1·2
	3·8	2·1	2·3	2·6	2·7	2·6	2·6	2·2	2·0	1·6	1·5	1·7	1·9	2·0	1·8
COWES ROAD	4·7	2·5	3·4	4·1	4·2	4·1	3·8	3·0	2·5	1·1	0·6	1·2	1·8	2·1	0·6
	4·3	2·4	3·1	3·7	3·8	3·7	3·5	2·8	2·6	1·5	1·2	1·5	1·8	2·1	1·2
	3·8	2·5	3·0	3·3	3·4	3·4	3·2	2·7	2·5	2·0	1·7	1·9	2·0	2·2	1·8
CALSHOT CASTLE	4·7	2·6	3·6	4·3	4·4	4·3	4·1	3·2	2·6	1·2	0·7	1·3	1·9	2·2	0·6
	4·3	2·6	3·3	3·8	4·0	4·0	3·7	3·0	2·6	1·6	1·2	1·6	2·0	2·2	1·2
	3·8	2·7	3·2	3·5	3·6	3·6	3·4	2·8	2·6	2·0	1·9	2·0	2·2	2·3	1·8
LEE-ON-SOLENT	4·7	2·7	3·6	4·4	4·5	4·4	4·2	3·1	2·5	1·1	0·6	1·2	1·8	2·1	0·6
	4·3	2·7	3·4	3·9	4·1	4·0	3·7	2·9	2·5	1·4	1·2	1·6	2·0	2·2	1·2
	3·8	2·7	3·2	3·6	3·7	3·6	3·3	2·8	2·6	2·1	1·9	2·0	2·2	2·4	1·8
RYDE	4·7	2·7	3·7	4·3	4·5	4·3	4·0	2·9	2·4	1·1	0·7	1·2	1·8	2·1	0·6
	4·3	2·7	3·4	4·0	4·1	4·0	3·7	2·9	2·6	1·6	1·3	1·6	1·9	2·2	1·2
	3·8	2·7	3·2	3·6	3·7	3·6	3·4	2·9	2·7	2·1	1·9	2·0	2·2	2·4	1·8
NAB TOWER	4·7	2·9	3·8	4·4	4·5	4·3	3·6	2·4	2·0	0·9	0·6	1·0	1·5	2·1	0·6
	4·3	2·9	3·6	4·1	4·2	4·0	3·4	2·5	2·2	1·4	1·1	1·8	2·2		1·2
	3·8	2·9	3·3	3·7	3·7	3·6	3·1	2·6	2·3	1·9	1·7	1·8	2·1	2·4	1·8
SANDOWN	4·7	2·0	2·7	3·2	3·4	3·2	2·7	1·5	1·1	0·2	0·0	0·4	0·9	1·3	0·6
	4·3	2·0	2·4	2·9	3·0	2·9	2·5	1·6	1·3	0·7	0·5	0·8	1·1	1·4	1·2
	3·8	2·0	2·3	2·6	2·7	2·5	2·2	1·7	1·5	1·2	1·0	1·1	1·3	1·6	1·8
VENTNOR	4·7	2·0	2·5	2·9	3·0	2·7	2·1	1·2	0·9	0·2	0·1	0·5	0·9	1·3	0·6
	4·3	1·8	2·3	2·6	2·6	2·4	2·0	1·3	1·1	0·6	0·5	0·8	1·1	1·4	1·2
	3·8	1·7	2·0	2·3	2·3	2·2	2·0	1·5	1·4	1·0	0·9	1·1	1·3	1·5	1·8

Note.—Area enclosed by pecked lines represents the period during which the tide stands, or during which a second high water may occur.
† Heights at Christchurch are for inside the bar; outside the bar, L.W. falls about 0·6 metres lower at Springs.

Fig. 3.2   This simple table is far the easiest way to work out depths of water on the Solent. It is self explanatory — you find the height of high water at Portsmouth today and choose one of the three figures given in the column labelled 'height rise'. You then select the time you are interested in and work down to the horizontal. The ringed area refers to the example on page 45.

the 24 hours, and approximately six hours between high and low water (Semidiurnal tides). For Diurnal and Mixed tides, you would have to work from other sources. Equally, freak tidal rhythms need special attention. Perhaps the freak tides best known to yachtsmen are those of the Solent, particularly now that so many competitors visit there from abroad. A double high tide gives a long stand of high, or nearly high, water, followed by a rapid fall. The easiest way to work out the tide levels there is to use the special table in *Fig. 3.2*. Details are given below.

CONVERSION CONSTANTS

To cater for those who have no tide table for a port they are entering, there is a simple system of referring the local time of HW, to that of a standard port for which tables are available. A commonly used standard port for southern Britain is Dover, which lies approximately at the spot where the tidal crests coming down the North Sea and up the Channel meet.

A pilot book might describe Cherbourg as: High Water −3 hours 17 minutes Dover. This means HW is three hours and 17 minutes *before* HW Dover; any constant saying + such and such a time HW Dover, would mean that HW was *after* Dover by the time stated. Solomon's Island, on Chesapeake Bay, is −4h 46m Baltimore: four hours 46 minutes before Baltimore.

This system of constants or 'differences' is handy and compact, though more liable to error than proper tables.

TIDAL STREAMS

Information on tidal streams (strength, direction and location) can be obtained from two sources: charts or tidal atlases. All charts have tables of tidal information, keyed to locations on the chart often marked by a letter in a diamond frame. Tidal atlases are contained in *Reed's Almanac*, and booklets are published for almost all the interesting areas of the world. They are often called 'Pocket Tidal Stream Atlases' though, in the case of the British Admiralty publications, which hoary old admiral had a pocket large enough to contain one I don't know — though thin, they have a tiresomely large page size. You need, of course, only buy the ones for those areas which interest you, and they do not go out of date.

A page from one for the English Channel is in *Fig. 3.3*. The arrows show clearly the direction of the tidal stream for each hour, and you can estimate the direction from the arrow accurately enough by eye when you need to plot the direction. The strength of the stream is given by the figures on some of the arrows. Look at the one just south of the Isle of Wight for three hours after HW

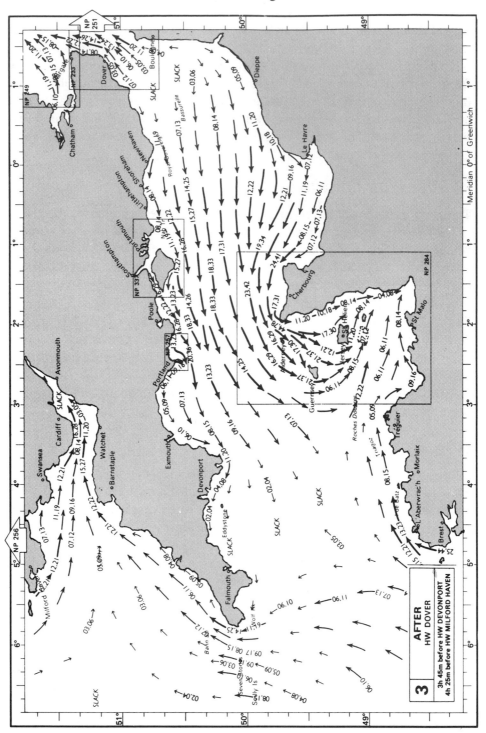

Fig. 3.3   The page from the Admiralty tidal atlas for the English Channel and Western approaches three hours after high water Dover. The comma between the pairs of figures is to separate the neap and spring rates. Each pair of figures is assumed to have a decimal point.

Dover, as given in *Fig. 3.3*; it says 16,28. The first figure is the neaps rate, the second the springs rate. For clarity the decimal point is left out, and the figures mean the neaps rate is 1·6 knots, the springs rate 2·8 knots.

For rates between springs and neaps, adequate accuracy can be obtained from interpolating by eye, because these figures can never be any more than a guide, they are so affected by weather conditions. If it were halfway between springs and neaps, the obvious interpolated speed is 2·2 knots. But if you are in the actual area and you see that the stream is running past a fisherman's lobster pot mark at obviously much less than this rate, do not hesitate to use what you observe — it is one of those days when the wind has affected the tide. The *direction* of the arrow is much more likely to be correct, though at times even that may be slightly out.

Some people think that the panels contained on charts are much more accurate about tidal stream strengths and directions, but this is confusing the issue. The tidal data is all derived from the same source for both tidal atlases and the panels on charts, from people observing and measuring the streams over a number of years, and then reaching an average. It is merely that the panels on charts *appear* to be more precise. They are just as likely to be quite wrong if the weather is doing funny things to the water.

WORKING YOUR TIDES

One of the most basic facts about sailing, where speeds even in big expensive boats are usually low and only in most unusual circumstances would reach double figures, is that you must, when it is possible, take advantage of tidal streams going your way. This is particularly so in narrow channels and beating to windward.

In tidal waters you can only make progress if you time your voyaging with the tidal streams. This is particularly important when making a voyage over a period of three or five tidal periods. The difference in time of arrival when you make a voyage with two tides helping you and one against, as compared with two against you and one with, is quite phenomenal. You can probably remember occasions early in your sailing career when you unheedingly set off for a sail and found yourself covering a tremendous distance, but mysteriously almost stopped when after an hour you turned round and decided to return. You had failed to find out what time the tide had turned. In power boats it may be unimportant, but when sailing you must *always* know the approximate direction of the tidal stream, and when it is going to change direction, even if you do not know its exact strength. As you make more ambitious passages you must learn to time your arrival at certain points to match the tidal stream.

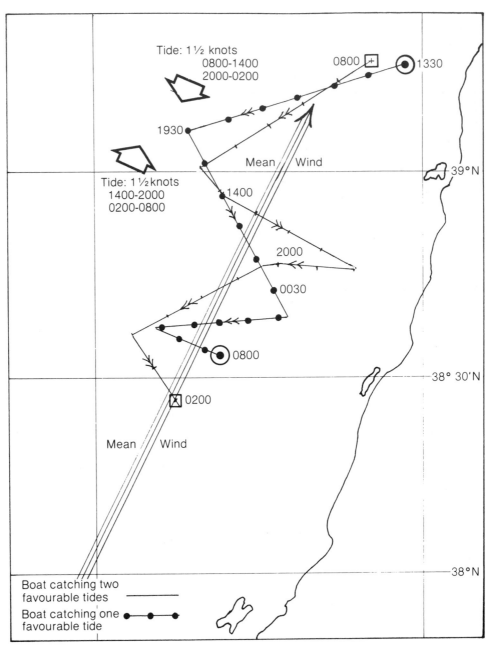

Tide: 1½ knots
0800-1400
2000-0200

0800

1330

1930

Tide: 1½ knots
1400-2000
0200-0800

Mean   Wind

39°N

1400

2000

0030

0800

38° 30'N

0200

Mean   Wind

38°N

Boat catching two
favourable tides

Boat catching one
favourable tide

Fig. 3.4   It is important to choose your time of departure so that tides work in your
favour. Here, the boat leaving at 0800 on an 18 hour passage carried two favourable
tides. The one that waited until 1330 had two against her and, at the end, is ten miles
back after sailing half an hour longer.

Heading off for Tidal Streams

When there is a tidal stream setting across your course, you must head up-tide to keep going towards where you want to be. You probably learned to do this automatically if you raced a sailing dinghy in tidal waters. But it is surprising how many people do not seem to be aware that they are being swept sideways by a cross current, unless they have a visible check like a buoy which they find themselves passing in crabwise fashion. You should always check which direction the tide is setting, and what its strength is; then you can make a rough estimate of what to head off. The greater your speed the less you need to allow. But when the wind is light and your speed is low in relation to the tide — it can often in fact be less than the speed of the tide — you need to allow a large angle, perhaps more than 40 degrees.

Calculating the angle off as exactly as possible for passages out of sight of land is one of the main arts of the navigator under sail. It is dealt with in Chapter 5.

Solent Height of Tide Table

In view of the extreme simplicity of the Solent double tide table which is reproduced in *Fig. 3.2*, and the large numbers of yachts of many nations which race in the Solent during Cowes Week, it is surprising how little known and used this table is. It has to be used in conjunction with a tide table for Portsmouth giving the height of tide for the day and the time of high water. With these two factors, a fairly accurate depth can be found for anywhere in the area covered by the table. A certain amount of interpolation is necessary but, since the range in this area is not large, this is not difficult. Admiralty Tide Tables and *Reed's* have recently changed to a much more complicated graphical system for the Solent.

EXAMPLE 3.   On a day when high water Portsmouth is at 1420 hrs, with a height of 4·2 metres, what is the depth above chart datum at Lymington at 1200 hrs?

The time for which the height is required is between two and three hours before HW Portsmouth, so the height will be found in the area of the table ringed. The height of tide at Portsmouth is 0·1 of a metre less than 4·3, so you would only be out a very small amount if you took the figure for 4·3 metres. The figure for two hours before Portsmouth is 2·3 metres, and for three hours before is 2·0 metres. The time you want is in fact $\frac{20}{60}$ of the way from two hours to three hours — one third. One third of the way between 2·0 metres and 2·3 metres of course gives you 2·1 metres.

If you are worrying that you more or less skated over the fact that HW at Portsmouth was 4·2 metres instead of 4·3, look at the figures for the day when the height at Portsmouth is very low, only 3·8 metres. If you used them, the height you would get would be 2·0 metres — the width of your hand less, and not really much to worry about! After a little practice, this kind of visual interpolation becomes automatic for both the height of tide and the times.

The only snag to watch for with this table is that you must make sure to use the same basic time throughout — British Summer Time or GMT for both time factors. If you take a GMT table for Portsmouth and use a BST required time of tide without correcting it, you will be quite a lot out.

Young's Tidal Depth Estimator

If you are one of those people who hate even the most elementary addition and subtraction, there is a simple short cut to tide levels which works reasonably well in places where the tidal pattern is an ordinary curve. Called the Young's Tidal Depth Estimator, it is illustrated in Plate 1 and can be bought quite cheaply. It is small, flat and stows easily. All you need is the range for the day, obtained by subtracting low water level from high water level. You set the pivoted arm against the range, and read off the rise above low water level against time along the arm. To get rise above datum you must add low water level to this.

This modest and effective device is about as accurate as the twelfths rule of thumb, and easier. I have carried and used one for years in the large tides of North Brittany. It should be emphasised that it works only on normal tide curves, without hummocks or bumps where there are stands at high or low water. It definitely is no help in the Solent, and should not be used there. As with the rule of thumb, a generous safety margin should be allowed.

EXERCISES

3.1.   You are in an area where the range of tide for today is 6·4 metres. The height of low water is 1·2 metres. It is two hours after low water. What is the present height of water above chart datum?

3.2.   You are approaching a river in a boat which draws 6 feet, and there is a bar which has a depth of 3 feet at LAT. It is two and a half hours after high water, on a day with a range of tide of 16 feet, and a depth at low water above datum of 2·1 feet. (a) How much water is there over the bar now? (b) Allowing an additional safety distance of 4 feet to your draft above calculated depth, what is the latest time after high water that you can safely cross the bar?

3.3.   Top of springs was on the 17th; today is the 21st. Your Tidal Atlas shows an arrow with *12,34* written against it, which is close to your projected track. What strength of tide would you allow?

Answers are in the Appendix, page 298

4
Lighthouses

A lighthouse is any lit seamark, from the small automatic lamp on the end of a little mole, flashing a meek light of modest range, to a lofty tower incorporating a noble light and a helicopter landing platform. Lighthouses are as valuable in the daytime as they are at night, because they are designed to make it easy for the navigator to check his position by them, being prominently situated and painted for easy identification. Their position is accurately plotted on charts with a star and a magenta or purple blob, together with details depending on the scale involved. A passage chart, for instance, will give details only of powerful lights useful to ships on passage or approaching a coast; a large-scale chart will give all lights, because there are few things so confusing at sea as finding a flashing light that the chart does not mention.

You may, if you are at an early stage of your cruising and navigating career, think that you do not need yet to know much about lighthouses, because you do not aim to be at sea in the dark. But suppress this feeling because, ever since man first took to the sea, the world has been full of people who intended not to be at sea in the dark — but suddenly there they were, discovering just how dark darkness can be.

In olden times it was plain blackness which was the problem. Nowadays, as more people discover every year when the wind dies and the engine just will not start, the trouble in coastal waters is *excess* of light. Seaside resorts and towns, industrial complexes, oil refineries and even coastal roads, blaze like film premières, frequently absorbing into invisibility the quiet little flashing light of the buoy you want to pick out. If you mistake for a moment a car with headlights on, driving down a road lined with trees, for a flashing light, you are not the first person who has been fooled.

This is why the site and characteristics of lighthouses are chosen with some care — though there are always people to point out with scorn that on such and such a coast there are two lights of the same characteristic within a short distance of each other. Those who sail in the region of the Channel Islands are often puzzled why the French make Cap de la Hague, the big light on the

48

northwest of the Cherbourg Peninsula, and Ile Chausey, only some 40 miles to the south, both flash once every five seconds.

Generally however, characteristics of lights are well chosen. The aim is that ships approaching a coast from far offshore, perhaps uncertain of their position within some miles because they have had no sight of the sky for days due to overcast, and perhaps they carry no radar, can approach cautiously on soundings, identifying any light they see with certainty. All major lights carry an identifiable sound signal too which goes into action in bad visibility.

LIGHT LISTS

While charts give some details of lights, it is much better, when you really need to use and identify lights, to check them from a current light list. *Reed's Almanac* gives a good light list for British and northwest European waters; the American edition of *Reed's* covers the eastern seaboard of the USA. Further afield, the British Admiralty list of lights is published in sections covering the whole world. The US Coast Guard publishes lists of American lights. For a small boat all are bulkier and more expensive than *Reed's*. Sometimes you may have to rely on a local authority list, which means struggling with a foreign language, but again *Reed's* is likely to be helpful here as it has a valuable four language glossary — five, if you include English.

LIGHT DETAILS. A light list tells you the following details of a light, in convenient tabular form:
1. Name
2. Position
3. Description
4. Characteristic, including colour and sectors
5. Visibility
6. Height
7. Sound signal, if any
8. Radio beacon, if any

There will also be additional general detail where necessary and, when a light does not show through the complete 360 degrees (a common feature on coastal lights that have high ground behind them), the arc of visibility.

CHARACTERISTIC. Going through these light details more closely, points 1 and 2 are self-explanatory — position is given in latitude and longitude. Point 3 just says what the light structure looks like. Point 4, the characteristic, is the most important. In addition to saying what the light flashes or occults and in which colour(s), it will give the period, the time between each of its complete performances. This is the most valuable aid to identification, and a stopwatch, or at least a watch with a centre second hand, is helpful in checking the timing. The period is taken from the start of each characteristic to the start of the next. It is *not* the interval between groups of flashes. So remember to check your watch from the start of each series to the start of the next.

VISIBILITY. Point 5, visibility, is undergoing a muddled period at the moment until British metric charts are general, and there are in any case a number of misconceptions widely current. Some people think that it is the *geographical visibility* i.e. the point where the curve of the earth cuts it off and, on older charts, this could normally be assumed for powerful lights. The observer's height of eye is taken to be 15 feet, approximately five metres (this dates it, because it takes the average deck on which the mariner is standing, to be 9 feet above sea level) so, if your height of eye is lower, which it is sure to be in a small sailing boat, a correction has to be made to obtain the theoretical distance at which the light is visible.

But older charts also make some allowance for the power of the lamp and the fact that it may be coloured, arriving at the calculated *luminous range.* Older charts are supposed, in theory, to state the visibility of a light in whichever of these is the less. This they sometimes notably fail to do.

A further range has now been established, the *nominal range,* which is being used on all metric charts. This is the luminous range when visibility is 10 nautical miles.

At present Admiralty Light Lists will give both the geographical range and the luminous range. *Reed's* is in process of changing over to the nominal range system as metric charts come into use, but the process is likely to take some years.

You see why I said the situation was muddled. The only reason I have emphasised it, is because of the widely quoted misconception that light ranges shown on the chart are derived solely from the height of the light and the curvature of the earth, so that a light coming up over the horizon gives you an accurate distance off, provided a correction has been made for height of eye.

HEIGHT. The height of a light is from the level of high water spring tides to the centre of the lamp. The height of lights is of great value in daytime fixes by vertical sextant angle (Chapter 7). You can also calculate from it the geographical range of a light, if you think that what is charted is only the luminous range. The easiest way to do this is from a convenient table in *Reed's* called 'Distance of Sea Horizon in Nautical Miles'. You simply add together the height of the light and the height of your eye, and read off the distance from the table against the height.

Because the height of a light is given above the level of high water springs, for those of no great height (say under 60ft or 20 metres) in areas of large tidal range, allowance may need to be made for the state of tide. Where the tide at the moment of observation is, say, 20ft or 6 metres below high water springs, you would have to treat a light whose charted height was 13 metres as one of 19 metres (before correcting once again for your own height of eye). As explained on page 115, this need not be of any concern when taking a vertical sextant angle.

SOUND SIGNALS.   These are emitted by major lighthouses in thick weather, using a variety of sounds, ranging from an explosive signal, through various types of siren and horn to the old-fashioned bell. They will have a time characteristic as a further aid in identification. It is not possible to describe sound signals really well, but the list below will be a rough guide. The word in brackets is the usual contraction on charts:

Diaphone (Dia) — low note ending in grunt.

Siren (Siren) — medium power, may be high or low.

Tyfon (Tyfon) — medium note like ship's siren.

Nautophone (Nauto) — electronically produced high note.

Reed (Reed) — High note of low power.

Electric Foghorn (EF horn) — Powerful combined note, medium pitch.

Gun (Gun) — self explanatory. Some acetylene guns give a useful bright flash

Explosive (Explos) — These go off in mid air, short distance from light.

Sound signals in Morse Code will have Mo with the letter or letters and the time interval added to the description in the light list.

Although sound signals are a tremendous comfort when it gets really thick, little reliance should be placed on them for accurate fixing. Sound reflects off cliffs and banks of fog inconsistently and you have to be very close indeed before you can say to within 20 degrees of accuracy what its bearing is. All that can be said for them is that they are better than nothing.

RADIO BEACONS.   Presence of a radio direction finding or radar beacon on a chart is shown by a magenta or purple circle round it. No further information is given on the chart, it just invites you to go and seek the details from the proper source such as a list of radio beacons, or a radio beacon chart. Details of using radio beacons are given in Chapter 10.

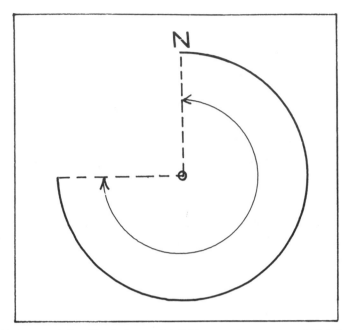

Fig. 4.1   Lights are defined by their arc of visibility seen from seaward. This light will be described as being visible from 180° through north to 090°.

ARC OF VISIBILITY.   When the light is obstructed by land, the light list will give its arc of visibility. This is defined as a bearing from seaward, not as a direction from the light, e.g. a light invisible to anyone in the area between due north and due west because of high ground would be described as showing 'from 180° through north to 090°' (see *Fig. 4.1*); these bearings are always given in degrees True. Occasionally, as in the case of Portland Bill, the characteristic of the light changes as it is cut off by its invisible sector.

COLOURED SECTORS.   Many lights show different colours in different directions to emphasize channels or isolated dangers. These also are defined as bearings from seaward, in degrees True. Charts show the arcs of the different coloured sectors. If you suddenly find yourself going from a white sector of light into a red or green one and you are not expecting it, check the chart quickly. The change of sector is there for a reason, and you might be standing into danger (*Fig. 4.2*).

LIGHTSHIPS.   Lightships are drawn in outline on the chart at the centre of the circle round which they swing to their chains, and the light characteristic

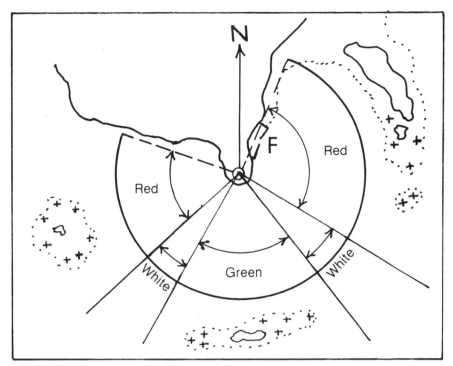

Fig. 4.2   This light has coloured sectors whose bearing from seaward will be defined in the light description. Lights usually (though not always) have a white light shining over the safe sector and red or green over dangerous sectors. Don't ever assume a green sector is necessarily safe.

will be given in the same way as any other light. They are painted red in British and most European waters, but some lightships are black. Sometimes lightships are taken off station for maintenance and replaced by buoys.

LANBY BUOYS. Owing to the high cost of maintaining lightships, and the resident crews' dislike of the way merchant ships home directly at radio beacons on them, to the extent of running them down, they are being replaced by Lanby buoys (the name is derived from Large Automatic Navigation Buoy). These are enormous objects, unmanned, with a lattice light-tower some 40 feet (12 m) high standing on a 40 foot diameter float. The characteristic will normally be the same as any lightship which the buoy replaces.

5
Elementary pilotage —
Bearings

In estuaries and sheltered waters with recognised shipping channels there is no reason ever to be in doubt about your exact position, for you are seldom more than a short distance from a buoy or beacon. Provided you know that you are on the safe side of the buoy in question, there is no need to worry except about a ship coming up on you. But many small anchorages that appeal to the sailing man have only minimal navigational aids, and you need to know your position exactly before you make the entry. The same applies when taking a short cut through a narrow and mainly shallow channel that would never be used by big ships.

So, when sailing down a broad well-marked channel, it is a good idea to practise checking your exact position by the many methods available, even though you know where you are: that is a familiar buoy 100 yards away, and you can tell from the tide going past that it has not broken its moorings and started to drift — a not unknown event.

Position checks are done with landmarks, the compass, a chart and perhaps a sextant — and I am not referring to navigation by the stars. One of the most valuable instruments for inshore position checking is the sextant. Echo sounders can also give a position check where there are suitable steep underwater contours.

Observation of a landmark with a compass designed to take bearings, or lining up two landmarks, gives you a **position line,** or **line of position,** which can be plotted on the chart, and somewhere along which you lie. When you have more than one position line you are beginning to define your location quite accurately. But a common error for beginners is to think that two crossing position lines are enough, and that you are where they intersect. It would be nice if this were so but, life being full of disappointments, you must realise that inaccuracies nearly always creep in. So whenever possible you should obtain at least *three* position lines, and these will intersect, not at a point but making a triangle known as a **cocked hat**. The size of the cocked hat will immediately give you a check on the accuracy of the position lines and, if the cocked hat is small,

54

Plate 2. A dome-top compass, with a cover for the dome to cut out unwanted reflections, and internal gimballing. This one is a Sestrel Major, made in Britain by Henry Brown and Son. It can be fitted with an azimuth ring and prism for particularly exact bearings, though normally the centre pin will be used. A model that can be mounted in a place free from magnetic interference, with a repeater unit in the cockpit, is also available. Caps for recesses to hold corrector magnets can be seen just above the mounting screw holes. *(Photo: Henry Browne and Son).*

the result is known as a **fix**. I will return to fixes later; at this stage we need to look at how we obtain a position line, which it is often convenient to contract to PL or, by Americans, to LOP.

TRANSIT OR RANGE

If as you are sailing along you observe that two charted and easily identifiable objects, like a lighthouse and a television transmitter aerial pylon, are in line, they are known as being in transit — usually called simply a **transit**; the American word is **range**. If on your chart you draw a pencil line through the

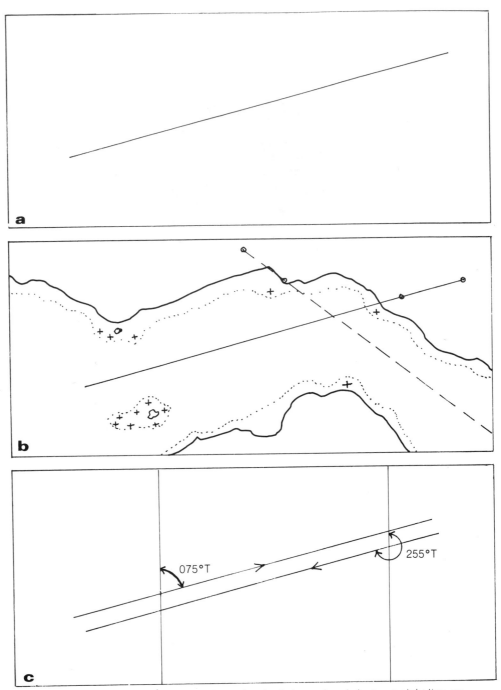

Fig. 5.1   What's in a line? Like everything else, it all depends. **a** is just a straight line on a blank bit of paper. **b** is a line that is defined both on a chart and on the surface of the earth: it is a transit of two objects in line, Americans call it a range. Here it shows the way into a river. **c** is a line on a chart that has a measured direction relative to true north;

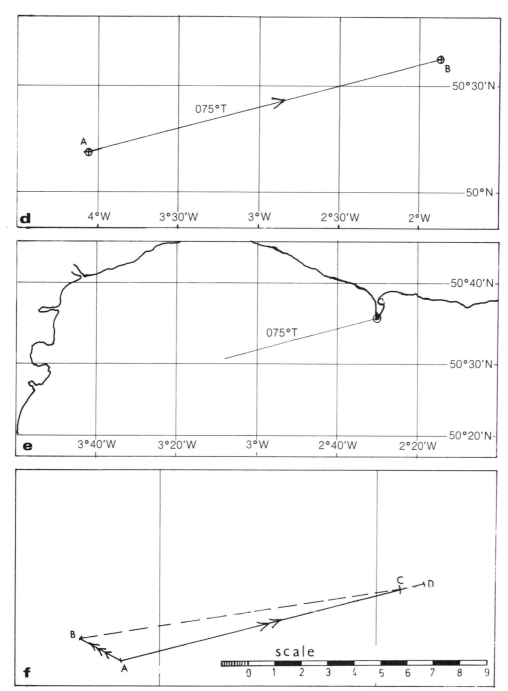

Fig. 5.2 At **d** the line has acquired a specific direction from the arrowhead on it, and a length defined by the positions shown at A and B. At **e** the line has become a position line, being a bearing taken of a lighthouse (and corrected from magnetic to true). At **f** the line has become one of the components of a vector triangle.

two objects and on out to sea, you have a line on which you can say with certainty you were at the moment they came into line with one another. This is the best of all position lines, provided certain conditions have been fulfilled. These are:

1. There is no possibility of error in identification.

2. The objects chosen are compact on the chart and give a reasonably clear aiming line. The lighthouse and television pylon mentioned would be excellent for this, but a large rock covering a considerable area on the chart would not, unless it had a sharply defined vertical edge that could be readily distinguished. Buoys, which move around on their chains with the tide, should not be relied on for a proper transit.

3. The objects are a satisfactory distance apart in relation to your distance from them — ideally this separation distance should be large. If the objects were half a mile apart, and you were about two miles from the nearer, the transit would be good — if you were six miles off it would not.

FIX BY TRANSITS.   If you keep your eyes open you can in most waters find objects suitable for giving a transit or range at almost any time, and you will find that the chartmaker is obliging in this way. He marks a number of objects as 'conspic' (conspicuous) when he thinks they may be useful to the navigator. Except that recently-erected buildings have an infuriating way of not being marked on the chart, while 'tall tree, conspic' has a way of falling to the woodsman, the system works well. So when you find that you are approaching one transit, a quick look round will often show you are also on or close to another. If the time lag between being on the two transits is small, you have one of the best of fixes, and one of the few on which reliance may be placed when derived from only two position lines.

This business of seeing and using transits or ranges is one of the most important things in pilotage, and can become vital in waters infested with offlying rocks. You will find beacons have often been put up in particular spots to act as part of range marks for boats on various approach routes. You may also find that the chart has the transit lines drawn and identified, sometimes with little sketches to aid identification.

TRANSITS OR RANGES AS LEADING LINES.   Besides their value as components in a fix, transits have particular value as guides through a narrow entry, especially when the tide is setting sideways across the entrance. By keeping two objects — perhaps specially erected beacons or signs painted on houses — carefully in line through setting the ship's head off for the tidal stream, you proceed safely down a known line, regardless of what the current is trying to do to you, and where the boat is actually pointing. This is much easier and much safer than approaching on a steady compass course, even if the course has been adjusted for the effect of the tide. Such entry and exit transits are called **leading lines,** and they are particularly valuable to the small boat man. They work equally well at night if identifying lights are put on them.

Sometimes the inexperienced are confused over which way to put the helm when a drift off a leading line is noticed. Since it is the rear object which appears to move as you drift off the line, it is best to make your correction in relation to this. To return to a leading line towards which you are heading the rule is:

If the rear landmark has moved to the *left* of the front one, turn to the *right*.

If the rear mark has moved to the *right*, turn to the *left*.

CLEARING LINES. There is a development of the transit known as a **clearing line**, which is much used in inshore pilotage when there are such things as underwater rocks about. Looking at *Fig. 5.3*, a sailing direction might say something like 'Galleon Head open of Snape Point leads clear of Mackerel Rocks.' This means that, if you can see Galleon Head out to seaward of Snape

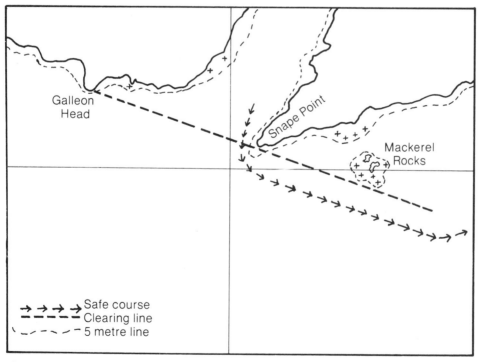

Fig. 5.3   Clearing lines are a simple and practical way of indicating a safe track past a danger. Here, if Galleon Head can be seen past Snape Point, you are clear of Mackerel Rocks.

Point, you are on a safe line to go past Mackerel Rocks without fear of grounding. There are other ways of obtaining clearing lines, both with the compass and with a sextant, as we shall see later.

ORIENTATION OF TRANSITS OR RANGES.   When you draw the line of a transit or range on the chart, you need to be able to define its direction. This is done by stating its angle in relation to **True North**, which is the direction of the northern end of the axis on which the earth rotates. All Mercator navigational charts contain a grid of latitude and longitude, and the north-south lines point to true north, and the east-west lines are at right angles to them. So with an ordinary protractor, you measure the angle where your transit line cuts a north-south line, and express it as an angle reading clockwise from north. West, for instance, is 270°. Angles having less than three figures indicating a direction, are normally expressed with a zero preceding them for clarity, so east is 090° not just 90°. North is expressed as 360°, not 000°.

The reason for emphasizing the description true north stems from the existence of **Magnetic North** which, as pointed out earlier, is in Canada and thus many hundreds of miles from the northern end of the earth's axis of rotation. The fact that the earth's magnetic field creates this unfortunate irregularity, so that you have to introduce a correction to your compass reading which varies according to where you are on earth, is tiresome, but need not be a worry. For the moment, just bear in mind always whether you are dealing with true or magnetic north, and on writing them down add T or M. Later, in sailing directions, you may find directions given in magnetic, but the custom is growing of defining everything in true, which simplifies many things.

At this stage you can draw against the angle measured on the chart its direction. Obviously it has *two* directions, according to which way you are looking, but it is usual to define the direction of shore objects from seaward.

RECIPROCAL BEARINGS

This business of defining the direction of a line may seem confusing, so it is best to get it quite clear as soon as possible. The point to remember is that an object's bearing is always the exact opposite of where you lie in relation to it. If you are in a boat due east (true) from a lighthouse on an isolated rock like the Eddystone, its bearing from you on a compass, corrected to bring it to true, is 270° — not 090°. It is surprising how many beginners get puzzled over this, and when they are trying to plot the bearing, draw a line from the light running in the direction 270°, which of course puts you on the wrong side of Eddystone altogether. What you need for the plotting is the angle exactly opposite to 270°,

Plate 3. The Sestrel Moore compass for cabin top mounting is very handy for taking bearings with the sighting vane attachment shown. The markings go round the edge of the card as well as on top against the normal lubber line, and beginners sometimes find this confusing. Although the cabin top mounting is very convenient for freedom from deviation and for taking bearings, it is inclined to catch lines. *(Photo: Henry Browne and Son).*

called the **reciprocal** of the bearing. It is easily found by adding or subtracting 180° to or from your bearing. Some compasses made for taking bearings also show the reciprocal.

USE OF THE COMPASS

Massive tomes can be written about the magnetic compass, and some knowledge of its character and vagaries is inseparable from navigation. But deep knowledge of the compass usually begins with statements about its inherent errors so that any faith you may have in the instrument is destroyed, especially when infinite complications in correcting or allowing for these errors are also included. All this alarming sea lore is necessary in large *steel* ships. It is much less applicable in a small fibreglass or wooden boat, even if she has an iron keel and an engine.

So at this stage I am going to tell you just the basics, saving such necessary additional information until Chapter 13. You can get valuable use out of the compass without knowing all its quirks, providing you remember certain rules. I am assuming your boat has already got a compass, and you are stuck with a particular type. If you are going out to buy one, do not fail to read Chapter 13 before you do so; a compass is not a cheap item, and for what you spend you want to get the most convenient and suitable instrument.

Unless you have been very unlucky and been landed with an antedeluvian ex-naval boat compass, your **compass card** will be marked in degrees up to 360°, which is north and probably has a fancy arrow on it. In the event that you have a card subdivided into four sectors of 90°, or the old-fashioned 'points' of the compass without having degree markings too, throw it away as soon as you can, read Chapter 13 and go out and buy yourself a new one. You can get quite a good one for little more than the price of a good meal for four people.

The Magnetic Compass

So here is a basic box of facts about the magnetic compass, that you must really know. Purists will, I am sure, squeal in indignation at this supermarket-type package deal of compass lore but, in the early stages of a sailing man's career, it is better to be sure of the basic facts, than to forget some of them because they have been buried in a mountain of more complicated matter, much of which is irrelevant to the small boat. I am numbering the list, because I think it may help to keep the details in your memory.

1. The small boat magnetic compass is an assembly of small magnets attached to a card which is marked in degrees up to 360°, pivoted on a jewel so that it rotates freely, the whole being immersed in fluid to damp the movement. The 360° or north arrow will, *provided no steel or iron has been placed near the compass*, always point to **magnetic north**, which we have seen is different from **true north**; the angular difference between the two is called **variation.** Variation differs in various parts of the world, but does not alter at any one place, except over a period of many years, regardless of the boat's heading. Your chart will tell you the variation for the area you are navigating, and it can also be obtained from *Reed's*. If you go to waters strange to you, always check the variation.

2. As a boat rotates round the compass card, which basically remains with its north arrow pointing steadily at magnetic north, the boat's heading can be read off a mark or wire attached to the bowl, close against the card, aligned

with the fore and aft line, and called the **lubber line.** The whole compass needs to be gimballed, either internally (i.e. the card on its pin) or externally (i.e. the whole assembly pivots), to allow the card to remain approximately horizontal as the boat rolls and pitches.

3. Small boat compasses may be divided into four basic categories
   (a) A bowl in which the heading is read off the card directly at the lubber line — the best ones have a domed top for magnification.
   (b) A grid type in which parallel wires are set to the desired course on a lubber line, and then a north/south line on the magnet system is kept between and parallel to them. A variation of this type for large boats with lots of power has a grid-type reader in the cockpit, taking its reading from a magnetic unit sited in the best place to avoid extraneous influences.
   (c) A so-called vertical compass, where the boat's heading is read as a bearing directly off a rotating ring which passes behind an aperture.
   (d) A bulkhead compass, which is a modified form of (c).
A variation of type (c) is one which may be held in the hand, and has a sighting system or prism so that it can be aimed at a landmark and either the bearing read as above, or else the lubber line seen against the card; it is known as a **hand-bearing compass.** Its stowage position and the place where

Plate 4. The beginner usually finds it easier to hold a course on a grid compass like this one made by Henry Browne. The verge ring is set to the required course, and then the card aligned with the grid. Only very rough bearings can be taken. *(Photo: Henry Browne and Son).*

it is used must always be well away from the steering compass, because the two sets of magnets will seek each other in preference to the north magnetic pole, thus causing false readings on the steering compass.

With certain types of compass, which have a domed top with a high pin in the middle, the operations of ship's compass and hand-bearing compass can be combined if they are suitably mounted.

4. The steering compass must be mounted so that it is easily visible to the helmsman in his normal position and, above all, so that it is well clear of any steel or iron which will affect it, or any electronic devices such as echo sounders, instruments such as ammeters, loudspeakers, torches (don't forget metal long-life batteries), or winch handles. Stainless steel should affect it very little, but some of it can also be guilty. If the steering compass is stowed below when not in use, it must always be mounted in the same position when on deck. This is because the magnetic effect of any large lumps of iron or steel, unavoidably close, will have been eliminated when the compass was swung in that position, and corrected for such influence. The hand-bearing compass, on the other hand, may be used in any position, provided it is not within three or four feet of any large iron or steel influence. Beware, therefore, boom crutches, outboard motors, fuel cans, tools, lifelines, beer cans, even your own harness hooks will upset it if they are ferrous.

5. The magnetic field of the boat, caused by all the iron and steel in and aboard her, creates an error to the compass known as **deviation**, which varies *according to the heading of the boat*. In a wooden or fibreglass boat, if the admonitions in paragraph 4 above have been carried out, these errors should be small, but the navigator should always be aware of the possibility of the deviation having suddenly increased or changed because new gear has been put aboard (such as a new anchor in a cockpit locker).

6. When a boat or compass is newly-installed, and at least every two years during her life, a professional compass adjuster should be employed to 'swing' the compass — that is to discover the deviation on all headings. His fee should also include **adjusting** the deviation found so that on any heading it is reduced to less than two degrees, and he should provide a deviation card showing any error remaining. Adjustment is done by attaching small corrector magnets to the compass, or moving built-in correctors, and *should never be changed* except by a qualified adjuster. The boat should be in her standard seagoing condition when the compass is swung and adjusted. You should be given a card showing the deviation on at least every 45 degrees of heading; if the figure on any heading is more than two degrees, insist that you

are dissatisfied and want the adjuster to do some more magic with the correctors. If he still cannot reduce the deviation, you will have to allow for it whenever you use your compass, as described in Chapter 13. But in a wooden or fibreglass boat it is a poor compass adjuster who cannot bring deviation down to less than two degrees when the compass is properly mounted, and this small error can be ignored most of the time.

7. As soon as possible after your compass has been swung and corrected, find two transits or ranges near your own home port, as near as possible at right angles to each other. At a time of no tide or current, point your boat along each, first bow towards it, then the stern, and note carefully what the compass reads for each of the four headings. Then occasionally when leaving or entering your home port, check what your compass reads when steady on these transits — one is usually enough, but do not always make it the same one. The compass reading should be the same as it was immediately after you were swung. If it has changed more than one degree, steel or iron has been stowed differently, someone has been rough with the compass, or has a steel object in his pocket, or the inherent magnetism in the vessel has changed and you need to call the compass adjuster again.

8. If you have a hand-bearing compass, do the same thing, though you will not have to sail along the ranges, just get on the correct line and point the compass. If your steering compass has no deviation, you should get the same readings on both compasses for the transit lines. The reading is magnetic, and varies from true by the amount of variation.

9. If you ever have to take bearings with a steering compass which has an appreciable amount of deviation — more than one or two degrees on any heading — this must be allowed for when plotting, and you must use the deviation for the *heading of the boat*, not for the angle of the bearing.

10. Always treat your compass and its mounting with the utmost respect. Being at sea with a shattered compass is very little fun.

11. If the compass or its mounting ever has to be removed, it should always be put back in *exactly* the same position, into the same screw holes, even if the latter have to be lined with filler or epoxy resin glue. If different screws are used, check each one carefully with a magnet to be sure that it is non-ferrous.

If you think that this box of compass do's and don'ts is a load of rubbish, let me mention a little cautionary tale. I was coming out of the Hamble river once in a large and expensive yacht, bound for a race in which we were due to cross the English channel twice. I happen to keep in mind that the transit of Calshot

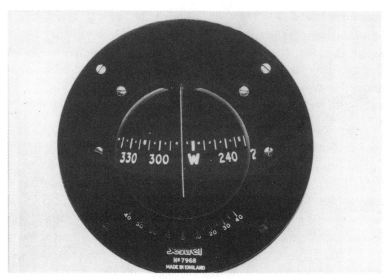

Plate 5. The bulkhead compass is specially convenient once you get used to seeing the lubberline *this* (aft) side of the compass, not the far side as usual. Frequently one is fitted each side of a hatchway to make it easier for the helmsman. It is important to make sure that there is nothing just the other side of the bulkhead which will make the compass readings go haywire, like a radio or echo-sounder. Many bulkhead compasses can be read from both sides.

Castle and the television mast in the middle of the Isle of Wight is 195°T, but the large and reliable make of compass on board was registering 16 degrees of error. Hasty checks around the cockpit revealed no transistor radios, pliers or anything similar lying around, but a careful look did show that the lubber line did not appear central to the boat's fore and aft line. Detaching the compass disclosed that the screws holding it down had been removed at some time and the compass rotated about four degrees. Because the original screw holes had become dubbed, new ones had been drilled. This would not have been such a disaster if three of the eight original chromed brass screws had not been replaced by chrome-plated steel ones. Quick packing of the original holes, replacement of the three errant screws, and a hasty swing on a couple of ranges and the hand-bearing compass, showed that the main instrument was back to its normal happy condition (the magnet used to check the screws was in fact the loudspeaker of a transistor radio).

Applying Variation

Before you can make proper use of the compass and the chart, you need to understand how to apply variation — the difference in angle between true north and where the compass needle north arrow points, due to the earth's magnetic field not being properly aligned with its axis. It is a permanent correction that has to be applied *every time* you use the compass. Variation has been plotted, and is known for all areas of the earth. It changes very, very slowly, about one degree in every 15 years or so. The only reason you need to know about the change is that you obtain details of variation from your chart, which will say something like 'Varn 7° 05′ W (1977) decreasing about 4′ annually'. If you are using the chart in 1981, you can see that the variation will have decreased by 16 minutes. Since for plotting you can ignore any angles of less than half a degree, until about 1990 you keep right on using the same variation as in 1977: 7°W.

Variation in north-western Europe at present is between five and ten degrees West, but in some parts of the world it grows to more than 40 degrees; even five degrees is more than you can ignore.

At this stage it is wise to fall into the habit of using certain phrases when changing courses or bearings from true to magnetic and vice versa.

When changing from true to magnetic, call it **converting.**

When changing from magnetic to true call it **correcting.**

I know there is a large body of opinion among American navigators which likes to say uncorrecting rather than converting. But this is the worst kind of gobbledigook, that should be stamped on in the interest of plain language. So remember:

When heading for the true, you are **correcting.**

When going away from true, you are **converting.**

Say it over to yourself a few times until it has stuck and you will find life simpler.

The same rule applies if you have to allow for deviation. You apply the **conversion** for variation to the true heading, reaching magnetic; then you **convert** to compass course by applying deviation.

When converting, therefore, you go: True — Variation — Magnetic — Deviation — Compass.

When correcting you go: Compass — Deviation — Magnetic — Variation — True.

There are two cheerful phrases that will help you to remember this, taught me by an American friend who said he picked them up in the US Navy.

Converting

TIMID VIRGINS MAKE DULL COMPANY

Correcting

CAN DEAD MEN VOTE TWICE?

I am sure any would-be navigator who has spent any time trying to convert a timid virgin will have no trouble about changing from true to compass course.

The key to applying variation lies in whether it is defined as west or east, the description being derived from the direction the compass needle points in relation to true north. When variation is 7° West, it means the compass needle is pointing west of true north by seven degrees. So to steer any True course, you have to add seven degrees on to it. You want to steer 090° True. What you must read on the compass (on which all deviation has been eliminated) is 097°M. And if you wanted to go due south, 180°T? — 187°M. So westerly variation is also defined with a + sign when converting. From this one can frame another useful memory guide.

Whether Converting or Correcting:

    Anything west, magnetic best.

    Anything east, magnetic least.

Best of course means higher. Do not let the change at 360° confuse you. If you wanted to make 358°T in an area where the variation is 7° West, what would you steer? — 005°.

Do not make the mistake of having another little rhyme when correcting back to true, when of course the arithmetic will have to be *reversed*. In an area with the same variation, you take a bearing of 124°M. Magnetic is best, so subtract to get true —117°T.

But suppose you have flown off to a part of the world where the variation is

Plate 6. A repeater unit, the Brookes and Gatehouse Halcyon, which gives a convenient grid reading from a remote master installed where it is free from any deviation. *(Photo: Brookes and Gatehouse)*

11°E and chartered a boat there. You want to steer 340°T. Anything East, magnetic least, so you subtract and steer 329°M.

Again, in the same far-off area with 11°E variation, you obtain a bearing of 062°M. Magnetic is least, so you *add* the variation and your bearing is 073°T.

PLOTTING BEARINGS

Suppose you take a bearing of a lighthouse, 345°M, 338°T and want to plot it. For this you need the reciprocal of the bearing, for which you either add or subtract 180° — 158°T in this case. You can then orientate a 360 degree protractor on the object of your bearing, and lay off a line at 158°. A lot of people save the trouble of working out the reciprocal, by laying a straight edge across the protractor and marking the reciprocal directly. A proper navigational protractor does the job for you.

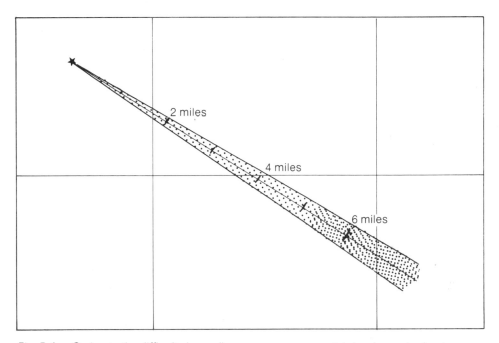

2 miles

4 miles

6 miles

Fig. 5.4   Owing to the difficulty in reading a compass accurately in a bouncing boat, even if the instrument is exact, there is always an area of doubt on any compass bearing. At seven miles distance, this error can be over a mile across. This accounts for the inexactitude of all compass bearing fixes, and the very large errors in D/F radio fixes (which are often taken at distances of over thirty miles). Thus, when taking any fix using a compass either directly or attached to a D/F radio, you should always use the nearest possible suitable object.

Plotting a Fix

Suppose for any reason that you want to return to the exact spot where you lie now — perhaps your anchor is snagged in something on the bottom, so that you want to cut the chain, buoy the end and come back at low water springs in three days time, when you may have a better chance of recovering it. You must take an exact fix.

First of all, are there any good transits or ranges? Yes, there is a beacon over there exactly in line with a house which you find is marked on the chart as 'conspic'. That gives one good position line. The only other objects suitable to give you lines crossing at a good angle stand alone; you will have to use compass bearings. You take careful bearings, while still at anchor, of a lighthouse and a church spire. Corrected for variation, with the transit they produce a nice small cocked hat; on the chart you are using, only about 50 yards across. You should have no trouble in relocating your buoy, provided you make a careful note of the figures and the objects you used (so you can repeat them correctly later).

The easiest way to return will be to get yourself on the transit, in a position you know is offshore of the point you are seeking, and then motor gently inshore along the transit, checking bearings as you go. Don't overshoot and go aground!

Fix by Compass Bearings

The technique of taking a fix by compass bearings should be standardised as much as possible. If you always do things the same way, as a drill, there is less likelihood of your making a silly mistake, such as applying variation the wrong way when perhaps you are tired. A typical routine using a hand-bearing compass is:

1. Check the objects you are going to use to be sure that the bearings they provide will cross at a good angle. Make sure they are on the chart — frequently a conspicuous object like a new power station may not be. Take a piece of card or notebook and a pencil on deck with which to note the bearings; never try to remember them. Choose a good sighting position, clear of magnetic interference.

2. Take the first bearing and note it down, writing M against it to remind you that it has not been corrected for variation. Repeat the process for the other two objects, always writing one bearing down before taking the next. A small delay between sights will not matter in open water; note an average time.

3. Correct all three angles for variation, writing them down with T after each one.

4. Plot each position line carefully on the chart, orientating your protractor over the object you have used for your bearing. It can reduce the chance of error if you mark the chart at the angle of the bearing, and then extend the line back out to sea through the object; if you prefer, you can merely plot the reciprocal by adding or subtracting 180°. It is not necessary to draw the line the full length as has been done for clarity in *Fig. 5.5*, as it merely messes up the chart; a short line in the general region of where you are is enough.

5. If the resulting cocked hat is large, work out in your mind which of the bearings was the most likely to be in error, and check your plot to find which

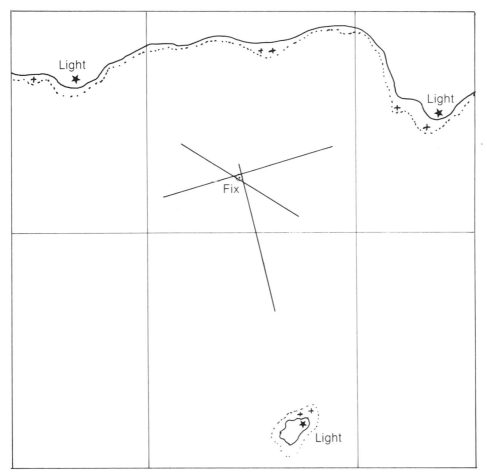

Fig. 5.5   This is the ideal kind of fix which you will find you seldom get in real life. The bearings come to a nice small cocked hat, and you are so positioned that the angles of cut are good for all of them.

two position lines cross at the smallest angle. Your location in the cocked hat is likely to be away from this angle and towards the other two. Place a dot with a circle round it on the chart where you consider your fix has put you, and write against it the time you took it and how good you thought it was: '1620. Fix. Compass. Good.' The length of the position lines you draw on the chart should be enough to indicate the objects used for the bearings.

Why a circle with a dot in it? This is the convention for a fix and saves time while plotting, enables you to return to the chart later and rework if necessary, or allows the navigator in the other watch to interpret your work without waking you up. There are also conventions for a Dead Reckoning Position (a cross) and an Estimated Position (a triangle with a dot in it). The DR position is based solely on course, speed and time; the Estimated Position takes account of tide, currents, leeway and anything else which may affect your position. These three are conveniently in alphabetical order in degree of accuracy: a DRP is not as accurate as an EP, which in turn is only a best estimate and not as good as a Fix; the cross becomes the triangle and finally the circle.

Interpreting Cocked Hats

Having obtained your cocked hat, you must interpret it to work out where you are in it. It is unlikely you are right in the middle, because of the different distances of the various objects you have used, and the angle at which the lines cut. The principle to follow is that you are in the middle of its *area* and, if in doubt, towards the corner where the lines cut at the largest angle: if the lines all cross at about 60° you are closest to the line on the best bearing, which is usually the nearest object.

Fig. 5.6 is based on a sketch chart such as might be found in a pilotage book, or a cruising article in a yachting magazine. Note, however, that though much simplified, the sketch contains most of the information that a normal chart would give. Fix A is a typical good compass bearing fix. Provided the boat was not tossing too much, the position is likely to be accurate to within a mile, perhaps even half a mile. It is one you can lay off a new course from with confidence.

Now let's look at Fix B. This is obviously a poor one, only just better than nothing at all. The distances from the tower and the island are considerable, so these bearings are likely to have large inaccuracies and, worst of all, the bearing lines cross each other at much too fine an angle. The bearing of the light is better, because the object is closer, but the key point you want to know, how far out you are from the headland, is in great doubt.

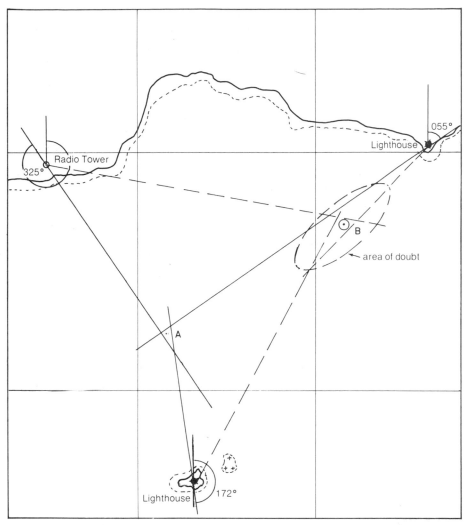

Fig. 5.6   This compares a fairly good fix from three compass bearings at A, with a poor one at B. The fix at A has two of its bearings crossing at a right angle, and the third at rather a fine angle; for this reason the fix has been placed closer to the angle where the good cut occurs. The fix at B is poor in every way because of the fineness of the angle of cut, yielding a large cocked hat; the oval area of doubt is large.

Returning to Fix A for a moment. You will notice that the fix has been drawn right in the cocked hat. This is because all the bearings were fairly good, and they cut at excellent angles — the cocked hat is almost an equilateral triangle. You can draw a circle round this fix with a radius of half a mile and say with some certainty that you are within it. This is an aspect of navigation that many people tend to overlook. All fixes, except two or perhaps three transits taken and plotted with extraordinary exactitude, put you in an *area*, not a point on the chart. There's an old saying that the only man who knows *exactly* where he is lies impaled firmly on the only rock on the chart.

Fix B has a large area of doubt, the elliptical area enclosed by the dashed line. It is narrower that it is long, because the bearing of the light is quite good.

You can if you want draw in on the chart your areas of doubt, so that you can see where they add together to put you in potential danger. But it is better not to, for it messes up the chart unnecessarily and can worry any member of the crew who takes a look at it. But it is important to keep in your head your areas of uncertainty round each fix, and above all its *shape*, according to the quality and nature of the different position lines which make it up.

This business of areas of doubt of course applies to passage making as well. However carefully you worked out and plotted your allowances for tides, there is always a considerable uncertainty after, say 24 hours out of sight of land. If you see a landmark on the other side and obtain a fix, even a poor one, your area of doubt is reduced.

ANY INDICATION, FROM ANY SOURCE, CAN USEFULLY BE USED TO CONTRIBUTE TOWARDS REDUCING DOUBT ABOUT YOUR POSITION.

Sometimes even the sense of *smell* can be useful, though it is subjective and unreliable, and should never be used without confirmation from another source. Oil refineries and depots put out a well-known stench that often extends for miles downwind. As a pleasanter thought, I might mention that I was once helped to find the island of Sark in bad visibility by the scent of flowers, which was quite noticeable in June in a light wind six miles from land.

EXERCISES

Work out the following exercises; the answers are in the Appendix.

5.1.   You are in an area where the variation is 8°W. You wish to steer 225°T and your deviation card says that your deviation is 3°E on SW. What course should you steer on the compass to make good 225°T?

5.2. In the same boat, on another occasion, you are heading 220°C in roughly the same waters. With the steering compass you obtain a reasonable bearing of 227°C on one landmark, while another member of the crew is getting bearings of two others with the handbearing compass; he gets 162° and 265°C. State the true bearings you used to plot the fix.

5.3. You are tacking against an east wind, in a boat with an off-centre compass giving 6°W deviation on north-east, 8°W on east and 3°W on south-east. On starboard tack you find you can hold 048°C after allowing for leeway. Variation in the area is 6°W. What is (a) Your true course on starboard tack and (b) on port tack, assuming your boat tacks through 90° by compass?

6
Dead reckoning

With this simple grounding of pilotage and fixing methods, many will start thinking of going further offshore, perhaps even out of sight of land — navigation by 'dead reckoning'. I am all in favour, provided you do not stop reading here. There is plenty more you need to know, but the basic principle of dead reckoning — some people prefer the more correct but prissy phrase 'deduced reckoning' — is absurdly simple.

It is the same principle you would follow if you had to go in total darkness to collect something you had left outside the house. You know you must go half left as you leave the door, walk about three paces, and then there are three steps down. From the steps you turn right, and about five paces will bring you to where you have left that spade, garden saw, or whatever. If you had one, you might even have thought how handy a luminous compass would have been, to get you back. In practice, of course, you either leave a light on in the house or take a flashlight.

But the principle remains the same. *You keep a check on the direction in which you move, and you measure how far you have gone.*

If you have no distance-measuring instrument when travelling in a boat across water, it is easier to measure or estimate speed rather than distance, and then convert the time you have travelled at that speed into a distance. A variety of devices are made to measure speed in boats, none of them totally accurate. But even an estimate will give you something to work on, and experience of your boat will make your estimates fairly accurate. In default of anything else, a simplification of the Dutchman's Log will do. Drop over the bow something which floats, and time it as it passes any measured distance down the side. Divide the distance travelled in feet by the seconds taken, and multiply the result by 3/5 or 0·6; the result is speed in knots.

$$\frac{\text{Distance in feet}}{\text{Time in seconds}} \times \frac{3}{5} = \text{knots}$$

COURSE AND TRACK

The word 'course' is rather loosely used afloat to indicate the direction a boat is travelling, and it is necessary to define it more precisely. **Course** is the direction of the boat's heading, and can be defined as True, Magnetic (after variation has been applied) or Compass (after both variation and deviation have been applied). But what the navigator needs to know, in areas of currents and tidal streams, is the line he makes over the seabed. I am going to follow flying practice and called this **track,** although it is also commonly called 'course made good'. When there is no current or leeway, **course** and **track** coincide. The line you draw on the chart from Port A, where you are now, to Port B where you wish to go is actually a track, although you will constantly hear people using terms like 'the course from A to B'. When you start making allowances for tidal streams and currents you will have to be more precise in distinguishing between them. At the moment we will go along with the widely-used generalisation for course, remembering only when marking course or track on the chart, you mark a **course** with **one arrow,** and **track** with **two arrows.**

So the principle of dead reckoning is that you draw a line on the chart down which you want to go, and measure its angle in relation to true north — let us say as in *Fig. 6.1* it is 145°. You correct this figure for variation, and then you have the heading to maintain on the compass. In the Virgin Islands as shown in *Fig. 6.1* variation is 10° West, so compass course is 155°M. I will assume your compass has no deviation.

Knowing or estimating your speed, you can make marks along this line which will tell you where you have reached at any given time. Suppose you are making six knots, as assumed in *Fig. 6.1,* using the scale of the chart at the level where you are, mark off nautical miles along your course line. At the end of one hour your position will be six miles along the line. This is your Dead Reckoning Position, usually shortened to DRP. It is convenient to mark the time against each plotted point. One hour later, assuming speed and direction have remained the same, you would be 12 miles along the line. What in fact you have decided to do, however, is to turn west and sail round Peter Island before dropping anchor for a swim.

It is at this stage that would-be navigators sometimes say 'Is that all? It's simple.'

Not that simple though. Because the brutal fact is that it is most unusual to proceed straight down your plotted line at a steady speed. A number of factors such as tidal stream, current or leeway are striving to push you aside, and they all have to be measured or estimated and allowed for as accurately as possible. In the Sir Francis Drake Channel in *Fig. 6.1,* although the rise and fall of tide is small, the tidal stream and current are considerable.

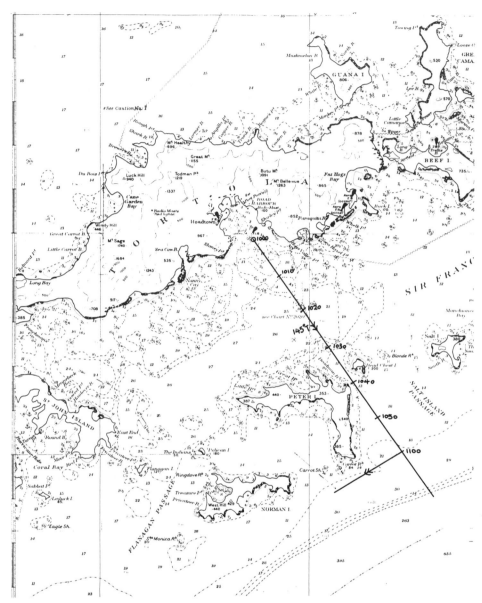

Fig. 6.1 The whole principle of D R navigation is demonstrated here. You draw a line
on a chart, measure its direction by protractor (in this case 145°T) and then set a course
on the compass that will take you down this line, checking your speed and calculating
how far you go in various units of time. One of the virtues of a DR plot like this is that, by
drawing it out, you can see where your actual progress varies from the plot, and you can
get an indication of your future travel.

In addition to all this the wind hardly ever allows sailing boats to stay travelling at a steady speed for long — which is why they are much harder to navigate properly than power cruisers, which can usually choose and maintain course and speed.

It is the delicate judgement of and allowance for these diverse factors which make navigation an art and not a science. It must by nature be imprecise. Even the aid of a well-adjusted radar set, which really small boats seldom carry, does not turn navigation into a precise and routine business, as many 'radar assisted collisions' have testified.

This book cannot conjure up for you the judgement necessary to become instantly a fully skilful navigator, any more than a text book can teach an art student to become another Leonardo. But it can, and I hope will, give you the necessary knowledge to find out and make allowance for the imponderables in a way that will enable you, while maintaining a due respect for the hazards of the sea, to go afloat in safety while you acquire the experience which makes an inspired navigator.

Plate 7. These two compact and efficient French handbearing compasses have become very popular. The Opticompas (right) has a top reading as well as its prism reading, so it can be put on the chart table as a tell-tale or course indicator. The rubber cases make them rugged enough to put in the pocket, but you should never steer or stand near the steering compass with one in the pocket or round the neck. Both have Beta-lights, for use in darkness. *(Photo: Channel Marine)*

WHAT YOU NEED FOR PLOTTING

Before you can start to do any navigational plotting, even practice at home, there are certain things you require. They are:

1. Suitable practice charts. You already have, I hope, a large scale chart of your home waters. Using practice charts when doing practice work at home is an economy compared with real charts, they cost only one tenth of the price. But when going to sea always use a proper chart. When you have got your eye in with plotting, you can get a fairly small scale chart that will allow you to plot passages from your local port to spots you might like to visit, such as the foreign coast across the water.

2. Soft pencils, eraser, dividers (one-handed ones shown on page 227 are best), pair of compasses, 18 inch transparent straight-edge or scale, 360 degree protractor, fair sized sheets of paper for drawing triangles.

3. *Reed's Almanac.* If you are only practising, even an out of date edition will do. If you are sailing in the western end of the English Channel a publication called *Channel West and Solent* will be found most useful.

4. A chart table — but if you want to be authentic keep it to a *small* table. If you do your 'homework' on the dining table, you may find doing the same on a chart-table less than a quarter the size is very difficult.

If you want to start off with the tools that you will need for the real thing (and getting used to them, right from the start, is a good thing), I give details in Chapter 12. Whatever you buy should be compact for easy stowage. There are a number of plotting devices which you may find useful in a small boat, and I enlarge on the subject in Chapter 12. But for the moment stick to a 360 degree protractor. If you are buying one specially, get a square one with parallel lines marked on it of the type called a Douglas protractor after its inventor; a plastic ruler to slide it along is useful. The American air plotter is nearly as good. (See *Figs. 6.2–6.3*).

At this stage you have the keen pleasure of finding that those tedious hours you spent at school doing geometry which, unless you are in a line of business like architecture, was never any use to you, had some value after all.

It is only very elementary geometry: measuring and laying off angles, using a pair of compasses to draw intersecting radii, and measuring distances with dividers. But getting the knack of doing so quickly, neatly and accurately will make your navigation more accurate too, and learning to do the necessary drawing with speed will reduce the amount of time you have to spend bent over the chart table, perhaps when the boat is bouncing about. If your stomach has a tendency to mutiny on a harsh beat to windward, as mine has, this is all to the good.

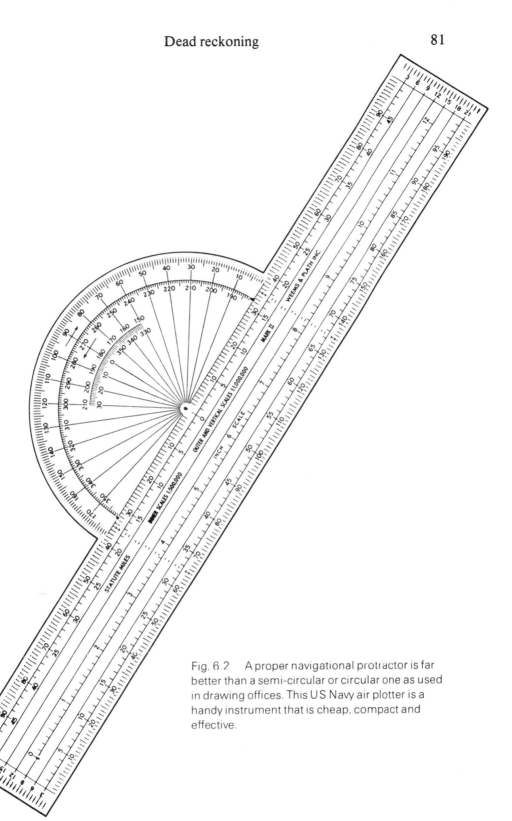

Fig. 6.2   A proper navigational protractor is far better than a semi-circular or circular one as used in drawing offices. This US Navy air plotter is a handy instrument that is cheap, compact and effective.

Give yourself some practice laying off courses, selecting suitable lines clear of dangers and measuring what they are against a meridian or parallel. Make a habit of labelling each line as you plot it, with its direction and the fact that it is true — not corrected for variation; modern practice is to do all plotting in true. Remember that the lines you want to make good over the seabed, regardless of where the boat's head points, are in fact **tracks**, and should be marked with two arrows. The **course** you select to make good any track, allowing for tidal set, you mark with one arrow.

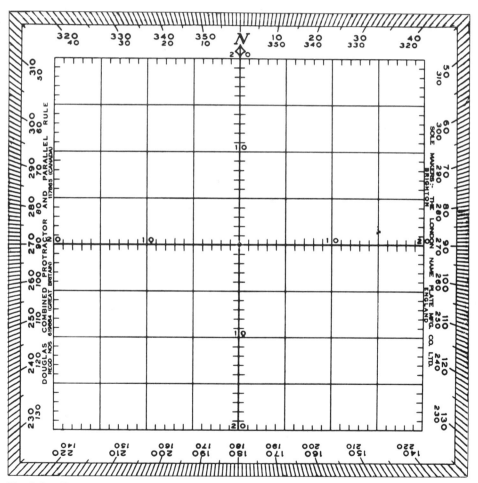

Fig. 6.3   The British made Douglas protractor is probably the best of all for the navigator with only a single plotting instrument. It is cheap, does everything the navigator needs, and is easy to stow; it is available in 5 ins and 10 ins sizes. A ruler to slide it along is useful.

ALLOWANCE FOR TIDAL STREAMS

We discussed earlier part of the problem of allowing for the effect of tidal streams when landmarks are in sight. Usually when approaching a port or a channel in a cross-tide, a transit pointing out the correct line makes things easy. Offshore the effect of the tidal stream is just as strong, but there is no transit or range to help you be sure that you are sailing along the line you want. The correct allowance has to be made by adjusting the course you steer on the compass.

A third of the time in a sailing boat is usually spent beating to windward, though it often seems more, and the wind will divide the navigational problem into two basic situations.

1. You are close-hauled, so you have to sail the best direction you can make in relation to the wind. The navigator records the average course made good, and plots the effect of tidal stream or current to obtain track and ground speed.
2. The wind is free enough for you to sail in any suitable direction to allow for tidal set. You then work out a course to steer to achieve the desired track on the chart.

A power cruiser is normally always in the second condition, which is another reason why navigating under power is easier. In a sailing craft it is not always clear which condition prevails until after you have worked out the effect of the tidal stream.

Finding the Tidal Stream

To correct for tidal streams or currents you must know as near as possible their speed and direction for each hour. I have already given details of the sources of these, and all I can say now is that the tide diamonds on some charts always seem to be spread so thinly that you have to work from one which is demonstrably not in the right place as far as your journey is concerned. The speed information on tidal atlases is not much more liberal.

Scattered among the arrows of the average tidal atlas are figures for the rate of the stream. These figures are given in knots and tenths of a knot, first for neaps and then for springs. In *Fig. 6.4,* which shows a page of the Channel Island area related to HW Dover, look at the figures on the arrows between Alderney and the French coast. The one to the west says 21,50. This means that at neaps the tide runs at 2·1 knots, and at springs at 5 knots. On the other side near the French coast it runs harder, and the figures here are 28,68 — 2·8

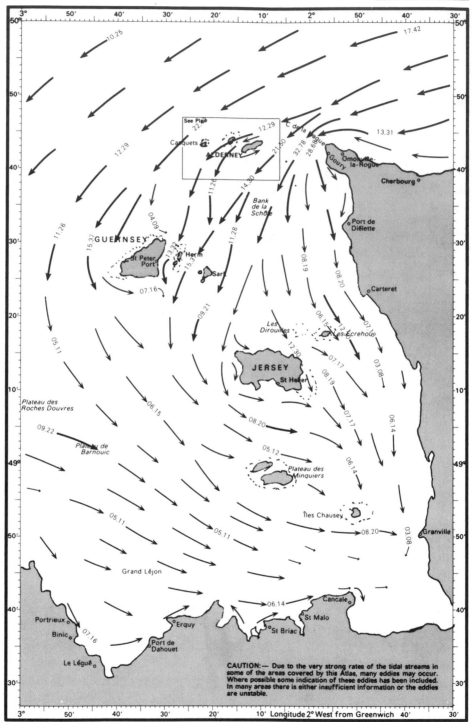

Fig. 6.4   A page from the British *Admiralty Tidal Atlas for the Channel Islands* shows how fast the tide runs in this popular area.

knots at neaps and 6·8 knots at springs; it reaches 7·8 knots in the middle. Which explains why it is a waste of time trying to sail through the Alderney Race without working your tides.

Note that tides are always presented as going *towards* the direction by which they are described — a tidal set of 100° is flowing eastwards. The alert reader will complain here that winds are always described by the direction *from* which they are blowing. This is just one of life's tiresome inconsistencies.

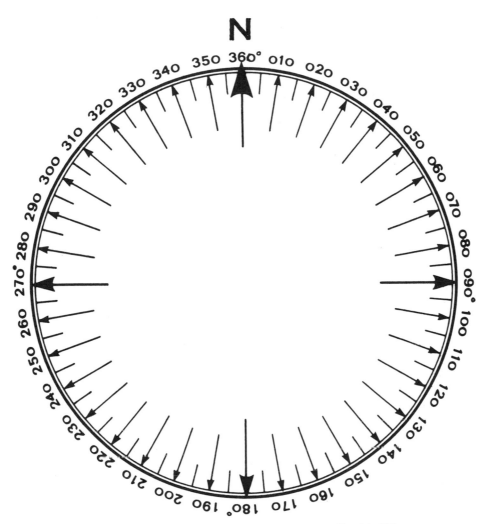

Fig. 6.5   Always try to keep in your mind's eye a compass rose like this. When conditions are bad, if you can visualise a course to within ten degrees until you can spare time to go below, it is much better than having to abandon the deck and get to work with a protractor.

Interpolation by eye for days between neap and spring rates is quite accurate enough for our purposes, and it is usually simplest to do it in decimals. If the spring rate is 2·4 knots and that for neaps is 1·6 knots, the rate half way between the two periods will be 2·0 knots.

To obtain the direction of the stream given by a tidal atlas you can, if you want, put a protractor against the arrow you select. But you will soon find yourself preferring to estimate the angle. This is one of the important disciplines to master when learning to become a navigator — always have a sort of giant protractor in your mind's eye that will, with practice, enable you to look at any line drawn on a chart and say to within ten degrees what direction it is pointing. *Fig. 6.5* is aimed at helping you to achieve this.

SPEED AND DISTANCE MEASURING

We have already seen that some way of measuring speed or distance is of great value, and a variety of devices have been invented to do this. The device is usually called a 'log', a name believed to be derived from the distant past when speed was measured by throwing a piece of firewood over at the bow, and timing by counting pulse-beats how long it took to reach a measured distance to a point on the poop. Later the log was cast astern in the form of a flat drogue-board which stayed stationary in the water uncoiling a reel of line — hence measuring the speed in knots, because the line was calibrated in length by knots tied in it at specific distances apart. Later still, in the 19th century, the log became a rotator trailed astern, the line being connected to a meter which mechanically converted the number of turns into miles run. This system is still in use, being more economical than the latest electronic logs (if you don't count the odd rotator taken by fish) and as accurate. Mechanical and electronic logs measure speed or distance run *through the water* and not over the ground, though there is a complicated system for big ships that measures speed over the ground in shallow water.

Electronic Logs

Electronic logs have improved greatly in the last twenty years, but many are still subject to error from the external impeller catching weed. Best of all are likely to be relatively recent electromagnetic or Doppler-effect devices, which have no external moving parts. They still suffer, however, from the fact that their external fittings are vulnerable to heavy-handed boatyard workmen too free with the paint, or from the growth of fouling. Logs are a case where the application of electronics to boats has been less than conspicuously successful, the old-fashioned rotator, or 'Patent' log, being often as accurate, and simpler to maintain as well as requiring no battery. But the electronic log is certainly more convenient to read.

Whatever the system of log, it must be calibrated properly for the boat in which it is used. In the trailed rotator log this is usually a matter of getting the length of line right. With an electronic log the calibration is done to allow for distortions of the waterflow close to the hull surface caused by air bubbles and irregular flow where the impeller or sensor operates, and careful allowances must be made for the effect of tidal streams during calibration runs. The best way will usually be to take the mean of two runs, up and down tide.

For the sake of DR plotting, I will assume now that you have a well calibrated reliable log, or else are working on a well judged system of speed estimation.

TRIANGLES OF VELOCITY

In school mathematics books, triangles of velocity, or vector diagrams, are usually introduced by a simile of a man rowing across a river at such and such a speed, pointing out how he doesn't end up at the spot opposite, but a certain distance downstream, according to the strength of the current. This is actively misleading, because it suggests that it is only currents running at right angles to your course which matter, and that there is a set distance in which the problem of working out the angle to steer can be resolved. The problem, in fact, is open-ended — at all times in tidal waters, except for a few minutes at the turn, the stream is carrying you somewhere; even when you are stationary in the water you are not stationary relative to the ground beneath, unless you put down an anchor — when you will once again no longer be stationary in the water.

Looking at *Fig. 6.6* let us assume that you are leaving point X shown, on a course of 270°T, making three knots through the water. At the end of one hour, with no tide, you would be at Y. But suppose, for the appropriate time, that the tidal atlas contains an arrow as shown, and let us also suppose that today it is neaps. The arrow shows the rate of the tidal stream to be 1·5 knots with its direction exactly the same as yours, namely 270°. After one hour you will not be at Y, but will have been carried on to Z as shown at **a**. Your speed over the ground has gone up from the three knots you are making through the water to $4\frac{1}{2}$ knots over the ground. If the tide had been in the opposite direction, but still exactly parallel to your course, your speed over the ground would have been cut from three knots to one and a half knots. This again makes the point raised under pilotage, about always travelling with as much favourable tide as possible.

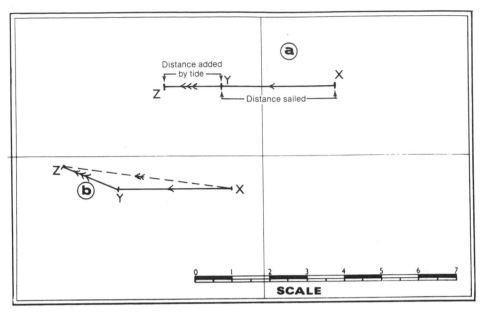

Fig. 6.6   In tidal waters the tidal stream is always carrying you somewhere, and you
are not going over the ground straight down the line you are pointing or at the speed
you are going through the water. At **a** you are heading 270°T at three knots for one
hour, which takes you from X to Y. During that time the tide is running 270°T at 1·5
knots, so you have been carried on to Z. This is a situation which seldom occurs, it being
much more common for the tide to be setting a bit across your course as at **b**. These are
'poor man's vector triangles' done to the scale of the chart; it is much better to do them
on a larger scale using speed as your scale.

Suppose, however, that the tide is not directly with or against you, but is
somewhat across your course as at **b** in *Fig. 6.6*. Only a proper triangle of
velocities, working on the correct tidal stream for the time in question, can tell
you what your actual direction and speed over the ground will be. This triangle
is a geometrical solution to the coastal navigator's main problem.

The solution depends not only on the accuracy of the factors used — and we
know some error is likely to creep in over the tidal streams — but also on the
accuracy of the drawing. Working on the average passage chart, which is
pretty small scale, an error of one degree in drawing will put you one mile out
after 60 miles. And this one degree error was one that, unlike the imponderables
such as tides, could easily have been avoided. So don't become confused in
your mind by the fact that everyone tells you that it is not possible to steer a
compass course to one degree. Perhaps not. But it *is* possible to plot to one
degree of accuracy, so do so whenever you can, even though you know that

your Estimated Position is only the middle of an area of greater or lesser size in which you consider you lie.

Having obtained our tidal direction and rate — suppose it to be 100°T, 2 knots — we must now apply it to our course.

Applying Effect of Tidal Stream

Some people like to plot on squared paper, but most use the blank backs of charts, drawing on them a few parallel lines to represent meridians, and at least one horizontal latitude line to make a base for measuring angles. When drawing triangles of velocity you need to make your basis one of **speed not distance**, because your plotting will hardly ever be done in convenient hourly chunks. If you work to a speed base, it is simple afterwards to convert figures like three knots for 49 minutes into a distance; you can use *Fig. 6.7,* or a pocket

Plate 8. This compact and economical dome-top compass made by Ritchie of Massachusetts is typical of many good small boat compasses. The sailing man should always check when buying this type of compass whether it has internal gimballing, those made for power boats often do not. There must be enough gimballing to allow 40° angle of heel at least. If the internals of the compass do not allow this, external gimballing must be used. *(Photo: Channel Marine)*

calculator, or the conversion table from *Reed's* or, if you are mathematically minded, work it out in your head.

For our first example, we will take the first of the two basic situations mentioned earlier, namely where you are close hauled and have to sail the best course you can in relation to the wind. As navigator, you get from the helmsman a report of the mean course he has averaged while sailing at six knots, and you want to plot where the tide has taken you. The time elapsed may be one hour, but more often it turns out to be an irregular time like 48 minutes, and you are drawing a plot because the wind has changed.

Let us assume the wind is just west of south allowing you to make 158°T on starboard tack. Draw on your paper a line in the correct direction, mark it with 158°T and the single arrowhead denoting a course line, as in *Fig. 6.8.* You can make six knots so you measure off six units to your scale; always make your scale large. In this case we will label the starting point A and the end of the six units B. From B draw your tide **vector** (all lines showing direction and speed are vectors) in the direction it is going, 100°T in our case, and mark off two units to

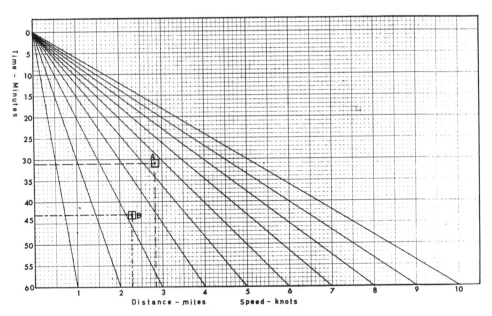

Fig. 6.7   This graphical method is one of the simplest ways of working out speed, time and distance problems. The broken lines with their point at A solve the problem: you have travelled for 31 minutes at 5·5 knots, how far have you gone? Going vertically downwards gives you a figure between 2·8 and 2·9 miles. At B you have to make 2·3 miles and your speed is 3·2 knots; how long will it take you? Go horizontally to the time scale — 43 minutes.

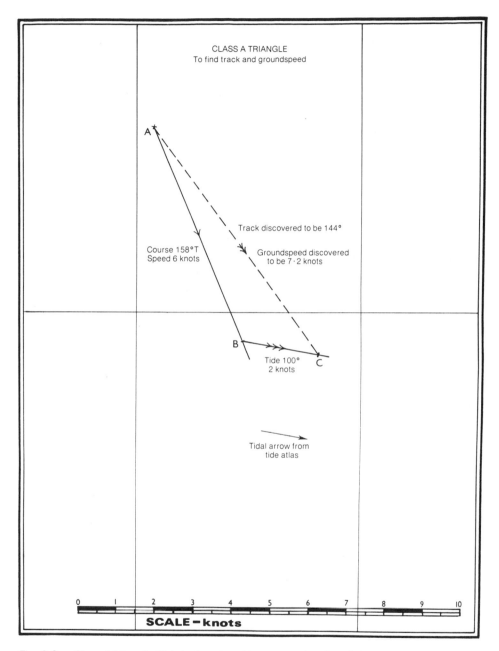

CLASS A TRIANGLE
To find track and groundspeed

A

Track discovered to be 144°

Course 158°T
Speed 6 knots

Groundspeed discovered
to be 7·2 knots

B

Tide 100°
2 knots

C

Tidal arrow from
tide atlas

0 1 2 3 4 5 6 7 8 9 10

SCALE – knots

Fig. 6.8   Class A triangle. This is the triangle you use when beating to windward or travelling in a power boat, when the effect of tide or current are not yet known. You plot the course steered from A to B, and then lay off tide or current from B to C, *down tide*. The broken line joining A and C is then the track, or course made good, and its length indicates ground speed.

represent 2 knots. The convention for a tidal vector is three arrows, so mark it accordingly. Let us call the end of it C.

Since you have not worked to the scale of your passage chart, C would *not* be your position even if you had drawn the triangle on the working chart. But, by joining AC and measuring its direction with the protractor, and its length to the same scale used for the other two vectors, you obtain your **track** and **speed** over the ground. The track you should have found is 144°T and the ground speed 7·25 knots.

You can now lay this track as a line directly on your plotting chart. Using the scale of the chart, you can plot on the chart your EP by marking off the time you have travelled along your track at your known **ground speed**. If you do this *before* you set off on course 158°T, you have the added advantage of seeing where you will actually travel, and can amend the course to avoid dangers. You can plot this line ahead of you, provided you remember that the tide is constantly changing in both strength and direction. It is likely to be significantly different after one or two hours, so you must then draw another triangle; the resulting track and ground speed will be different, depending on the change of tide or current.

Making Good a Desired Track

Now suppose that, instead of thrashing along close hauled and trying to hold up to 158°T, the wind is free so that, far from only making good a track of 144°T or even 158°T, the southerly wind has veered round to the north west so your starboard tack will let you steer right round as far as 270°T if you want to. You can thus decide what southerly track you want to make good and steer accordingly — the second of our two basic situations, in fact.

Turning to the passage chart, you rule a line between the breakwater at your departure point and the first large buoy in the estuary of your destination, to establish the track between the two; let us say that it is 168°T. There are no dangers such as shoals or overfalls on the way, so you decide that you can go direct. In these conditions your boat will make six knots. Draw this track on the back of the chart or on whatever sheet of clean paper you are using for plotting triangles of velocity, starting at point A once more (two arrows to identify it) as in *Fig. 6.9*; do not draw the line to any specific length (for you do not yet know your ground speed, and you can no more put boat speed through the water onto a track line than you can put speed made good over the ground onto a course line).

From point A, draw the tide vector (three arrows) towards the direction in which it is flowing; its other end is found from the speed of tide and gives point

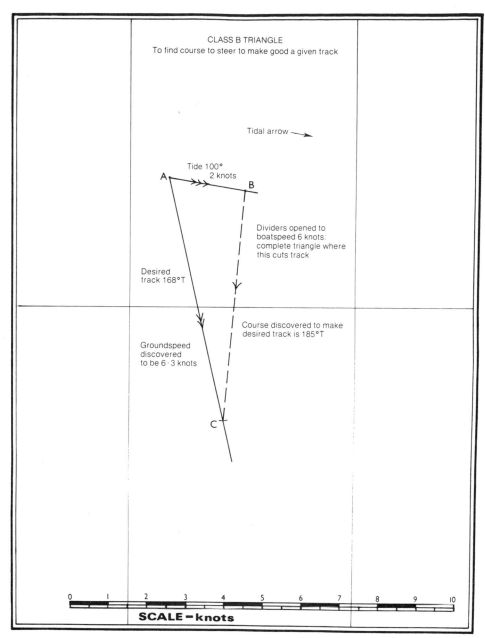

CLASS B TRIANGLE
To find course to steer to make good a given track

Tidal arrow ⟶

Tide 100°
2 knots

A   B

Dividers opened to
boatspeed 6 knots:
complete triangle where
this cuts track

Desired
track 168°T

Course discovered to make
desired track is 185°T

Groundspeed
discovered
to be 6·3 knots

C

SCALE – knots

Fig. 6.9   Class B triangle. When in a known tidal stream or current, you want to find
the course to steer to make good a given track, you use a Class B triangle. Note that the
tide is set off from point A, the starting point, as position C is yet to be discovered.

B. Opening your dividers or compasses to your speed through the water *to the same scale* (i.e. six units on the scale), lay the point on the end of the tide vector at B and describe an arc cutting your track. This is slightly easier to do with the pencil of a pair of compasses, but it is also quite simple with dividers, just making a small prick in the paper at the point where the arc cuts the track. Mark this point C, and join up B and C. BC is now the course you should steer to make good the track you want — 185°T in this case — and your ground speed is the length of AC, *measured on the same scale as the other two vectors*. It works out at a little under 6½ knots.

Triangle Classes

You have now resolved two types of triangle. The first, which from here on I shall describe as a Class A triangle, is one in which you know your course and boat speed through the water, together with the direction and speed of the tidal stream, and you require to know the track and ground speed. The second, which I shall call a Class B triangle, is one in which you know the track desired, the speed made through the water and the rate and direction of tide. You want to know the course to steer to make good this track and the groundspeed. Both types of triangle have their special uses.

From this it is clear that any triangular vector diagram of this nature has six characteristics: three directions and three speeds. If you know any *four* you can discover the other two by drawing the triangle (by using trigonometry you don't need as many as four, but this book is not for trig lovers).

This brings us to a further triangle, which I will call a Class C — you know your track very exactly between two fixes (A and B in *Fig. 6.10)*, and this also gives you your groundspeed; you also know the course you steered and your speed through the water, which can be plotted as A–C. From these four factors you can obtain the direction and strength of the tide, C–B.

The Class C triangle obviously has not got as many uses as the Class A and Class B, because the tide quickly changes rate and direction, and it only tells you what it was doing in the past. But on occasion it can be useful in inshore racing, or when approaching a mark in offshore racing where enough landmarks are visible to give you good fixes, provided it is realised that its answers are only short term.

A lot of local sailors may say knowingly 'What a longwinded way of going about it!' The answer to this is that a lot of knowing sailors frequently misjudge how far they need to stand on before tacking for a buoy lying in a strong current; you can see dozens of them any day of light wind. And in any case it is harder than you might think to judge the speed of the tide past a buoy —

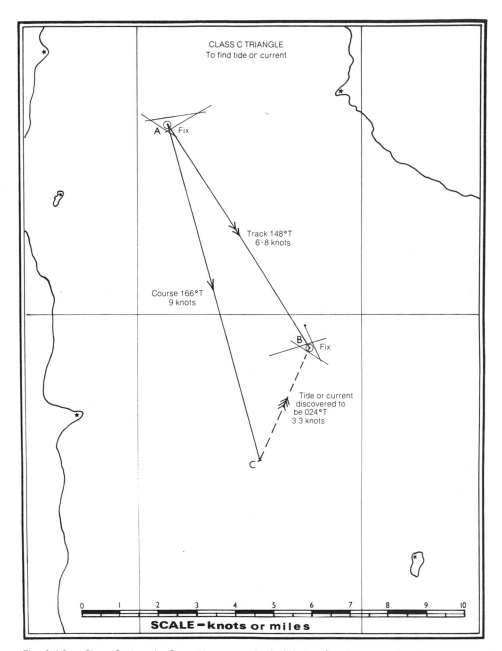

CLASS C TRIANGLE
To find tide or current

A ⊗ Fix

Track 148°T
6·8 knots

Course 166°T
9 knots

B ◇ Fix

Tide or current
discovered to
be 024°T
3.3 knots

C

0 1 2 3 4 5 6 7 8 9 10

SCALE — knots or miles

Fig. 6.10   Class C triangle. Sometimes, particularly in confined waters when frequent fixes are possible, you can find out what the tide is doing by working a triangle from two fixes (which give your track and ground speed), and then adding your course and speed through the water.

anyone who thinks he can be accurate to half a knot is a miracle man. And quite a few offshore races in light winds have been won by navigators who did quick Class C triangles. So don't reject it as valueless.

It is obvious that for general purposes while cruising, when many people try to keep off windward work, the Class B triangle is most frequently used. But the time always comes for a turn to windward, and then you must immediately appreciate that the situation calls for Class A. A great many books on navigation written for those who thunder about the sea with powerful engines almost entirely ignore the Class A triangle. The man under sail must *never* do this. The Class A triangle tells you your track and most of the time, particularly when dealing with transferred position lines, it is essential to know your track.

Tide Change on Passage

During a passage the tidal stream disobligingly does not remain constant. It varies in strength, and usually direction too, throughout the whole of the tide cycle, flood and ebb; at the turn, it will usually completely reverse its flow after a brief period of slack water. In some areas, instead of a reversal of flow after a time of slack water, the direction of tide will steadily change with a rotary motion, and there is no actual slack water. The words 'flow' and 'ebb' tend to be misleading and, though often used, they are in fact localised expressions. In the Solent, for instance, there is a tendency to speak of the 'ebb' having set in, meaning that to the west of Cowes the tide is running to the west. But in fact the level of water is often still rising and it is still flooding up Spithead and Southampton Water. For Long Island Sound, *Reed's* gives a special table for ebb and flow.

The majority of offshore passages are made with tidal streams or currents more or less at right angles to your course, and it is better to develop the habit of thinking of the water as 'eastgoing' and 'westgoing' or 'northgoing' and 'southgoing' as the case may be. The key thing to work out immediately is the time at which a tide reverses its direction. Lots of navigators write themselves passage check lists, and one of the most prominent things on them is a point like 'Tide turns to west at 0425 hrs'. This is an excellent idea, because it enables you to keep in mind as well as on your plot the direction of your actual motion, which it is far too easy to fall into the error of thinking is straight along the direction in which the bow of the boat is heading.

A point arising from this moment, when the tide reverses direction, is the way that for long periods of a tidal cycle the stream usually runs in approximately the same direction and, except at the first and last hour, at approximately the same speed. This can sometimes be used to cut down the number of triangles you have to draw, because you can average similar tides for two or three hours. If during this three hours the wind, and your resulting speed, change a great deal, you have to start again. On a six hour passage, for instance, it would be quite reasonable to do a bit of averaging where the tidal atlas or tidal table on the chart gave you these figures:

2100 — 078°, one knot
2200 — 088°, 1·9 knots
2300 — 091°, 2·1 knots
2359 — 093°, 2·1 knots
0100 — 094°, 1·8 knots
0200 — 099°, 1·1 knots

You could draw one triangle for the first two hours averaged together at 082°, 1.4 knots; the next two hours at 092°, 2·1 knots; and the last two hours at 096°, 1·5 knots.

Slightly greater exactitude might be achieved by plotting for the first and last hours at the figures given, and averaging the central four hours. Either method will cut down the amount of time spent working at the chart table without introducing too much inaccuracy and, since sometimes conditions are bound to be bumpy and unpleasant, you will appreciate any way of reducing chartwork.

By careful study of your tidal atlas you will soon see ways of averaging your tides to reduce work. But resist the temptation to do as many people do on what is hoped will be a 12 hour crossing with the tidal streams directly across the track; they assume the tides will cancel each other out. In a sailing boat, a 12 hour passage in which she proceeds at a steady speed in an unvarying wind is unheard of. The wind weakens round dusk or dawn, picking up again later, quite small cloud changes vary the wind, and even the trade winds vary during a passage of some hours.

It is a fallacy that has appeared in print, that allowing tidal streams to cancel each other out will get you to the other side faster. It will not, even if the wind does remain constant — try working it out on a chart of a suitable passage — the Needles Channel to Cherbourg is very suitable. Correcting at least every two hours, thereby keeping closer to the rhumb line, will always get you there faster, and it keeps you in a better position to take advantage of any change in circumstances.

I am not saying that you should stick to the shortest line between where you are and where you want to be in all circumstances — there may be excellent reasons (such as a forecast change of wind) for selecting a track to one side of the rhumbline, and I shall have something to say later about what is usually called the strategy of a passage. But do not let the tide shove you about freely because you are too idle to correct for it, it is the beginning of sloppy habits that will one day land you where you had no wish to be . . .

There is another aspect of tidal streams that seems to embarrass inexperienced navigators. All the time they are out of sight of land they allow handsomely for tidal streams; but the moment they, or perhaps their helmsman, see their target they tend to act like a horse sighting the stable door, and point straight for it. The tide will still go on swishing you away, and you might find yourself tiresomely at sea in a failing wind for hours longer than you intended, when you hoped to be sampling the fleshpots of some foreign port. If there is no prominent landmark like an offshore rock to demonstrate by its transit effect that you are sliding sideways, it may be some time before you notice. You would not be the first navigator to announce proudly to the family: 'There's Cherbourg', only to say crossly two hours later: 'I've changed my mind, we're going to Alderney instead.'

Keep to a Drill

It is wise to decide on a set way of doing your plotting and triangle drawing and stick to it. The tidier and more legible any marks made on the chart are, the less the chance of error and the longer the chart will last because, when the passage is over, you will have to rub them all out ready for the next trip. *Fig. 6.11* is quite a good example of how not to do it. Some good habits are:

(a) Note the direction of any line you draw on the chart against it immediately, always in true.
(b) Work to the largest convenient scale when drawing triangles, and *always use a speed, not a distance* scale.
(c) Mark your course with *one* arrowhead, your track with *two* and the tide with *three*. Quite often the tide is going faster than your speed through the water and, if you were checking back on your triangle, you might make a mistake.

Working on Chart Scale

When going to windward some people regard completing a separate Class A triangle as a waste of time, and they draw a 'poor man's' vector diagram to the scale of the chart. They mark in their course, add the tidal arrow, all in exact scale to the chart, and say that their position at the end of one hour is at the end of the tidal arrow — at C in *Fig. 6.11*. This has two disadvantages:

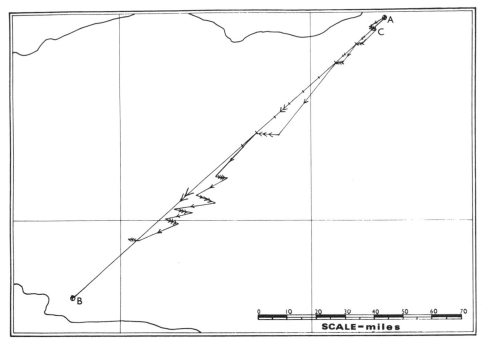

Fig. 6.11   This is a 'poor man's vector diagram' done to the scale of the chart. The triangles are so small that they introduce unnecessarily large errors, cover up important points on the chart for taking fixes as at C, and make it difficult to identify important characteristics of wind or tide conditions. They should be avoided.

1. You do not complete the triangle and find your track and groundspeed, which it is important to know when planning strategy to get to a certain point to windward, or when you want to **transfer** a position line, a valuable aid to fixing that we come to in Chapter 7.

2. Most charts used for plotting passages are on a fairly small scale, so that both ends of the passage can be included. Consequently any vector diagrams done to the scale of the chart will be so tiny that gross inaccuracies are likely to creep in.

The chart in *Fig. 6.1*, with a scale of about an inch to the mile, is about the smallest scale at which it is possible to do good triangles straight on the chart. There are occasions, however, when this method comes in handy. Suppose you have held on a steady course and speed to windward for four hours in open water — an unlikely though not impossible situation. If you then add the tidal arrows for those four hours onto the end of your course arrow, working to the scale of the chart, the end of the tidal arrows give you your position much more

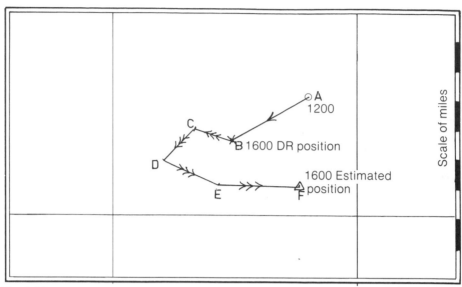

Fig. 6.12   The only poor man's vector diagram which is useful is when you are almost becalmed in open water, and changing tides are carrying you about. Say that from A at 1600 you have ghosted along until at 1600 your DR position is at B. You can then draw vectors for the tides during this period to the scale of the chart, making your estimated position finally at F. This should never be done if there are any dangers nearby. You should remember that you have not travelled directly from A to F, but have been carried about all over the place.

quickly than by working out your Class A triangles, and transferring the result to the chart, *which should always be on as large a scale as possible.*

This can be called a Multiple Class A diagram, if you like definitions. You could find it useful in conditions of light air, when you are out of sight of land, but when you know that the tide is whistling you about the place. Suppose in *Fig. 6.12* you have made good, you reckon, no better than about three miles in four hours, on course 240°T (maybe you have no engine, or it has broken down). Meanwhile you are in an area where the tides sometimes run at over three knots. Use the largest scale chart you can, plot your starting position A, add the line of your course and distance travelled to B; then add your four hours of tide to C, D, E, and F. Your estimated position at the end of four hours is at F. But you must realise that this is a very low grade EP, since any one of those tidal arrows may be inaccurate. All you can say for it is that it is considerably better than saying your DR position is at B.

The other point to remember is that your track is *not* AF — you have been swishing about all over the place at the behest of the tide. For this reason never drift about unthinkingly for long periods when there are dangers around to which the tide can carry you. If you idled about as supposed in *Fig. 6.12* somewhere close to a major reef, you would be in trouble, and you would have asked for it.

Leeway and Surface Drift

Besides the effect of tidal stream, there is another factor which makes a boat become diverted from her heading — leeway. Particularly noticeable in sailing boats and motor sailors going to windward, it is the tendency for the wind to blow the boat sideways through the water (*Fig. 6.13*). In a tubby, shallow-draft boat with a lot of windage aloft combined with little grip on the water below, it might under some conditions affect the resultant course by as much as 15 degrees. This angle-off varies with the design of boat, the helmsman, the wind and sea conditions, and the course being steered relative to the wind, so there is a good deal of fine judgement in estimating it correctly.

In periods of strong winds there is a further factor known as surface drift — the wind getting hold of the surface layer of the water. It is less critical on a boat with a deep keel, but all sailing vessels are subject to it in winds over about force 5 and, in strong winds, power boats and even large steamships are also vulnerable.

Since estimation of leeway and surface drift is dependent on many factors, it can only be judged in each individual case. But the table on page 102 gives a starting point to work from.

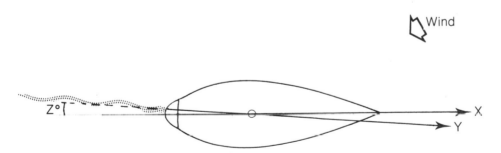

Fig. 6.13   Allowance for leeway is important to a good plot. In a sailing boat going to windward as here, the boat's head is pointing at X; her actual direction through the water (her wake course) is towards Y. To estimate the angle of leeway it is quickest to assess the angle Z between the boat's wake and her centreline. Leeway applies to power craft too. It is best to enter it in the deck log as an immediate estimation, and the navigator can then work from a course after leeway.

APPROXIMATE ANGLE OF LEEWAY AND SURFACE DRIFT COMBINED

Strength and direction of wind

Type of boat	Light airs		Force 2 to 4		Force 4 to 7		Force 8 to 10	
	Forward of beam	On or aft of beam	Forward of beam	On or aft of beam	Forward of beam	On or aft of beam	Forward of beam	On or aft of beam
Fine-lined deep keel racing craft	3°	2°	2°	1° or less	5°	3°	8° to 10°	4°
Well designed offshore racer 40 feet long	4°	3°	2°	1°	6°	4°	12°	5°
Tubby twin keel sailing cruiser 28ft long; draft 3·5 feet (1m)	10°	5°	8°	4°	15°	10°	25°	15°
Displacement motor cruiser with steadying sail; about 35ft long (under power)	nil		4°	6°	5°	18°	20°	25°
High-speed light planing power boat 35ft long under power (speed cut over Force 7)	nil		2°	nil	2° or less	2° or less	20°	30°

It would not surprise me if the table roused howls of disagreement or even fury, but it is based on considerable personal observation and experience. There are various points to note:

1. Leeway will always be worse with a poor or inexperienced helmsman, especially at night, and with those who tend to pinch going to windward.
2. The sharp rise in the leeway angle above force 7 is due to the addition of surface drift, combined with probable reduction of the boat's speed through cutting down sail.
3. The large leeway angles at low speed are the ones to note most urgently, because these are the conditions when they are most often forgotten.
4. With a sailing boat the leeway angle decreases as she comes off the wind to a reaching condition, with a power boat it increases.

The traditional way of assessing a boat's leeway angle is to estimate by eye the angle between her fore and aft line and her wake, but this is harder to do than it sounds, and will take no account of surface drift in strong winds.

I am guiltily aware that quite a few years ago I rushed into print with a statement advising people to ignore leeway in boats with good windward performance, because of the tendency of such craft always to make good a course a little better than the compass heading, thus cancelling out leeway. I can only plead that my change of outlook is due to:

(a) wider experience in many different types of boat and sea conditions.
(b) the way boats generally have become lighter and beamier, and have smaller keels, so they tend to make a bit more leeway.
(c) more precise evaluation of sailing craft performance factors through the increased use of electronics.

APPLYING LEEWAY. You can apply leeway either to the **course**, or the discovered **track**, but be careful not to apply it twice. Always enter in the log the amount of allowance made for leeway, and better still enter a course after leeway, what Americans sensibly call the wake course.

SURFACE DRIFT WHEN AHULL. It is especially important to make as correct as possible an estimate of surface drift when lying ahull in heavy weather. Under these conditions, when chartwork is difficult and the mind somewhat numbed, it is common to estimate only the *visible* sideways (or partially sideways) movement through the water — many boats lying ahull make noticeable forward motion, and some even work to windward. But, in addition to this, the whole surface of the sea has a leeward motion, whose effect varies only with the boat's draft. It will be much more marked in craft of shallow draft, even when they have a large keel area. It is keel depth which counts in this case. If you are familiar with your boat's response to lying ahull, you can make your calculation of the effect of surface drift in various strengths of wind above force 7 while you are ashore or snugly at anchor, and note it down in some easily located place such as inside the cover of the logbook for various strengths of wind.

I personally — and this is a highly personal thing between a man and the gods of wind and water — would allow, in a boat of six feet draft lying ahull, one knot at force 8 and two knots at anything over force 9. I would increase the figure by 50 per cent for a boat of four feet draft. These wind forces mean nearly continuous average strength, not just occasional isolated gusts, and with any luck you will never meet them anyway. Although the amounts are not large, you are likely to be subject to them for a number of hours.

This surface drift figure must be added to your calculation of what the boat is making, which is largely dependent on any sail you may be carrying and the underwater hull shape of the boat you are in, corrected for the tidal stream, and then plotted. Unless you are in wide open water, many miles from any danger, which includes shipping lanes, always plot a position at least once every hour when lying ahull, unless catching up with sleep to avoid exhaustion has become more urgent.

TRAVERSE TABLES

Those with any knowledge of mathematics may be wondering at all this elementary geometry and untidy lines all over a nice new chart, knowing that with trigonometry the position can be calculated without drawing any lines. The traditional way of doing this is with traverse tables, which are lists of resolved right angle triangles which enable you to work out your latitude and longitude after making a certain distance on a certain course. They also enable you to find out the course and distance to steer to go from one place defined by latitude and longitude to another. Old salts lay great faith in traverse tables, though they were really only a crutch for people who could not, or would not in the case of mean owners of coasters, buy the proper charts.

There are a considerable number of snags to traverse tables that you should at least be aware of, and it is now realised that they are obsolescent with the provision of proper charts for all parts of the world. The snags are:

1. A course worked out by traverse table does not tell you that it passes

over, perhaps onto, or dangerously near a hazard such as an isolated shoal, outcrop, or even an oil rig. You still need a passage chart.

2. They are only valid for distances between about 50 miles and 500 miles. Below the smaller distance use of the chart is a must, and the system on which traverse tables are constructed does not allow them to be used for distances over a few hundred miles, because of the curvature of the earth.

3. There are many different ways of presenting traverse tables, but many of them (including those in *Reed's*) save space by working them only for a 90° quadrant, so they require tricky adaptation for the other three quadrants, which I have seen people make into a source of error. Best of the 360 degree traverse tables are probably Bowditch, the incomparable *American Practical Navigator*. But this is a bulky and expensive volume that not everyone has space for and can afford to carry.

These are quite considerable snags for the coastal navigator. However, traverse tables, thoroughly mastered, have a value for those making ocean passages well away from any land, when a 24 hour run can conveniently be worked out on a plotting sheet to a Lat and Long which is then logged, without marking up the small scale ocean chart with close-together marks. Instead the chart will be marked at, say, three day intervals.

Many people are put off traverse tables by the mysterious phrases used in them particularly when, as is usual, they are contracted, often without any punctuation. The phrases are:

Dlat, or sometimes even **Chlat;** these are the contractions for difference of latitude or change of latitude. If a ship sails from somewhere on latitude 48° 30′ N to 51° 20′ N the Dlat is 2° 50′. This is 170 nautical miles.

Dlong or **Chlong:** this is the same thing for longitude. A snag arises here though — an angular distance in longitude cannot be expressed directly in nautical miles due to the way meridians of longitude converge at the poles. To use the traverse tables it is converted to **Departure:** this is a figure in nautical miles for the difference in an east west direction between two longitudes. It is obtained from the tables or by applying a trigonometrical formula to the longitudes and the middle point between the two latitudes concerned, known fairly simply as **Midlat.**

Largely because snag 1 above makes traverse tables unsuitable for the kind of coastal navigator this book is aimed at, I am saying no more here about them. If you have them, or study them in *Reed's*, you will find they are not unduly difficult, and have their uses when you get on to astronomical navigation and ocean voyaging.

A good scientific calculator can be used as a substitute for traverse tables.

EXERCISES

6.1. You wish to reach a point 32 miles away, which lies 245°T from your present position. The wind is south west exactly, and the tide is setting 160°T at 2·1 knots. Assuming your boat speed is 5 knots, what sort of triangle should you draw?

6.2. In the same circumstances, which is the better tack to start on?

6.3. After one hour the tide has turned and is setting 340°T at 1·2 knots. The wind has also veered to north west. What should you do, and what sort of triangle should you draw?

6.4. You are steering 170°T and making 2·4 knots through the water. The tide is setting 280°T at 4·2 knots. What is your (a) actual track and (b) ground speed? And (c) what class of triangle have you drawn?

6.5. You have sailed for 1 hr 48 minutes, and your well-calibrated log says that you have gone 9·2 miles. What is your speed?

6.6. You have travelled for 51 minutes at 3·1 knots. What distance have you covered?

6.7. You estimate your speed at 6·7 knots. (a) How long will it take you to travel 12·6 miles? and (b) if, after 45 minutes, your speed drops to 4·5 knots, how long will it take you altogether?

Answers are in Appendix, page 299.

7
Fixes and the sextant inshore

Since all position plotting has to be done on the basis that it is open to error due to factors such as careless steering, tidal streams not running according to the book, or excessive leeway, it is important to take fixes whenever suitable landmarks offer an opportunity.

BACK BEARINGS

When making a passage out of sight of land, the most useful early fixes are from position lines taken soon after setting off, as a check that the tide is acting as predicted. These are usually taken over the stern as you leave the shore behind, and are commonly referred to as back bearings for obvious reasons. Don't wait to take them until land is disappearing from view. Plot a couple of good fixes before you have sailed four or five miles (most good navigators take them at least every mile or two until they are ten or twelve miles out, when the landmarks will be becoming vague). It is useful to have a firm idea of your track at the start so that you can compare the tidal set with the predictions; you need an accurate basis from which to set off into the blue.

As you get further out to sea, transits or ranges cease to be of much value, because the objects are hard to pick out and the spacing between them becomes too small in relation to your distance away. A basic characteristic of all compass bearings is that, the further you are from the landmark you are sighting, the less accurate will be the bearing, as shown in *Fig. 5.4*. If land is still in sight, however, there is usually one object reasonably close to give a single bearing, but other objects to give suitable crossing position lines dwindle away. You must remember that a compass bearing of an object 20 miles distant is very inaccurate.

Assessing the reliability of position lines derived from dwindling landmarks is one of the basic arts of the navigator, and is something which you must learn. Ideally, all position lines would be infallible, meeting at a precise point. In practice, of course, they are not and do not; if you ever get three or more bearings which meet at a point when plotted, you will have cheated somewhere.

VALUE OF THE SEXTANT

Suppose you are about seven miles out to sea heading 180°T. Earlier you got a good fix from back bearings, and nearly astern is a lighthouse on which you can still get a reasonable bearing, but the objects further to the west that you used for the earlier fix are now too far off to be reliable, and any bearings would give too fine an angle of cut.

If you had some means of measuring fine angles accurately you would still be able to get a fix of sorts. This task the sextant performs most satisfactorily. It also has a variety of other ways of giving you position lines.

Many people who ought to know better say that taking a sextant aboard a small boat is an encumbrance and a waste of time. In fact a sextant earns its keep most of all when cruising in confined waters full of rocks and offlying dangers. When avoiding or rounding specific dangers, which usually carry a mark with a charted height of some kind, by far the quickest and easiest check of safe distance off with the minimum of plotting can be made with a sextant, using what is called a **distance off by vertical angle**, explained below. The chief objection to the sextant for small boats, its cost, which used to be high enough to be prohibitive, no longer applies. An adequate plastic sextant for coastal use costs less than a compass or an echo-sounder; see Plate 25

From the photo you can see that the sextant has two mirrors, one fixed and covering the right half of a piece of glass so that you can look at an object partly through the glass and with the mirror close alongside. The other mirror is

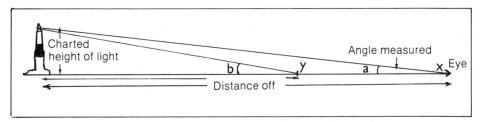

Fig. 7.1   When you approach any tall object — it may be a lamp post as you walk along the street, or a lighthouse as here — the angle it makes (mathematicians call it 'subtends') at your eye increases as you get closer. If you measure the angles **a** and **b**, the fact that **a** is smaller immediately tells you that **x** is further from the lighthouse than **y**. If you know the height of the object whose angle you are measuring (lighthouse heights are charted), you can immediately find out how far away it is, either by trigonometry or, more easily, from a table.

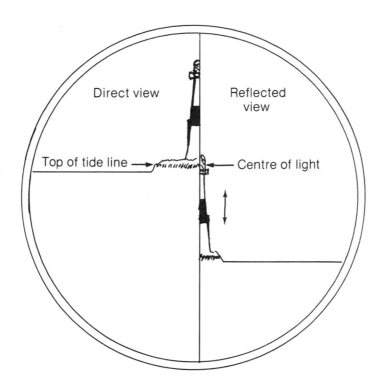

Direct view

Reflected view

Top of tide line ⟶ ⟵ Centre of light

Fig. 7.2   To measure the angle which a lighthouse subtends at your eye, you align the top in one half of the sextant horizon mirror with the base in the other half. A lot of people when first meeting the sextant think that the requirement is to make the images coincide, as with a rangefinder. It is not : when using a single object it is the *separation* which measures the angle.

attached to an arm that pivots and has a reading against a scale of angle. If you set the arm to zero, what is reflected in the pivoting mirror and the fixed mirror will continue what is seen through the clear glass, provided there is no error in the instrument. If there is any error, called **index error**, a straight line such as the horizon will have a break in it, and a small correction must be made to the reading. If you sight through the eyepiece or telescope and the clear glass, say at the foot of a lighthouse, and swing the arm until the top of the light is visible

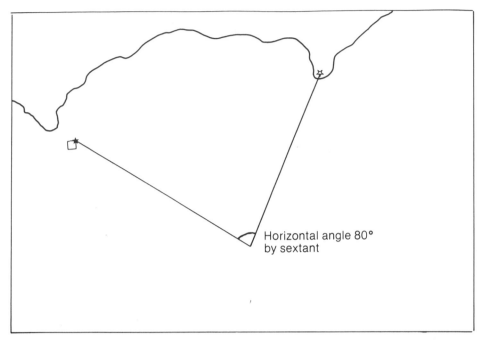

Horizontal angle 80°
by sextant

Fig. 7.3   If you turn the sextant on its side with the handle underneath, you can measure a
horizontal angle, which has special uses in navigation. Here you do make the two objects
coincide.

reflected through the two mirrors, you have measured the angle that the
lighthouse subtends at your eye, and you can read it off the scale. Even a cheap
sextant should measure angles to within one sixtieth of a degree — one minute.

At this stage we will ignore the mechanical details (see Chapter 14) and will
consider the sextant merely as a device for measuring angles with precision and
in a form handy for use at sea. It can measure angles in either the vertical plane
— up and down, as you will have seen in pictures of people 'shooting the sun'
— or in the horizontal plane, when it is turned on its side with the handle
underneath, to measure an angle between two objects in a plane parallel with
the surface of the sea. Not surprisingly, when the instrument is held upright, the
angle is a **vertical sextant angle** (see *Fig. 7.1 — 7.2*) and when it is held
horizontally it is called a **horizontal sextant angle** (*Figs. 7.3 — 7.4*).

Any angle measured with a sextant is much more precise than one derived
from a compass, and can be sub-divided more finely. Two bearings accurate to
one degree taken with a compass would be remarkable in a small boat, and
would have to be corrected for variation; they would be open to deviation to an

unknown degree, depending on where the navigator was standing in relation to magnetic influences. With a sextant, even in a tossing boat, it is not very difficult to measure an angle to an accuracy of one minute of arc; a high grade sextant for astronomical navigation will, when skilfully used, measure down to about ten seconds, a second being a sixtieth part of a minute (which in turn is a sixtieth part of a degree).

Corrections may have to be applied to a sextant angle for errors in the individual instrument, but they are less productive of trouble than variation and deviation as applied to a compass bearing. It takes practice to become

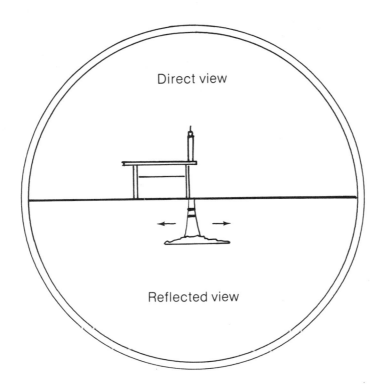

Fig. 7.4   With the sextant on its side, you measure the angle by looking straight at one object, and then swing the other by moving the sextant arm until they coincide in a vertical line.

Plate 9. The efficient and compact Brookes and Gatehouse Harrier speedometer and log, which has an amplified fine reading dial so the effect on performance of minor sail trim changes can be assessed. *(Photo: Brookes and Gatehouse)*

proficient but, once the knack of using the instrument is acquired, it is quick and easy. The chief error is called index error, illustrated in *Fig. 7.5*, when the sextant does not read an absolutely true zero.

Sextant Angle and Bearing

So let us return to the position discussed earlier, when you were about seven miles south of your main landmark and your second object was rather a long way off to the west (*Fig. 7.6*). You have a good compass bearing of the lighthouse at 008°T. Then take the sextant, which normally has a low-magnification eye piece acting as a mild telescope, turn it so that the handle is below, and measure the horizontal angle between the lighthouse and your secondary landmark, the tower. It will be simplest to sight the sextant directly at the object hardest to see, and then swing the arm to bring the more prominent lighthouse across until one is over the other, where the clear glass meets the fixed mirror.

Let us assume that the angle you have measured is 15° 10′, which you can safely take as 15°. You first plot the compass bearing of the light. You could, mathematically, get a bearing angle of the other object by subtracting 11° from your compass bearing, and then plotting in the normal way. But there is a much easier and more effective system. Draw an angle of 15° on a piece of tracing paper and lay it over the chart so that the line representing the compass bearing is over your plotted line. Slide the tracing paper up and down this line until the other line of the angle coincides with the object you sighted. Then prick through the point of the angle with the dividers and that is your position. Remember that, due to the fineness of the angle at which the lines cross, this is not a particularly good fix; it is merely much better than the result of two finely-crossing compass bearings, as shown in *Fig. 7.7*. The fix can also suffer from any error in the compass bearing that forms half of it.

DISTANCE OFF BY VERTICAL ANGLE. Suppose you are passing an isolated landmark such as a lighthouse on an offshore rock, whose height is charted. The larger the angle of the object at your eye, the closer you are to it (*Fig. 7.1*). But since you know the height of the object, if you measure the angle at **a** in *Fig. 7.1* you can find the distance between X and the foot of the

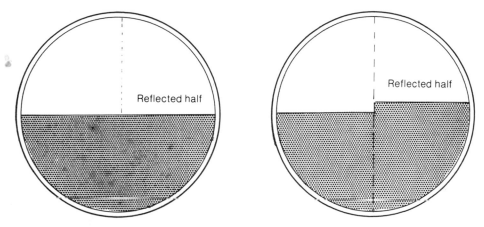

Fig. 7.5   To check a sextant for index error, look at a horizontal line at least two miles away — the horizon is usually best. Set the sextant to zero, and the horizon should look as it does at the left. If there is a break in the line there is index error (right). Its amount is the extent that the reading is out when you have brought the horizon into line. This amount must be applied to every sextant reading, and can quickly be done without any figuring. If the reading is less than zero when the horizon is straight, the correction is *off the arc* and should be added to all readings. If the reading is *on the arc* the correction must be subtracted.

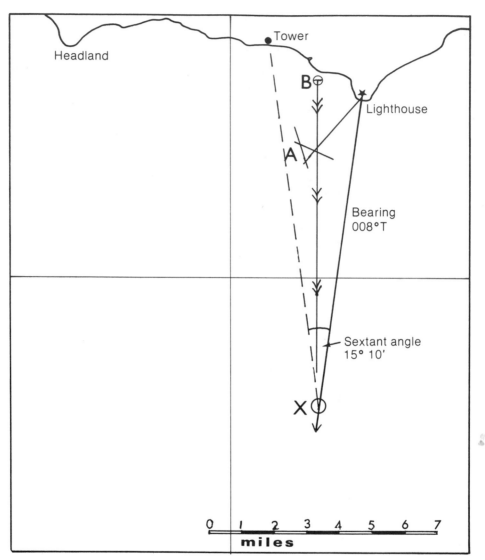

Fig. 7.6   If you have a single object of which you can obtain a reasonable compass bearing, but other objects are at too fine an angle or too far distant for accuracy, you can improve the fix by using the much more precise sextant for measuring the angle between two charted landmarks, such as the lighthouse and the tower in this example. Here you sailed from B and got a good fix at A. By the time you got to the region of X, the headland to the north west is no longer visible, and the tower is only just in sight. Measuring by sextant the angle between the lighthouse and the tower is much better than plotting two compass bearings. Plot the compass bearing of the lighthouse first, then draw the sextant angle on a piece of tracing paper, slide it up and down the bearing line, and prick through at the point when the western line is exactly over the tower. Remember that this is still only a moderate fix.

lighthouse. There are a number of ways of doing this, those who fancy their mathematics, or carry a scientific calculator with them, can do it by trigonometry. But since this book is for sailors who want no truck with trig, we will concentrate on easier ways.

The handiest is to refer to the 'Distance off by vertical sextant angle' tables in *Reed's* which allow for heights in either metres or feet. They can be found by looking up in the index 'Sextant, distance off by'. The tables run to several pages, and enable you to find distance off up to seven miles on objects up to 2000 feet, or 610 metres, in height.

Across the top of the tables is given a large selection of possible heights, in both feet and metres, and on each side is the distance off in nautical miles and cables for each angle tabulated. It is easy to interpolate when necessary, but the angles are accurate to one cable, 200 yards, by direct inspection.

Inman's, Nories' and *Burton's* tables provide them, but small boat sailors will find *Reed's*, all in one volume, the most convenient. Vertical sextant angles are sometimes referred to as 'masthead angles', because for centuries warships kept station on each other by measuring with the sextant the angle of the

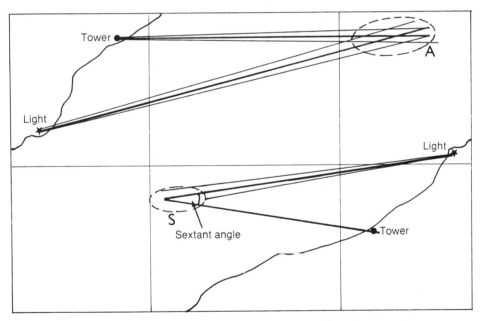

Fig. 7.7   These two fixes compare the virtue of two compass bearings crossing at a fine angle at A, and a compass bearing aided by a sextant bearing at S. The compass bearings have the cone of error indicated by the fainter lines, whereas the sextant angle fix can be regarded as almost precise and having only the error of the single compass bearing which comprises half of it.

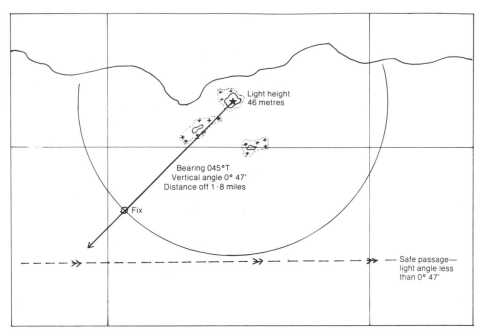

Light height
46 metres

Bearing 045°T
Vertical angle 0° 47'
Distance off 1·8 miles

Fix

Safe passage—
light angle less
than 0° 47'

Fig. 7.8   Where a landmark or lighthouse of charted height has dangers off it, drawing an arc of safe distance round it and working out the vertical angle for this arc from the table in *Reed's* is a most practical way of keeping a safe check. So long as the angle on the sextant is less than the calculated angle you are in safe water. A compass bearing combined with the danger angle can give a fix as shown.

mainmast of the next ship. The height of mast of all units was carried in each ship so that exact station could be maintained.

With your distance off known, you have the radius of a circular position line, which you can easily plot with a simple pair of compasses, even the schoolroom type will be good enough; see *Fig. 7.8.* If you have only a pair of dividers, these can be used, putting a series of pencil dots beside the rotating tip to give you a circular line.

FIX BY BEARING AND VERTICAL ANGLE.   The vertical sextant angle is valuable when rounding a headland marked by a light, which has offshore rocks at its foot. With your compasses plot an arc clear of all these dangers, and with a reasonable safety margin. Measure the radius of this circle then, using the correct height for the light, you can work back through the Vertical Angle tables to find the angle corresponding with the arc you have plotted. Set this angle on the sextant and keep it handy. Occasional sighting with the sextant will tell you that you are outside all the dangers, provided the angle of the light does not get any *larger*. If it has become larger, you are too close. If you work out any distance off, and have taken a compass bearing too, you have a fix, a kind very useful when passing an isolated light.

DOUBLE DANGER ANGLES.   Sometimes you want to round a point which not only has dangers nearby but also isolated dangers further off, with a navigable passage in between. You draw on the chart two arcs or circles of safety, working out the required angles, again from the table. Plot an approximate compass course to steer, but the sextant will show how you are lying without any plotting. If the inner angle is too large you are too close in,

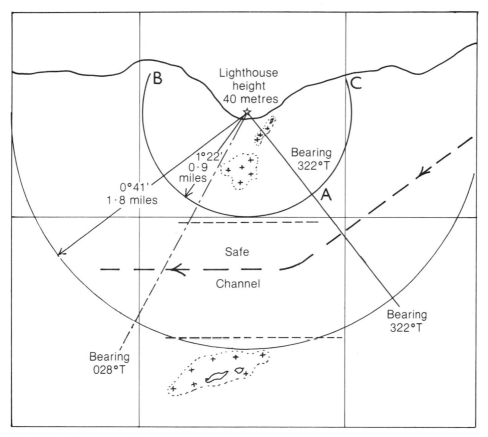

Fig. 7.9   Where you wish to pass between an inner and an outer danger, two safety angles can be set which, combined with check bearings, make the passage quite safe. The angles should always be written down, not just memorised.

and when the outer angle gets too small you are closing the offshore danger and must head inshore. Combined with bearings a very precise path through dangers can be plotted (*Fig. 7.9*).

Height of Tide

There are two aspects of vertical angles that should always be borne in mind when plotting. The first is that the height of any charted object is given above Mean High Water Springs. This condition only exists for a few moments, and only at spring tides. For exactness, the height of tide should be obtained and subtracted from the height of high water springs, and the figure obtained added to the height of the object on which the angle is being taken. Fortunately most seacoasts, whether rocky, sandy or cliffs, have a fairly distinct line which shows the 'top of the tide', the height above which only exceptional tides go. If this line is used when it is towards low water, the error will be only small. In any case, if an angle is taken to water level the distance off will be plotted as less than it really is, which can be regarded as a safety feature (*Fig. 7.10*).

The second, and sometimes more serious, error occurs because the basis of the sextant angle position line is that one pre-supposes a right-angled triangle which cannot always be achieved. In the case of a tall lighthouse standing upon a small rock, the situation is satisfactory. But in *Fig. 7.11*, where the point of sea level used as a datum is some distance towards you from the base of the object used for height, a considerable error can be introduced if the sextant is much above sea level. The warning applies mainly to big ships whose navigators cannot help being some way above sea level. But don't ever do as

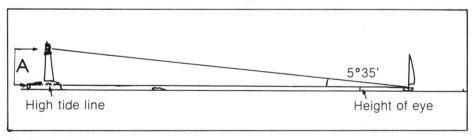

Fig. 7.10   If the tide is much below high water when a vertical sextant angle is taken, the angle should in theory be corrected for tide level, and also for height of eye above water surface. But the first correction need be no worry if you use as a base the dark line which almost invariably shows at 'top of the tide'; the second error in fact puts you slightly further away than you are and may be regarded as a safety factor. If you are taking inner and outer safety angles or are in a large vessel, the correction for height of eye can be found in *Reed's*.

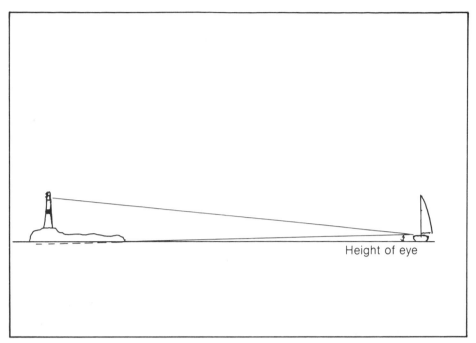

Fig. 7.11   The only time to be wary of a distance off by vertical sextant angle is when the sea level being sighted is much nearer to you than the top of the object.

someone I once read of did when entering a pass in a coral reef in the Pacific, where it is common to have a man in the spreaders, since a better view of coral heads can be obtained. He took the sextant with him for an angle on the light at one side of the pass. The considerable error that can be introduced in this way could be dangerous. The danger is only great when accuracy must be exact, and the object whose angle is being measured is high in relation to the distance off. For normal purposes the cockpit of a small boat is so close to sea level that results will be good provided the angle is taken carefully.

When measuring the distance off of a lighthouse, the height given on the chart is to the *centre of the lamp*, and this point must be used for measuring the angle. Some light towers have a considerable amount of structure above the centre of the light.

Horizontal Sextant Angles

There is a geometrical theorem that you may remember from your schooldays which says that angles in the same segment of a circle are equal. In other words,

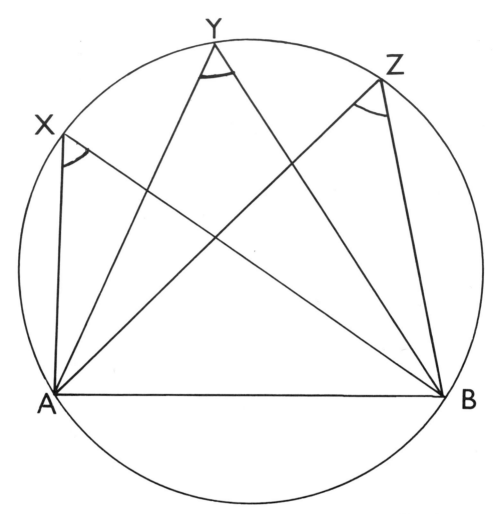

Fig. 7.12   There is a useful geometrical theorem which says that angles all based on the chord AB, as shown here, are equal. This is the basis of the circular position line, and the very useful fix by two horizontal angles.

if as in *Fig. 7.12* you draw the chord of a circle, and then draw a series of angles from the ends of the chord to any point on the larger segment of the circle, all these angles will be equal. So in *Fig. 7.12* angles AXB, AYB and AZB are all equal. This aspect of geometry is of great convenience to the navigator with a sextant checking his position against landmarks.

Suppose you are working your way along a coastline which is somewhat featureless, except for the occasional building. These are charted, but they are not tall enough for their heights to be given, and they are far enough off to give poor compass bearings. If you turn the sextant on its side, with the handle underneath, and measure the angle between two of these buildings, you can then construct a **circle of position** — a position line does not have to be straight — which, combined with some other position line, can give you a fix.

There is a variety of ways of constructing this circle. In a small boat one of the easiest is to draw the angle you have measured — let us assume it is 55° — on a piece of tracing paper, slide it about over the chart with the two lines always over the charted landmarks, and prick through the dividers for a number of positions. Joining up these pinpricks will give you your position circle adequately enough for rough purposes. More to the point, if somewhere on this featureless coast there are underwater dangers you want to avoid, you can draw on the chart a circle, passing through your two charted objects and clearing the dangers. Then draw to any spot on this circle two lines clearing the charted objects and measure the angle they make. Set this angle on your

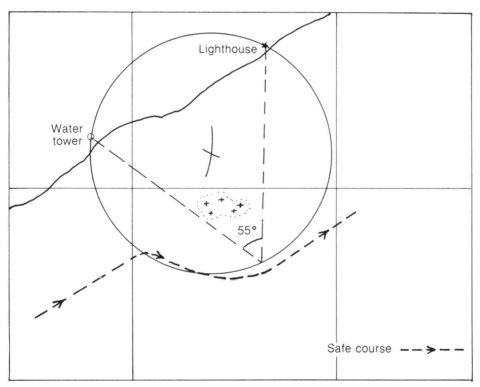

Fig. 7.13   Here a horizontal danger angle has been drawn and, provided that the sextant angle you sight is always kept smaller than the danger angle, you are a safe distance off.

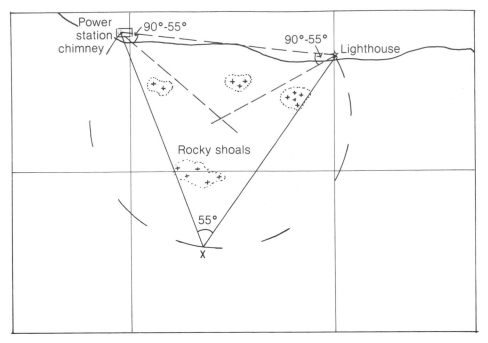

Fig. 7.14   If an angle of two shore objects has been taken and it is desired to construct
a circle of position, it is done by drawing a line on the chart joining the two landmarks
used. Subtract the sextant angle (here it is 55°) from 90°. The result is called the
complement which, for 55° is, of course, 35°. Using the line joining the two landmarks
as baseline, draw two angles of 35° as shown by the broken lines. Where they intersect
is the centre of the position circle.

sextant, and it becomes a clearing angle in the same way as a vertical angle.
Provided you sail so the angle never gets *larger* you are safely outside the circle.

Fig. 7.13 shows how to construct the circle. With compasses open to a bit
more than half the distance from the charted objects to the danger, and using
the charted objects as centres, draw two arcs. The offshore point where they
intersect is the centre of your circle, which you draw using the same arc. The
first time, you may misjudge your circle and make it too big or too small and
have to alter the opening of the compasses, but you will quickly get the knack.

To construct a circle of position from a horizontal sextant angle by plotting
is also pretty simple. Again let us assume an angle of 55° (*Fig. 7.14*). Draw a
line joining your two charted objects. Subtract your measured angle from 90°,
which gives you what is known as the **complement** of the angle: 90 –55 = 35°.
From each end of the line you have drawn between your charted objects, draw
out to sea an angle of 35°. Where these lines intersect is the centre of your
circle, and the radius is of course from the centre to the charted objects.

Reed's Almanac gives a series of tables under the heading 'Horizontal sextant angle fix' for constructing circles of position quickly, but the method is only marginally quicker than plotting the circle.

INSTANT FIX BY TWO SEXTANT ANGLES

If there are three objects visible, and you can measure with the sextant the angle between the middle one and each outside one, you can quickly and easily obtain one of the most accurate and easily plotted fixes available to the inshore navigator. It is variously known as the **horizontal sextant angle fix** or **station pointer fix** after a device called a station pointer which is used to make its plotting quick and easy. In America they are called three-arm plotters. But, since they take up space in small boats and good ones are expensive, a simple piece of tracing paper or the matt surface of a square navigational protractor (Douglas type) will be just as effective and quick.

Suppose (*Fig. 7.15*) you obtain angles of 41° 52′ between the middle and lefthand objects, and 25° 10′ between the middle and righthand objects. Draw these angles on a piece of tracing paper, or on the matt surface of your protractor (with a protractor you only need to draw two, because you can use the north/south line as the middle one). Then place the middle line over the middle object on the chart, and slide your drawing about until the outer two

Plate 10. The Walker SAT-NAV 801 made a breakthrough in compactness and ease of use in small boats for satellite navigation using US Navy Transit satellites. Right round the clock there is no period of longer than an hour when a satellite will not be in position to give a very exact fix, and the machine keeps track of DR between fixes. If switched off to conserve power, it can give an accurate fix within 25 minutes (provided a satellite is in sight), even when only fed a very rough starting position. The development is likely to make Loran C obsolete. *(Photo: Thomas Walker and Son)*

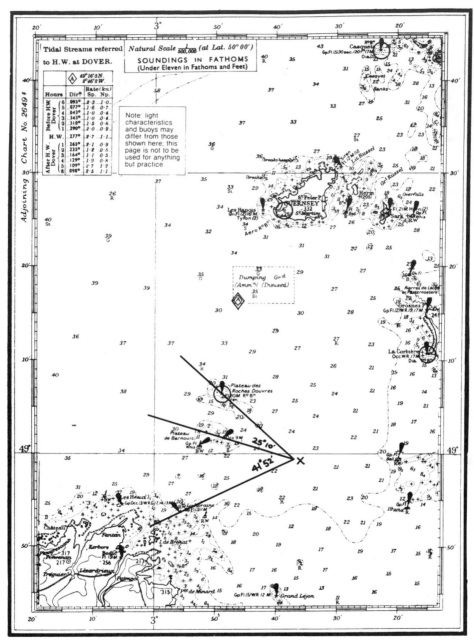

Fig. 7.15   If you can measure the angles between a centre landmark and two others, one each side of it, you can obtain the easy and precise horizontal sextant angle fix. Here the angle of 25° 10′ between Roches Douvres light and Barnouic light, and a second angle of 41° 52′ between Barnouic and La Horaine, have been measured. By setting a three-armed plotter (called a station pointer) to the angles, or drawing them on a piece of tracing paper, and then sliding whichever you use around on the chart until they are over the three landmarks, you get the position at X, which you prick through with the point of the dividers. It sounds clumsy and haphazard, but is actually simple and accurate.

lines coincide with the relevant objects. When the lines are 'on', prick through the point of the angles and that is your position — at X.

Until you have tried it you may think this sliding things about on the chart is rather a clumsy way of doing things, but actually it is easy. The important thing is to start off by aligning the middle line on the middle object. Using tracing paper or the protractor no lines need be drawn on the chart. I once met a man who refused to believe, theoretically, that by this drawing of angles there was only one possible position it applied to. I too, not being a theoretician, could not prove it in a Euclidian way, but I could and did demonstrate it to him so that, after some repeated attempts to prove I was talking drivel, he accepted it. If you do not believe me (and the thousands of seamen who have lived for centuries by this method) try it for yourself.

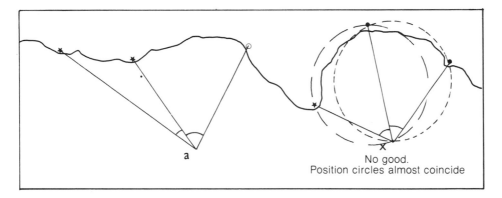

a

No good.
Position circles almost coincide

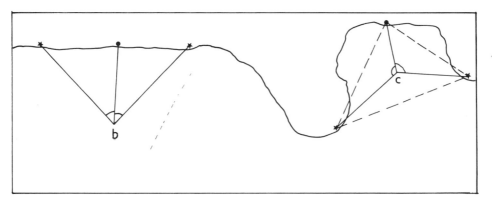

b

c

Fig. 7.16   Owing to the geometrical construction of the circles which make the horizontal sextant angle fix, it is essential that landmarks are picked which have a certain relationship to each other. They must never be in such a position, as in **x**, that one circle goes more or less through the landmarks and your position. They can be in a straight line as in **b**, or the middle object may be closer to you, as in **a**, or you can be in the centre of the triangle formed by the three landmarks as at **c**.

The tables in *Reed's Almanac* can also be used to construct circles of position if you have no tracing paper, no matt surface protractor and no station pointer, but in these circumstances I feel it is unlikely you would have *Reed's* — or a sextant or a chart, come to that.

STATION POINTER.   If you have a station pointer, sometimes called a three-arm plotter (you can get reasonably cheap ones in plastic), you merely open the arms to the required angles, and again slide it about on the chart until you are 'on' with your charted objects, pricking through the position at the centre (Plate 19).

The horizontal sextant angle fix is delightfully simple and avoids all the fiddling with variation, and perhaps deviation too, that use of a compass involves. There is really only one snag to consider with this method of fixing — the possibility that the landmarks you select might provide angles that construct circles almost coinciding. This in effect means that the three landmarks you have chosen, and yourself, lie on approximately the same circle. To avoid this you need to be sure that the three objects selected are in an approximately straight line, or at least with the middle one closer to you than a line joining the other two.

If you choose a middle landmark that lies the further side of a line joining the other two, you will be in danger of constructing the unwanted single circle on which all three points and your own position lie. So always check carefully on the chart to avoid this. *Fig. 7.16* shows the three satisfactory cases, and one that gives a bad fix.

When the only objects that offer are in this annoying situation, the best thing to do is to construct a single circle of position from one angle as described above, and then turn it into a fix by adding compass bearings as necessary. Remember that they must be corrected for variation certainly, and perhaps deviation too if the steering compass is used.

Sometimes a good fix can be obtained from a vertical sextant angle circle combined with a horizontal angle, using as one of its landmarks the object like a lighthouse that you have used for your vertical angle.

TRANSFERRED POSITION LINES

There are occasions on a passage when a single object offers a reasonable position line, but there is no means of crossing it immediately with another line — perhaps it is dark, or the object is something whose height is not charted, so the sextant cannot be used for distance off. This is when a **transferred** position line is valuable; it enables you to shift any position line you have taken until an

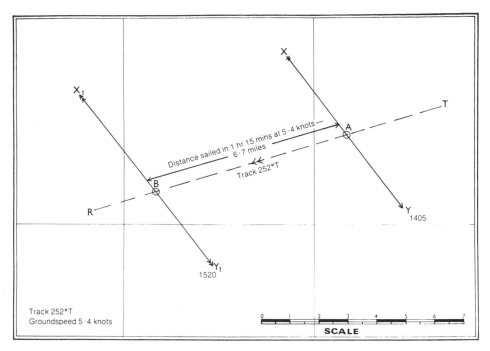

Fig. 7.17   Transferring a position line or line of position. If there is only a single object in sight to obtain a position line from, and you have no sextant to get a distance off, you can 'transfer' this PL until such time as a means of obtaining another line of position occurs. You must work out your track and ground speed (by a Class A triangle) before you can do so. You obtain the line XY by taking a bearing of the lighthouse X (323°T) at 1405. You are steering a course which gives you a track of 252°T, at a ground speed of 5·4 knots. At 1520 another landmark comes in sight, or you decide that the lighthouse bearing has changed enough to give a decent cut, so you take the new bearing and complete the fix by transferring the original PL forward to your present time. At any point along XY you draw a line TR which is *parallel* to your track — remember, it is *not* your actual track, but parallel to it. Using your groundspeed, you work out the distance you have sailed between 1405 and 1520 — 6·7 miles at 5·4 knots, giving you point B. Through B you draw a line $X_1 Y_1$ parallel to XY, and mark it conventionally with a double arrow at each end. Your second PL from the lighthouse or some new landmark gives you what is called a running fix; (see *Fig. 7.18*). Provided you always work out your correct track and ground speed, you can transfer a line of position for a period of several hours.

opportunity occurs to obtain another, **provided your track is accurately known.** By convention a transferred PL has a double arrow at each end, see *Fig. 7.17*.

RUNNING FIX.   A fix made with a transferred PL is called a running fix. In *Fig. 7.18* you are sailing in the direction AB, a course of 212°T giving a track

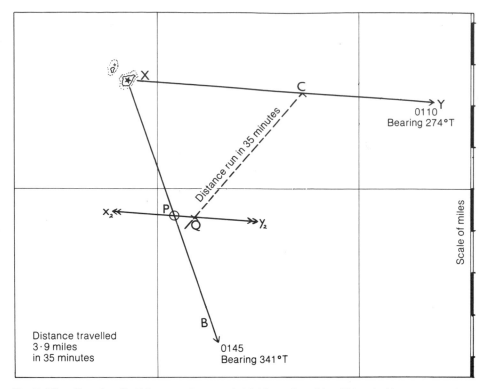

0110
Bearing 274°T

Scale of miles

Distance run in 35 minutes

Distance travelled
3·9 miles
in 35 minutes

0145
Bearing 341°T

Fig. 7.18   Running fix. When you have an initial line of position XY and either a second source of a PL comes into view, or the angle of the first object has changed enough, you can get a fix by transferring your first PL along any line parallel to your track. Where the position lines cross is the fix at the time the second PL or LOP was obtained. Here the line CQ is parallel to your track and you have used Fig. 6.7 to work out the distance travelled in the 35 minutes between bearings. The first bearing XY is then transferred as X_2Y_2 to point Q (which, at a ground speed of 6·7 knots, is 3·9 miles away), and where it cuts the second bearing XB at P is the fix (with the track, of course, running through it parallel to the arbitrary track you have drawn).

of 220°T, when you take a bearing at 0110 of the only light in view, which gives you a bearing of 274°T and is drawn as XY. You sail on for more than half an hour, and at 0145 you take a second bearing of the same light, which now bears 341°T.

Now from *any point* on your bearing line XY, you draw in a line parallel to your track. Measure off down this line the distance you travel between 0110 and 0145 — it works out at 3·9 miles to the point marked Q. Through this point 2, draw X_2Y_2 parallel to XY and marked conventionally with an arrow at each end pointing away from the middle of the line. This is your position line transferred, and where it crosses the second bearing at P is your position at 0145.

It is not necessary to take your bearings at any exact hour, the landmark might be popping in and out of mist, or a rainsquall. You take it when you can, and using your groundspeed, the scale of the chart, and a speed and distance table, you transfer the position line for exactly the distance necessary for the time since you took the first bearing. Position lines can be transferred for a brief period, as here, or for longer periods up to several hours, though this becomes complicated because of the change of tide.

Whatever you do, you must always transfer your position line in a direction parallel with your **track.**

Working on the same basis you can transfer two position lines until you can get a third, giving you a cocked hat. There is not much advantage to this, for error tends to creep in that is not in the actual bearings. When you come to astronomical navigation, as I hope one day you will, you will find transferred position lines very valuable. Since you will then probably be working out in the open ocean, where there are only ocean currents less subject to irregularity than tidal streams, your track will be more accurate too.

There are certain points to watch when transferring position lines, because there are traps which are easy to fall into. The first is when you decide to work out triangles in order to make good a constant track. You must remember that, if there is much change of direction and rate in the tidal stream during the period you are doing the transferring, your groundspeed will alter. It must be worked out each hour at least, or the error may become large.

USING SECOND LANDMARK.   The bearings used in running fixes do not all have to come from the same object. You can transfer a bearing of one object until a second object comes in sight giving a good cross bearing. You can mix sources of transferred PLs too.

It is often suggested that a direct reading of a log, either electronic or operated by rotator, can be used to simplify the running fix, transferring the first bearing by distance run. But since the log reading has to be corrected for the effect of tide, this requires a triangle to be worked out in any case unless the tide is directly parallel with the course, either with or against. So I think it is safer to avoid this additional possible source of error.

Because lecturers and instruction manuals often illustrate transferred position lines with compass bearings, many people get the idea that only bearings can be transferred. This is quite wrong. Transits or ranges can be transferred in exactly the same way. They are, after all, both just lines having a

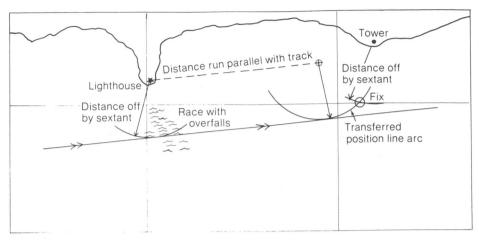

Fig. 7.19   Arcs or circles of position can be transferred in exactly the same way as straight position lines, except that you must plot the transfer line through the centre of the arc, and then inscribe another arc. Here you took the distance off by sextant, and then found that you were in such a seaway that a compass bearing was hopeless. Later on you obtain a second distance off from a tower. Transferring from the centre of the first arc for the distance sailed (using track and ground speed) you draw another arc. Where it cuts your second distance-off arc is a fix. You can improve it by taking a bearing (not shown) of the second object.

set direction — the source from which they are derived does not affect their transferability.

In the same way sextant angle circles of position can be transferred; there is the small added complication that the direction of track along which it must be transferred must be plotted through the centre of the circle (*Fig. 7.19*). But it is not very often necessary, because if you have a sextant as well as a compass, you can usually get a good fix as soon as you sight an object of charted height in daylight.

ROUGH POSITION CHECKS

Up to now we have talked mainly of PLs which, properly observed and plotted, can be of reasonable accuracy, and these should always be used when possible. But sometimes they are not available, and you have to use whatever you can, from whatever source available. Even though a position check may be so poor that you hesitate to flatter it by calling it a position line, a large number of these put together gradually point out each other's errors so that quite a reasonable estimated position can be evolved. It is a principle which occurs quite often in navigation, that information derived from a series of observations, none of which in isolation has much to commend it, averages out to quite a satisfactory result.

RISING LIGHTS.   The most widely used of the rougher checks is when you are approaching land in the dark, and you sight a lighthouse which you can identify. The chart will give the range at which the light will be seen but since, as explained in Chapter 4, this varies with a variety of factors, such as the power of the light, as well as its height, an equal variety of corrections will have to be used if anything like accuracy is expected. Chief of these is for your own height of eye, which is hardly ever the 15 feet assumed on charts. The other important one is to be sure that you are actually seeing the light and not its loom (its reflection from cloud or haze above it, which can often be seen for twice the range of the actual light). When in doubt, you can be more certain by sighting the light first from an elevated position, say standing on the cabin top. Then come down to cockpit level and see if it vanishes. If it does, you are between the two arcs you can draw for the two heights of eye combined with that given by the height of the lamp.

This should make it clear that a distance off by rising light is inherently inaccurate. But many navigators have succumbed to the human frailty of the false comfort in 'We know where we are now. That's Block Island light over there.' Even assuming that one can get a really first class bearing, distance off is likely to be an estimate, accurate only to within about four or five miles — scarcely a fix in the accepted sense.

ANGLE ON THE BOW.   There is a whole family of fixes based on the changing angle, relative to the boat's heading, of a landmark past which you are steaming or sailing, which will eventually give you distance off from the landmark. I dislike this method of fixing because it contains inherent flaws and inaccuracies which I think make it potentially dangerous. But since it is a hoary old standby in navigation books, I am mentioning it in case you hear others discussing this method, though only to warn you against using it where there is a strong and variable current, as is normal off any headland.

The most common of these fixes is known as 'doubling the angle on the bow.' Suppose, as in *Fig. 7.20*, you sight a landmark 30° on your port bow. If you maintain a steady course and speed until it is 60° on your port bow, you can now construct the isosceles triangle shown, and the distance made good AB equals the distance BC, due to the properties of an isosceles triangle. The key words are 'distance made good', because the plotting has to be based upon your track and ground speed, which off any headland will be almost impossible to

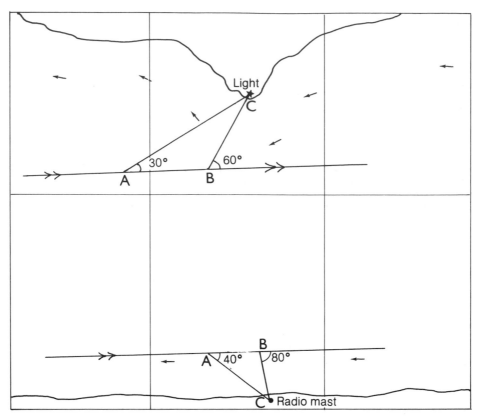

Fig. 7.20   There is a way of obtaining a very rough position known as 'doubling the angle on the bow', which I dislike because of its inherent inaccuracy. If you can keep to a steady known track and you sight the angle of a landmark from the bow at A, when you reach point B where the angle is twice the first, in theory CB equals AB. In practice the tidal stream round the headland will be doing something like the arrows show, so your track will have been most irregular near the headland. This method is a bit more reliable when heading along a regular coast as shown in the lower drawing.

calculate accurately because of the quick changes in the tidal streams. Since this system is normally recommended for use off headlands, it must be viewed with suspicion unless your rounding is many miles off, well out of the headland's effect on the tidal streams. It might however, be useful if working down a regular coast which has a prominent landmark like a power station or water tower.

Many people use the system, taking the first angle at 45° and the second when the landmark is abeam, which is somewhat easier to judge. But since the main aim of finding your distance off a headland is to clear any dangers off it, waiting until it is abeam is likely to be too late, so the system of doubling the angle as shown at the top in *Fig. 7.20* is better, choosing angles such as 35° and 70° or as convenient.

The further snag to this system is that really you need some kind of sighting system to measure the angle relative to your heading, and inaccuracies creep in here too. A proper azimuth device, for taking a bearing to the boat's fore and aft line is called a **pelorus**. It is bulky and in a small boat is hardly worth the stowage space since it is not often used. I found a compact one made by the Danish Limex company (Plate 26). Home made ones are often satisfactory, and I have heard of people using the ring of grid-type compasses. It is only when swinging a compass that a pelorus becomes essential.

Obviously, taking bearings on the compass is going to involve tedious calculations for variation and deviation. A better way is to use the compass card as a reference point, measuring round the required angle by eye. But this all pre-supposes a rock-steady course, another thing uncommon in a small boat, and is a further reason for looking at the system coldly. I have tried it often, and found it highly inaccurate. I would much prefer, as a navigator, to have a headland identified for me as being 'there', than to be misinformed by someone who has just doubled the angle on the bow that 'We are passing such-and-such point one mile and two cables off'; his estimate could easily be 50 per cent out.

CROSSING SHIPPING LANES. This can obviously be little more than a helpful indication, and it depends a good deal on proper identification of the particular ships seen. Certain ferries follow exact lines and times, and these are obviously more useful than casual traffic in the regular shipping lane. Hovercraft ferries are often some distance off their line in strong winds if they have to avoid shipping.

BEARING OF SOUND SIGNALS. The deceptiveness of sound signals in fog is well-known, the signal echoing off banks of fog. When there may be cliffs also reflecting the sound, the guide can only be taken as the very roughest. Often when a sound signal is heard, two members of a crew may differ by more than 90 degrees as to where they think it is coming from.

LINE OF SOUNDINGS. This type of fix can vary from very bad to very good, depending on the abruptness and alignment of contours on the seabed, but it is a much more useful way of obtaining a position line since adequate echo-sounders arrived in small boats. It is not very practical in a small cruiser under 30 feet to seek a change of depth from some 250 feet to under 100 with a hand held lead line — few people have the skill or strength to do it effectively. But it is a simple matter if you have an echo-sounder with suitable ranges. Sometimes, on steadily sloping shores, a similar depth, corrected for height of tide, will give you a rough position line. But it should be remembered that the contours on charts drawn from old surveys may show bays and peninsulas in the contours that can be misleading.

The most effective way to take a fix by line of soundings is to obtain by triangle the direction of your track, and from tide tables the present rise of tide. On a piece of tracing paper draw a north line, and a line showing the direction of your track. Choose a convenient time and speed scale for your present circumstances and the type of coast you are approaching. If it is steeply shelving and you are making eight knots, one a minute might be suitable, while if it is a gently shelving bottom and you are approaching at three knots, a sounding every quarter of an hour might be better. Correct your soundings by subtracting the present rise of tide and mark them in along your track line *to the scale of the chart you are using*. Then slide the piece of tracing paper with the line of soundings around on the approximate area of the chart where you think you may be, and you will very likely obtain a rough fix.

There are two points to remember. This method must never be used in bad visibility on a steep-to shore, and particularly approaching at right angles to the shore — you could run straight on. The second point is that a position check by soundings can only be achieved by intelligent study of the chart, and adequate changes of sounding on the bottom. You will never obtain a satisfactory check if the bottom is featureless. The change of sounding must be a reasonable percentage of the total depth — if you were in fifty feet, you would need a variation of at least five feet between each sounding to obtain useful information.

EXERCISES

7.1. It is a clear day and somewhere south of Guernsey you obtain bearings of 319°M of Les Hanois, 021°M of the centre of the southern part of Sark, and 093°M of Grosnez Point. using *Fig. 7.15*, (a) what is the latitude and longitude of the middle of the cocked hat obtained, and (b) how long in miles approximately are its sides? Take variation as being 7° west.

7.2. You obtain a vertical sextant angle of a light 49 metres high of 1° 32'. How far off is it?

7.3. There are rocks up to half a mile off a charted lighthouse of 64 metres height, and a single group of underwater rocks 1·4 miles off. What angles should you set on the sextant to make sure that, when going through, you remain in the safe passage between the inshore rocks and those lying further off?

7.4.   There is a prominent lighthouse within two miles of you, but no other close landmark, though you can see land some miles beyond the lighthouse. What is the best fix you can expect to get in these circumstances?

7.5.   The wind is force 3 just east of north, with driving rain and poor visibility. You are closehauled on port tack in tide setting 160°, 1·2 knots, and steering 075°C; variation is 6°W and deviation on this heading is 1°E. You reckon you are making 3 degrees of leeway, and your reliable log shows 4.5 knots.

Through a gap in the drizzle your crew gets a good bearing on a known lighthouse using the handbearing compass; this gives 040°T and then the weather closes in again. Twenty minutes later you get a glimpse of the same lighthouse still just forward of the beam, and you get a snap bearing over the steering compass of 015°C before the rain moves in again. How far from the light are you at the time of the second bearing?

Answers are in Appendix, page 299.

8
Passage making

Although you are making a passage whenever you leave your home port, most people think of a 'passage' as being a trip either out of sight of land, or at least to somewhere you have not been to before — new destinations, new problems to be tackled. To be able to make passages is after all the purpose of learning to navigate.

I hope you will not, however, behave like a surprising number of relative beginners, and choose for your first passage too deep an end into which to jump, so to speak. Having learned the rudiments of the navigator's art, don't feel that nothing less than an offshore voyage of a couple of hundred miles is what you need to stretch your legs. There is all the difference in the world between practising your plotting on the comfortably stable dining room table, and doing the same on the exiguous chart table of a small boat, which even in fine weather never keeps still.

Best make your early passages *along* a stretch of coastline so that you acquire experience while you have landmarks to keep track of your progress unless fog intervenes, and it is less likely to matter if you find that there are things you ought to know and be able to do, but somehow you don't and can't. This has happened to many before now — every year people set off for the first time, bound for a place only 60 miles away, and somehow miss altogether the great wide estuary they are trying to enter, finding themselves to one side or the other — but which side? Don't be discouraged if it happens to you, though I hope if you digest this book it never will.

ADVANCE PLANNING

The navigational success of a passage will depend greatly on the care taken over advance planning. Once you have passed the midway point it is no use thinking 'I wish I had a large-scale chart'. This is as foolish as waiting until a gale has blown up before pondering the desirability of a storm jib.

Advance planning for the navigator consists of two stages: making sure you have everything you need in the way of instruments, charts, pilot books, tidal information, almanacs and tables; and secondly, the work you can do before you actually put to sea.

Boat's Navigation Equipment

There is certain **boat's navigation** equipment that should be aboard and available at all times, as opposed to the **navigator's** equipment, which is often a matter of personal taste and depth of pocket. This boat's equipment, which I realise goes beyond the basic minimum mentioned in Chapter 12, consists of:

(a) Charts, almanac, tide tables and pilot books suitable for local sailing waters.

(b) A steering compass mounted and corrected so that deviation on any heading is not more than two degrees. If this cannot be achieved, the compass must be swung and a deviation card provided as described in Chapter 13. If the steering compass cannot be used for taking bearings, there must be a separate hand-bearing compass.

(c) A radio for weather forecasts and time checks — if possible a direction finding one.

(d) A way of keeping accurate time. In conjunction with a radio, an accurate and reliable watch will do.

(e) A good pair of 7 × 50 binoculars.

(f) Table or board (not less than 24 inches by 18), rigidly fastened, on which charts can be spread for plotting; dividers, protractor, magnifier, pencils and eraser.

(g) A barometer. The reading must be logged, preferably on graph paper, at two-hourly intervals to be of any value.

(h) Lead and line for finding depth of water. It should be carried even if the boat has an echo-sounder — they sometimes go wrong.

(i) A rough deck log — a small stiff-cover notebook is handiest — and, if you like to write up a proper log of your voyage as well, you will need a suitable logbook for this. What are sold as yacht logbooks are seldom satisfactory, and they are usually too bulky for convenient stowage. Again, a stiff-cover schoolbook, ruled off into columns, is far the best. A suitable series of column headings for the deck log, though they may not all be needed for the clean log, is shown in *Fig. 8.1*. It is important that two quite separate columns be made for 'course ordered' and 'course steered' because, unless this is done, inexperienced helmsmen, without meaning to be dishonest, will tend to write down the course ordered, even though

Date	Time EST	Log Reading	Course ordered	Course Steered	Course after Leeway
July 8	0800	Set to 0000	145°T 150°c	—	—
''	0830	2·9	150°c	145°c	147°c
''	0900	10.8	150°C	150°C	155°C
''	1000	17·1	150°C	145°C	148°C

Fig. 8.1   Here are suggested column headings for a simple deck log drawn into a hardcover school exercise book. Use both pages of the open spread, for cramming everything into a single page is too crowded. Make sure that all three course columns

subconsciously they know they have not managed to hold it. 'Course after leeway' becomes specially important in strong winds or very light winds.

Most desirable, though not absolutely essential, since they have to be weighed against the whole cost of the boat, are:

(j) Electronic echo-sounder, either driven off the yacht electrics or internal batteries. It should be the type with two scales, feet and fathoms, or in metres to read either shallow or deep water. For navigation purposes you need one that reads at least to 50 or 60 fathoms (300 feet or 100 metres) when the gain

Wind		Conditions & Sail Set	Speed	Remarks	Initials
From	Force				
.E.	3	Main and genoa	5·6	Free on port tack	JD
"	4	"	6·5	Wind increasing in gusts. Tending to gripe above course	JD
"	5	Main and No 2	6·7	Wind increasing Decide to reef main and reduce to worker	RD
"	6	main reefed and working jib	6·6	much easier to handle, + going just as fast. Luffing a bit in gusts	FJ

are completed, and see that it is kept up for every hour — every half hour if racing offshore. Keep it in a plastic bag, and make up the fair log from it later.

is turned right up; the kind that read only to a small depth are for inshore racing. Sound warnings, while convenient, are not essential.

(k) Distance reading log, or speed indicator from which distance run through the water can be derived. The distance reading log is better.

Navigator's Equipment

Things the navigator would check details of himself before any passage are:

(l) Charts of the whole area to be sailed over, of appropriate scale for

Plate 11. This shows the extreme compactness of the SAT-NAV 801, hardly bigger than the portable echo-sounder below it. *(Photo: Thomas Walker and Son)*

passage plotting and harbour entry, and also charts to cover any area you might be forced into by bad weather.

(m) That the almanac aboard is an up to date one, and carries adequate light lists, tidal information etc. In north west Europe *Reed's* will probably be adequate, but it does not, for instance, cover Scandinavia; the American edition of *Reed's* does for the eastern seaboard of the USA. In the English Channel a yachtsman's almanac called *Channel West and Solent* is a great convenience.

(n) If possible, take a sextant aboard, even if only a plastic one, and a station pointer if liked, and if there is room for it.

(o) Yachtsman's pilot books for the areas to be covered. Admiralty pilot books are of only limited help to yachts, being for the large ships — though this is being improved.

(p) Whatever special plotter or protractor the navigator prefers (see Chapter 12).

(q) A few sheets of tracing paper and graph paper, or a school squared paper exercise book. If you have room, some plotting sheets for vector triangles are useful, but the backs of charts are quite adequate if parallel lines are drawn on them in advance.

(r) Cards for deck list of lights, helmsman's orders etc — ordinary postcards or file cards do very well.

PLANNING THE TRACK

The simplest form of passage is when you have a free wind and can sail from your departure point A to destination B in a straight line, only having to make allowances for currents or tidal streams, and changes of wind which affect your speed. What you first draw on the chart is your desired **track**. Often this is conveniently across open water with no intervening dangers, and you just apply your tidal stream corrections by Class B triangles.

More often, however, your desired track will have to pass various dangers, which you must aim to leave at a safe distance. What comprises a safe distance depends on the type of danger and the present and forecast visibility. In *Fig. 8.2,* showing the passage from the south east corner of Guernsey to Tréguier, in Brittany, it is reasonably safe to pass Roches Douvres about four miles off, since it is an enormous lighthouse, which also carries a radio beacon. The Plateau de Barnouic has a smaller light and no radio beacon, and it also has dangerous outlying rocks marked only by a buoy, so you must allow a little bigger margin unless visibility were good enough to give you good fixes from Roches Douvres or your planned landfall mark, the big light at Les Héaux. This is pretty straightforward if you have a commanding wind or are in a power cruiser, even though the tidal streams in the area are strong.

Although the majority of navigational errors that get small craft into trouble arise from such things as tiredness combined with lack of practice, it is surprising how often people expose themselves to avoidable hazards in a simple matter like laying off the track on the chart.

Certain factors should never be forgotten when planning the line you are to take. To avoid nasty surprises, it is a good idea to make a little drill for yourself

Plate 12. The Lo-Kata 5 self-contained handheld D/F radio has an excellent performance, and a large electronically linked digital readout makes tuning in to the right station simple. The headphones with which it is used are not shown. Like all handheld sets incorporating a compass it must be used carefully away from magnetic influences.

after you have plotted and decided on a particular line, and ask yourself these questions:

1. What does this track look like in the event of thick weather closing in, and lack of wind or a recalcitrant engine deprives you of motive power?

2. Although the weather is good now, what is going to be under your lee in the way of hazards or ports of shelter in the event of unexpected high winds?

(a) In north west Europe *unexpected* high winds will usually be from the south west, veering to north west, from a sharp secondary depression that has wormed its way into the system without being detected. Strong winds from other directions are usually forecast.

(b) In American waters and the Caribbean in the summer and fall, the navigator (and the skipper) must be prepared for hurricanes. These occur on the east and the south west coasts, in the Caribbean and in the Gulf of Mexico. While their progress is often typical, and the warning broadcasts are good, they can be erratic, so that the prudent mariner will have a safe hurricane hole never too far away during the hurricane season. In addition, summer fog can quickly form off the coasts of the north eastern states, Canada, Washington and northern California. In the Gulf Stream, northeasters can build up dangerous seas, and often develop very fast. Mediterranean winds usually strike from the north.

The questions facing the navigator obviously have to be asked with a weather forecast in mind and, although forecasts achieve fame through their inaccuracy, when it comes to hurricanes and visibility, they are very good. If the forecast for your area says that visibility will be good, then it usually will be; if it says fog patches, there will certainly be some fog about. Where the forecasters cannot help being vague is the speed of travel of weather systems. Often a trough they expect slows down suddenly, they have warned of impending high winds, and lots of people lurk in port when they could have fitted in a nice passage, but the strong winds do not arrive until 36 hours later. This book cannot cover meteorology because it deals with such a wide area. Study the weather for wherever you are going to sail as deeply as possible.

Passage Principles

So never plan passages in isolation from present and forecast weather conditions. Here are some principles to follow when making a passage during which conditions have deteriorated from the sailor's dream of fair winds and good visibility:

1. Approaching a coast or danger in poor visibility, do so at a fine angle rather than a right angle. This greatly increases the chance of sighting and identifying off-lying buoys or marks and picking up landmarks when the coast is first sighted.
2. Never run towards a coast in strong winds or bad visibility unless you are quite certain of your position and the suitability of your destination. When in doubt, stay at sea until things improve.
3. Careful study of the chart *in good time* is the only safe way to approach a dangerous coast. Expecting to pick up a chart at the last moment and be able quickly to plot a course through a multitude of off-lying dangers is useless.

PREPARATORY WORK

Returning to the passage in *Fig. 8.2*, from St Peter Port in Guernsey to Tréguier, in Brittany, you find from the tide tables and atlas what time the tide begins to set southwards down the Little Russel outside St Peter Port, because

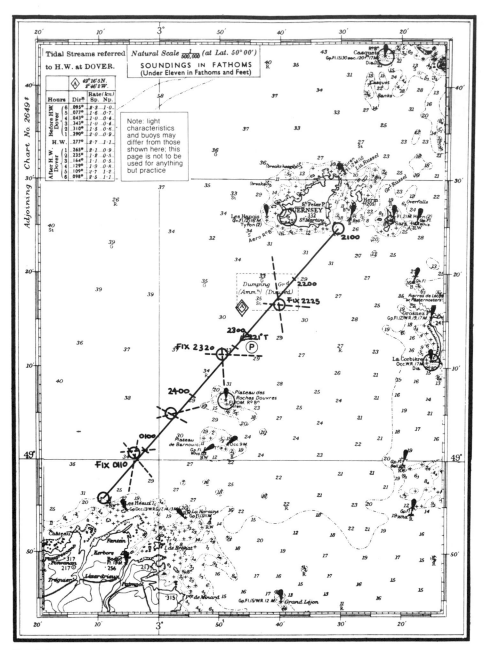

Fig. 8.2　This is the chart of the simple passage from Guernsey to Tréguier in Brittany, described on pages 143–8.

it runs so fast that you won't make much progress against it. Let us say the two times today are about 8.30 a.m. and then again at about 9 p.m. — one hour before HW Dover. You are checking this up just after breakfast, and decide that when you are ready you will have missed too much favourable tide to go now, so you will leave port at 8.30 p.m., almost slack water, and make a night passage. There are so many lights in the area that navigation is often easier after dark. You will have the last of the evening light to get clear of the Little Russel, the powerful lights in the area to navigate by, and daylight to help you into the entrance to the Tréguier River. The only question is whether to make a slight dog leg to give a larger offing to the west of Roches Douvres, but you decide you have allowed enough. The 38 mile passage should take about six hours because, if the wind drops light, you intend to run your motor to keep up an average speed of five knots, and you have timed your departure to gain from the tide. The present wind is a lovely force 4 north westerly, and should give you a perfect trip.

Looking at the tidal atlas you see that, on reaching the south east point of Guernsey at St Martin's point, you will have two hours of strong west going tide, after which it swings south west for two hours (hard in your favour), and then for four hours it runs eastward, with a bit of south, across your course but only a trifle against you. It only runs dead against you for about an hour (at four hours before HW Dover) and then not very strongly, as by that time you will be away from its hardest running area. Your chief concern, you realise, is likely to be that you will arrive early off Tréguier and, since you prefer to await daylight before going in, you may have to hang about for a bit. But better to arrive early and hang about a little than be late because of unforeseen delays.

Assuming a speed through the water of 6·5 knots, you plot your first three triangles (*Fig. 8.3*). The line you have laid off shows you want to make a track of 221°T all the way. Using a tide of 275°T 1·2 knots for the first hour, your triangle gives you a course of 212°T and a ground speed of no less than 7·1 knots. The series of triangles come out like this.

Time	Desired Track T	Boat Speed (kts)	Tide Dir. T	Tide Speed (kts)	Course T	Ground Speed (kts)	
2100	221°	6·5	275°	1·2	213°	7·2	(Triangle A, *Fig. 8.3*)
2200	221°	6·5	260°	2·4	208°	8·1	(Triangle B)
2300	221°	6·5	245°	2·7	211°	8·8	(Triangle C)

At this rate you will be due west of Roches Douvres after three hours. Being a prudent navigator you mark the point ℗ on the chart to remind yourself to check wind and tide and your speed carefully at that point, in case it might be wiser to go to leeward of Roches Douvres.

The key lesson from these triangles is the long strides you take when the tide is in your favour. If you go on at this rate, your DR plot tells you, you will be off Tréguier entrance at about 2 a.m., and will have to hang about until there is some daylight soon after 4 a.m., but you decide to press on in case the wind falls light, and jill about waiting for daylight when you are about five miles from your destination. In an onshore wind, it would be unwise to go any further inshore. During the hours of darkness you have taken several fixes shown in *Fig. 8.2*, and they have all put you exceedingly close to your planned track — experienced navigators will say cynically I have cooked the plot.

There is really only one thing to worry about on this very simple passage. Soon after 0100 the tide is going to turn and start running, first south-east, and then east. When you decide to heave to and wait, you must continue your plot and also allow for the tide. So the rest of your plot (the triangles are in *Fig. 8.3*) goes like this:

Time	Desired Track T	Boat Speed (kts)	Tide Dir. T	Tide Speed (kts)	Course	Ground Speed (kts)	
2400	221°	6·5	245°	1·3	216°	7·7	Triangle D
0100	221°	6·5	160°	1·2	230°	7·0	Triangle E

At 0115, after plotting the 0110 fix shown on the chart, you decide to heave to and just stem the tide for a couple of hours (you have a nice old-fashioned boat that, unlike present-day butterflies, heaves to in a civilised way). Since you have two or three good lights to keep an eye on, you decide you can average out the tide for the next two hours at 120° 2·2 knots. You lash the helm, with the boat heading 290° at 2 knots, but someone has to stay on deck keeping watch ready to let draw, since this is a busy area for fishing craft. Your final triangle, starting from the 0110 fix, is of course a Class A triangle, and it goes like this:

Time	Course T	Boat Speed (kts)	Tide Dir. T	Tide Speed (kts)	Track T	Ground Speed (kts)	
0200	290°	2·0	120°	2·2	176°	0·4	Triangle F

On this basis by 0400 you have travelled less than a mile from the last fix,

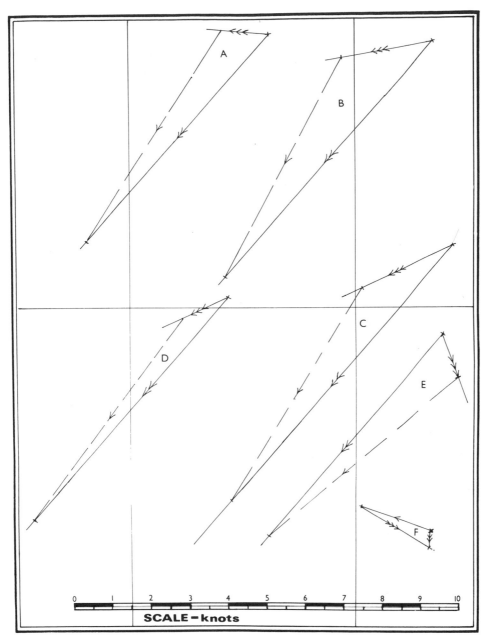

Fig. 8.3   Here are the triangles drawn for the passage in *Fig. 8.2*.

very nearly due south, and you are still so close to your planned track that I have not plotted this Estimated Position to avoid cluttering up the chart. You decide you would like to make a little more westing and a little less to the south during the hour in which the eastern sky begins to lighten, so you work out one more triangle mentally, assuming the tide is running almost due east at 2 knots. You steer 240° at 6·5 knots, and sight the buoy off Tréguier after half an hour, fine on the port bow.

This may seem an awful lot of work for a simple passage, but would have been vital in the event of bad visibility. Another thing you should study is an alternative plan, in the event of the wind falling light and your having to motor. Since people will be sleeping below you don't want to go at full blast, so you calculate your motoring speed at five knots. Your light wind plot would go like this for the first three hours:

Desired Track T	Boat Speed (kts)	Tide Dir. T	Tide Speed (kts)	Course T	Ground Speed (kts)
221°	5·0	275°	1·2	209°	5·6
221°	5·0	260°	2·4	203°	6·6
221°	5·0	245°	2·7	208°	7·3

This puts you four and a half miles further back along your track in only three hours sailing, although the courses are not very much different. It does however demonstrate how important changes of speed are to the navigator.

EFFECT OF SPEED

Let us compare the course and ground speed of two boats making 7 and 3 knots respectively. Both have an identical tide of 240°T 2.2 knots, and they are both trying to make good a track of 155°T.

	Desired Track T	Boat Speed (kts)	Tide Dir. T	Tide Speed (kts)	Course T	Ground Speed (kts)
Boat A	155°	7·0	240°	2·2	137°	6·8
Boat B	155°	3·0	240°	2·2	108°	2·24

These would be average conditions for a sailing boat — the wind has fallen light and Boat B's speed has been halved. To maintain the same track she needs to alter course almost 30 degrees. So when working out your course always consider at least one alternative for change of speed.

In some of these sample passages I have done neat hourly triangles for clarity. In actual fact most of the triangles you need to draw in a hurry are caused by **change of speed** and happen at irregular times.

PASSAGES TO WINDWARD

The big difference between the cruising man and the racing man is that the former thinks of a passage to windward rather as he views a visit to the dentist, while the racing man with a good boat, strong crew and good navigator regards it as an opportunity to carve up the opposition. It is very shortsighted of the cruising man to ignore the problems of windward work just because he hopes to avoid them. One day he will have to face them without the option. If you are a dedicated cruising man don't think of it as racing technique, but rather as a way of getting to a snug berth with good foreign food and wine ashore (I write as one who lives in Britain) instead of an extra 24 hours thrashing through a lumpy sea. You might, of course, be lucky and just by chance pull out of the hat the quickest way of getting to your desired destination in the teeth of the wind. But you are much more likely to choose wrong unless you do a good deal of hard work, in first planning your windward strategy (your long term aim), and then your tactics (what you are going to do in the short term).

STRATEGY OF CURRENTS

The effect of current or tidal stream on a windward-going vessel is the key to a passage in tidal waters or those affected by a geographical current or set. Although cruising navigators take into account such an effect on their position, they often do not pay enough attention to **planning** tidal strategy at the start of a passage, and they are not quick enough to detect when persisting in a wrong strategy is going to cost them hours of delay which could be reduced by careful thought.

Fig. 8.4 compares the passages of two boats, bound under sail from St Martin's Point on the south east of Guernsey, to the Pontrieux River (the entrance to which lies between the two big lights Les Héaux and La Horaine) both of which are marked with an X. They set sail from a point 1½ miles south east of St Martin's where the X is inside a circle and a square, at one hour before HW Dover on a day of normal spring tides. Since the tidal diamond on

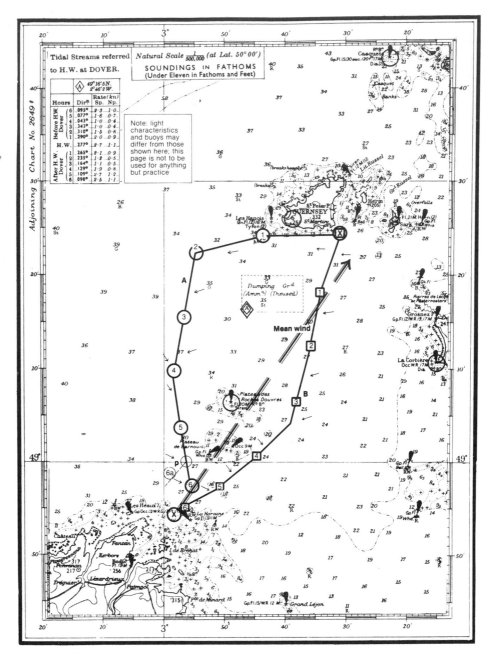

Fig. 8.4   The tracks of two boats, beating to windward from the same departure point to the same destination, as described in pages 149–155. One navigator thought harder and lee-bowed his tides, getting there much sooner.

the chart is not really enough to cover the whole area for the passage, I am taking the following streams from the tidal atlas.

Guernsey — Roches Douvres — Les Héaux

Time relative to HW Dover	Direction	Rate
−1	270°T	2·4 kts
0	265	2·5
+1	245	2·6
+2	245	1·8
+3	160	1·5
+4	150	2·5
+5	140	2·8

These are fierce tides, and there is an additional factor in that the dangers of Roches Douvres and Plateau de Barnouic are in the way and complicating life.

To avoid making things *too* difficult, I am going to assume that the boats are sister ships of virtually equal performance, with helmsmen equally skilled. The only difference between them is that one navigator thought harder, sooner. The wind remains pretty constant in mean direction from the south west; both boats work out that their average wind is in fact from 210°T. It is blowing about Force 4 at the start, enabling the pair to make their full windward speed of 5·5 knots, and continues to do so until HW Dover + 3, when it falls to Force 2 for three hours, before reverting once again to Force 4 (I know that winds never blow as tidily as this, but the rest of the book could be taken up with this example if we were to get too realistic). The effect of the force 2 spell is to reduce boat speed to 4 knots, *unless the tide can be brought onto the lee bow*, when half a knot is gained.

The distance, whether one goes east or west of Roches Douvres and Barnouic is very similar — 35 miles going to the west and 35·6 miles to the east. Boat A, whose EP each hour is marked with a circle, decides to go to the west, and Boat B to go straight south. Allowing for leeway, A can lay 260°T and B 170°T. So A is 40° off his direct line on his first tack and B, whose hourly EP's are marked with squares, is only 32° off. But this is before correction for tidal stream; who is being lee-bowed? B. The small arrows on the chart show the relevant tidal streams.

After a bit over five hours to windward, the final result shows that B gets to the target point nearly an hour ahead of A. In fact, since at A's point 6 he had a light wind and strengthening tide carrying him away, unless he called a powerful motor into play, he would almost certainly have been swept away to

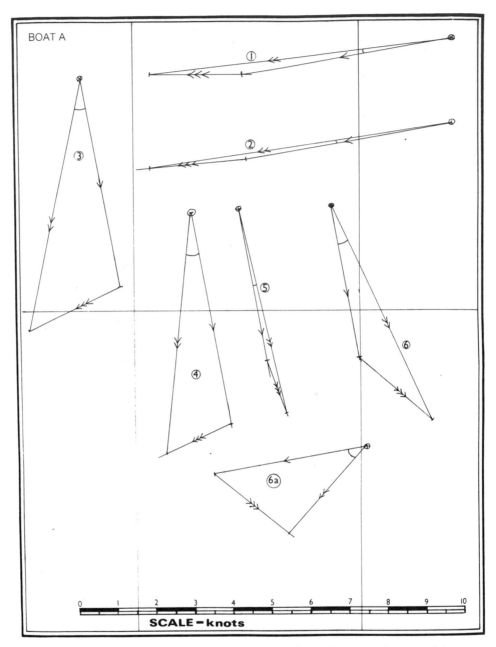

Fig. 8.5　These are the triangles drawn aboard boat A, which went to the west of the intervening rocks.

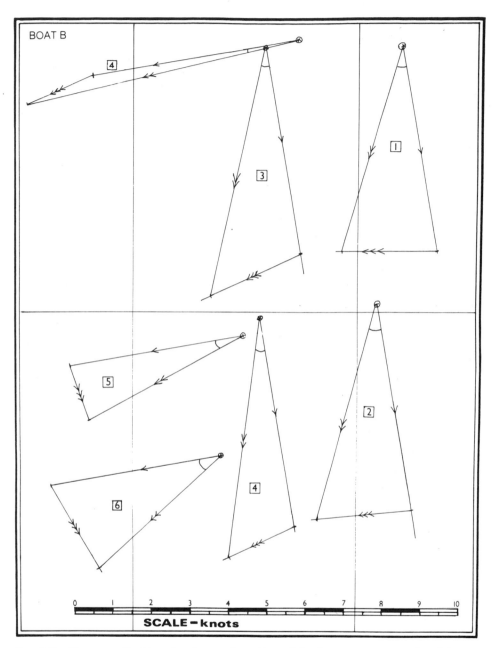

Fig. 8.6   These are the triangles drawn aboard boat B for the same passage. Careful study shows that he arranged his tacks so that he was always being pushed towards his rhumb line and towards the wind.

the eastward, and might not have made the entrance for hours. Soon after his point 5, B was still steering 260°, but the strong lee-bowing tide was carrying him south west towards his destination. He is already within sight of the leading marks and can use them to decide when to tack for the entrance without any risk of being swept away.

There are several reasons why B's performance is much more creditable than A's. Leaving at that state of the tide, B's decision to go the slightly longer way round Barnouic was wise, because the whole time he was rounding it, the tidal stream was carrying him *away* from it. By tacking as the tide turned south east, he kept the angle of his tacks to 45 degrees. Between his points 5 and 6, on the other hand, A ran a considerable risk, if the wind fell even lighter, of being carried onto the Barnouic area on an east-going tide.

A further point which, in order not to complicate things too much, I have omitted, is that B would almost certainly have been making better speed through the water during the whole passage, because he always had the tide either with him or on his lee bow, whereas A for much of the time had it on his weather bow, or taking him where he did not want to go.

In *Fig. 8.4* I have shown only the lines of the two tracks, indicating where each boat tacked, and the angles shown are those between their *tracks*. Their triangles are shown in *Fig. 8.5–8.6*. Although each boat made only one tack until almost at the end, B's course can scarcely be faulted. Navigationally he did everything right for the conditions. His tides were always pushing him *towards* his favoured track.

The vector triangles, all of course Class A, worked out hourly for each boat, with times excluded, are:

Boat A

	Course (T)	Speed (kts)	Tide (T)	Rate (kts)	Track (T)	Ground Speed (knots)
①	260°	5·5	270°	2·4	263°	7·9
②	260°	5·5	265°	2·5	261°	8·0
③	170°	5·5	245°	2·6	192°	6·7
④	170°	5·5	245°	1·8	186°	6·2
⑤	170°	4·0	160°	1·5	167°	5·5
⑥	170°	4·0	130°	2·5	154°	6·1

Boat B

	Course (T)	Speed (kts)	Tide (T)	Rate (kts)	Track (T)	Ground Speed (knots)
1	170°	5·5	270°	2·4	194°	5·6
2	170°	5·5	265°	2·5	195°	5·8
3	170°	5·5	245°	2·6	192°	6·7
4	170°	5·5	245°	1·8	186°	6·2 for 30 mins
4	260°	5·5	245°	1·8	256°	7·3 for 30 mins
5	260°	4·5	160°	1·5	240°	4·5
6	260°	4·5	150°	2·5	227°	4·3

There are other points about these two passages that should not be overlooked. A's idea of 'getting to the west' while the tide serves and while he can is an instinct with many people who sail in the English Channel, westing being something that does not come easily there. There is also the fact that a veer is always a possibility, and a wind swinging to the west would have got him there a lot earlier — he could have freed sheets and travelled a lot more rapidly. But if he was thinking of an approaching change of wind, he should have tacked to the south from his position south of Les Hanois at the end of his first hour, sailed for two hours on the favourable, lee-bowing tack and *then* decided whether to go east or west of Roches Douvres. He would then have been in a favourable position to tack to the west if the wind remained unchanged, as the tide turned onto his lee bow or, if the wind freed, to haul out. Later on, at the point on *Fig. 8.4* marked P near Barnouic, he could have saved himself from much of his error if he had tacked onto 260°, and he would then have made good the broken line marked 6a.

Chartwork Before and During the Passage

Before setting off (at whatever time) both navigators should have made normal preparations for a passage, with adequate instructions to the helmsman for times when the navigator has his head down. These would include one card showing characteristics of all lights and buoys likely to be seen, and another showing optimum courses (in this case making clear which track would go which side of Roches Douvres). On a windward passage the navigator will give more precise instructions than he would in a free wind. In Boat B in *Fig. 8.4* the navigator, if getting some sleep, would first take a fix on any lights visible and then write in the deck log or deck card something like:

'Beat to windward on starboard tack unless wind frees to allow 205°M, when keep steering 205°. Be ready to tack if wind puts you on course to port of 160°M. Tack to westwards will probably be made when Barnouic is about due west. Call navigator before tacking, if wind falls light, or visibility deteriorates. Log average course every 15 minutes. Take fixes on Roches Douvres, Les Hanois, Grosnez Point, La Corbière and Barnouic.'

An accurate estimate of the course achieved *must* be made. Inexperienced people usually name the course they point up to only momentarily during a freeing puff, or when perhaps they have pinched for a moment. Persistent pinchers are the navigator's despair, they destroy the boat's speed through the water and magnify leeway, often achieving a line 25° off what they have proudly proclaimed.

The speed estimate must also be as dependable as possible unless you have a log. These are surprisingly reliable when properly calibrated, until speed drops very low. When speed is low and the wind variable, it is not too frequent to log a speed or distance estimate every quarter of an hour — it prevents the form of self-deception so many people fall into of saying to themselves 'We've been sailing for four and a half hours, we must have made at least five miles.' If the deck log says firmly throughout that time 'Log reading nil, speed under half a knot' the navigator has no get-out, and cannot help realising the importance of plotting the tidal streams properly.

EFFECT OF WIND DIRECTION ON STRATEGY

When planning strategy for a windward passage of some length, say 40 miles or more, it is more important than with a free wind to bear in mind forecast wind changes — even if they never happen. There are some basic rules, which do in fact derive from well established inshore racing practice. It is curious how many people, even though they may be hot racing men inshore, forget first principles as soon as they are out of sight of land. They fail to choose the tack which enables them to point closest to the mark, they make themselves dead ducks for adverse wind shifts by making long legs out to the layline too early (see *Fig. 8.7*) and above all, when both tacks are otherwise equal, they fail to choose the one which keeps a tidal stream on the lee bow rather than the weather one. Our comparison of two boats above makes this point in the most extreme way; usually it is not so obvious, for there is often a shading of

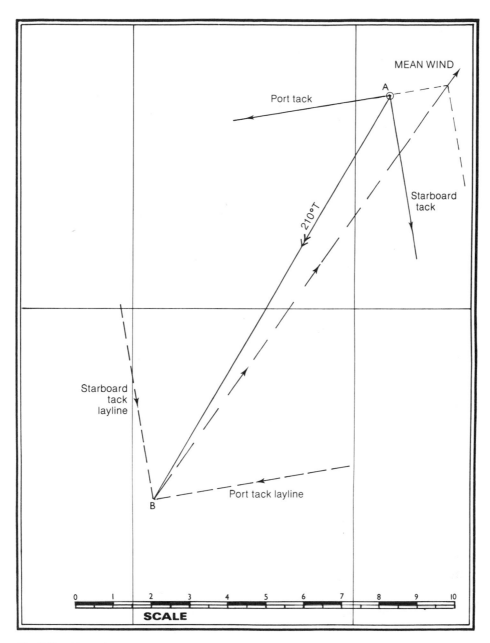

Fig. 8.7   If you draw in the mean wind from your destination, a transparent right-angle
like a Douglas protractor placed on it immediately shows you the true course you can
hold on each tack, and you can see which is the better initial tack. You can also see the
laylines by placing the right-angle over your destination. You never want to go right out
to either layline until quite close to the destination, because a shift of wind could put you in
the position of having overstood. Here, starboard is the best first tack if starting from A.

additional factors like the wind direction slightly favouring one tack or the other.

One navigator I know keeps a card stuck in a corner of his dressing table mirror, to his wife's oft-mentioned dismay. It says:

> ALWAYS
> Lay the tack nearest the mark.
> Keep the tide on the lee bow.
> Stay inside the layline.
> Climb up the wind shifts.

The last, of course, means slip in a quick tack when a shift of wind heads you, thereby suddenly favouring the other tack.

All these are inshore, indeed, dinghy racing precepts, but they apply just as much to the cruising man anxious to make a good passage — with the possible exception of the last one, because there is a limit to the frequency with which a 60 foot schooner can be flung onto the other tack just for a temporary advantage of some 15 degrees. So don't be ashamed to keep my racing friend's precepts in mind in this business of getting from A to B; they are good ideas for anyone going to sea under sail, racing or cruising. There is at least one more precept to add to the four above:

BEATING TO WINDWARD, HEAD TOWARDS WHERE YOU EXPECT THE WIND TO COME FROM

It is unusual for the wind to blow resolutely and steadily for the whole of a passage of 12 hours or more. The intelligent navigator, on hearing a forecast, might reckon the wind will veer (change direction clockwise) for several hours. Heading towards the side of the direct line which will be favoured after the shift will save much time. If the wind is approximately south-west, and you are beating for a point just south of dead to windward, normally the starboard tack is the better initial tack, putting you south of the direct line. But if a veer to the west is expected, it will be better to put in some distance on port tack. Then, when the veer arrives, you tack and find you are pointing much closer to the target. Obviously this must not be overdone — don't go so far that when the veer arrives you find you have overstood.

When the wind is free, the opposite principle usually applies. If you are on a fine reach on starboard tack and a veer is forecast, bearing away slightly and keeping to leeward of the direct line until the shift means you sail faster both before and after its arrival.

TACTICS

Tactics differ from strategy in forming the basis of your minute to minute plans, as opposed to the long-term scheme. This usually means taking into account the presence of other boats as well as the action of the wind, but at the moment we are only thinking in terms of making the fastest possible passage without regard to other boats.

The first thing is to establish the mean wind relative to the track you want to make good, and this can only be done with the compass. Since most marinas and small boat anchorages are sufficiently sheltered that even on a pierhead the wind is not doing what it is outside, your main decisions and a lot of your chart work cannot really be tackled until you are out at sea. Do not believe people who tell you that you can calculate the mean surface wind from what the clouds are doing — the wind at 2000 feet is not only blowing harder than at the surface, but in a slightly different direction. The most you can do is pencil in and mark your track, check what the tide is doing in various places along your route, write out deck cards listing tracks and lights likely to be seen, and do a little other preliminary work like getting the right charts handy. But not until you have established what the wind is doing right out to sea can you really get to work.

Once you are well clear of land, therefore, check the wind carefully by compass — not forgetting to correct for variation. Don't just make a casual check on one tack, but do a reasonable check on each tack, and try to make sure that you are not under some isolated dark cloud, which can often cause a temporary veering of the wind. Look at *Fig. 8.7* which represents a typical passage, the first line of which is 210°T. Let us suppose that after a quarter of an hour's sailing, well offshore, you establish that the wind is blowing around the mean direction of 215°T. Draw this line back from the destination point marked B, and label it clearly 'mean wind.'

Most good windward boats, near enough, will sail at 45 degrees to the true wind. If yours does not (hard luck), cut a rectangular piece of transparent stiff plastic and trim one end to form the angle she tacks through, perhaps 110°. Scratch a line bisecting the angle then, when this line is parallel to the wind direction, the sides of the angle give you the courses you can lay on each tack. Those whose boats will make 45 degrees to the wind, even allowing for leeway, can use any right-angle, such as the corner of a Douglas protractor or a school set-square. The Douglas protractor is better because, being square, it is easier to slide about the chart, against a straight edge, to the desired position.

Setting the corner of the protractor on the wind line so that its edge cuts your starting point with its diagonal aligned to the wind, you will immediately see

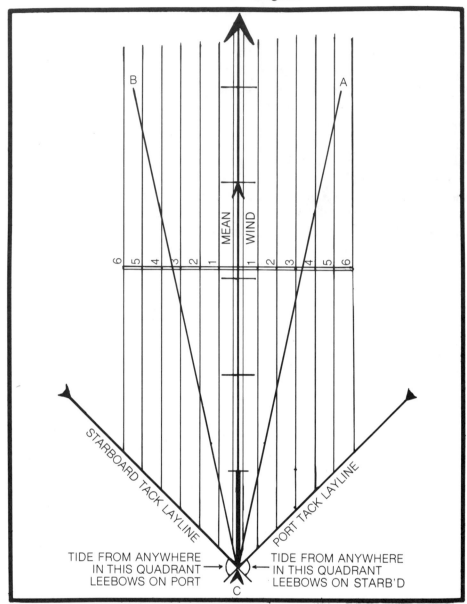

Fig. 8.8   For a long windward passage out of sight of land, a diagram like this, on a transparent overlay put on the chart, will quickly reveal which is the favoured tack relative to the target. After checking the mean wind carefully, the point of the arrow is placed over the target on a suitable scale of chart (the figures are only a guide, they cannot be to any exact scale) and the centre line aligned with the mean wind; then the favoured tack is the one which takes you towards the centre line. The diagram can be slewed around to check the effect of various possible wind changes. Draw a tidal arrow on the chart, and you can then see which is the lee-bowed tack, and how far off the centreline it pays to go to allow for the tide.

that the starboard tack lets you lie nearly ten degrees closer to the mark than the port tack. Let us ignore the effect of any current or tidal stream for the moment, so that we may only consider the wind. You are now provided with the laylines we discussed earlier. If your upwind mark is a long way off, you will be better advised to draw parallel lines some ten miles either side of the mean wind line until you get to within 25 miles or so, before drawing in the laylines themselves. Those who have trouble visualising their position in relation to the wind and their destination should find *Fig. 8.8* useful. When there is no tide, tacking towards the centre line gives the better tack.

Tacking on Shifts

Although the wind at sea is truer and steadier than wind over estuaries or land, where it is cut up and deflected by obstructions, there are still variations in direction as well as strength. Skilful tactical use of these shifts, which can sometimes only be detected on the compass, or occasionally by watching clouds, can gain a mile or more in a 20 mile beat to windward. I emphasize that these are relatively short lived shifts either side of a mean wind direction which remains basically the same, so there is no call for a revision of strategy such as we discussed earlier in this chapter. It is a matter of judging whether the better angle which the wind will allow by a quick tack, and for how long it will last, is worth more than the time lost in making the tack. In a cruising boat which, by racing standards, is shorthanded almost by definition, nobody wants to put in unnecessary tacks; on quite a lot of boats it means calling the other half of the crew out of his bunk. So, if you are not racing, don't get wildly enthusiastic about wind shifts that are small and of dubious duration. But, if a shift of ten degrees or more has persisted for longer than five minutes and the other tack is now visibly better, it is time to think of putting her about, whatever the inconvenience; sometimes it can make an hour's difference in the time of your arrival. Ten degrees does not sound very much, but it is really twenty degrees, since the improvement on one tack is matched by an equal disadvantage on the other. Again, a tacking diagram on tracing paper or transparent plastic immediately makes the situation clear.

Lee-bowing

Whenever you are sailing in tidal waters or a current, your progress on a beat to windward will be greatly enhanced if you so arrange your course that the tide comes on your lee bow rather than your weather one. Often greater attention to the helm so you can point up two or three degrees without losing any way will

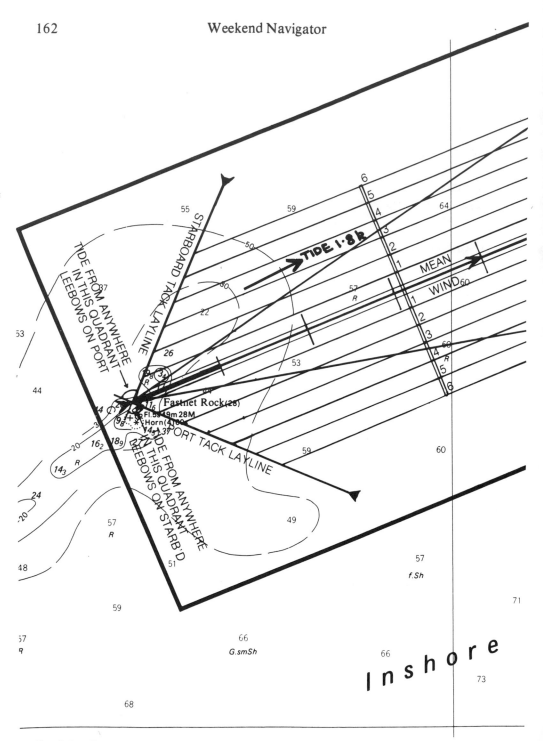

Fig. 8.9　The tacking guide placed over a chart of the approaches to the Fastnet Rock. The tide is drawn on the chart in pencil, and rubbed out the moment it ceases to apply.

bring the tide from the weather bow to the lee bow, and the affect is dramatic, as shown in *Fig. 8.10*. Pointing up just a tiny amount has improved Boat B's performance by almost half a mile dead to windward in a five mile beat compared with Boat A. Equally, failing to notice when you are lee-bowed usefully, and putting in a 'bad' tack can set you back an enormous amount, particularly when the tide is strong relative to your speed through the water (see *Fig. 8.11*).

Fig. 8.12 may be helpful for those who have trouble out of sight of land in analysing which is the lee-bowing tack. It is pretty self-explanatory. The thing to remember is that whenever it is possible to arrange that the tide or current is

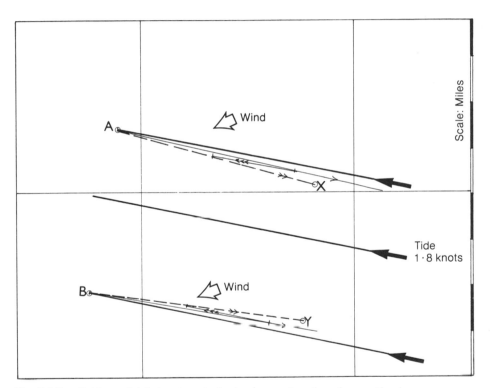

Fig. 8.10 Getting a tidal stream onto the lee bow rather than the weather bow can make a dramatic improvement in going to windward. The boat starting from A is not concentrating on his helm and the occasional freeing wind shifts; his average course keeps the tide about 3° on his weather bow, and he sags off to X. The boat leaving B has a keen helmsman, working and concentrating hard, and the sails are adjusted right. He points an average five degrees higher without going more slowly or making more leeway, and has the tide 2° on his lee bow, so he weathers up to Y. If one takes the distance AX and BY as being about five miles, boat B has gained almost half a mile dead to windward over A.

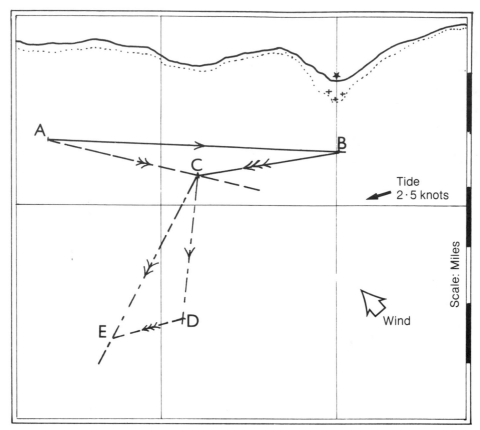

Fig. 8.11   Some people never seem to grasp that they are on a disastrous tack for making headway until they have done their progress great harm. Here a boat steering in the direction AB starts to worry about giving the point a wider berth, regardless of the fact that the tide is making his track AC and keeping him well clear to windward anyway. He unwisely tacks at C, is no longer lee-bowed, and is soon back almost level with his starting point. Always remember that in a tideway any sailing boat is virtually never going exactly where the bow points.

pushing you *towards* the wind it will improve your performance. In *Fig. 8.12* any tidal stream or current in the lightly shaded arc BC will be weather-bowing and therefore adverse. From B round to C through F it will be favourable if you are on the correct tack. But the key sectors are the small darkly shaded ones EC and BD, when the stream is just on the lee bow if you are on the correct tack.

Lee-bowing has a double benefit. Not only does the stream push you up to windward, but it tends to increase slightly the strength of the apparent wind, which in light airs is particularly useful.

FREQUENCY OF FIXES

The big professional books usually insist that fixes should be taken frequently, and add 'when speed is high', or some such phrase. Well, if you are blinding about the seas at 30 knots in a powerboat, you need to take your fixes pretty sharpish and often. But they can be equally important in light winds. Even if you are only making half a knot through the water, but you are swishing through the Race at the end of Long Island Sound with a four knot tidal stream under you and the wind is in the same direction and almost the same strength as

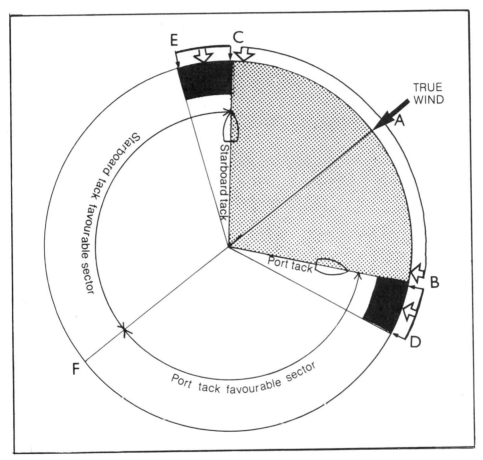

Fig. 8.12   Another diagram which will help you to assess which tack is likely to be favourable. Any tidal stream from the sector CAB will be unavoidably against you, but from B round to C through F it will favour one tack or the other. It is important to make an accurate analysis of the average wind direction, not taking a momentary lift on one tack or the other as being the mean. Going to windward, it is the heavily shaded sectors where a lee-bowing tide is most valuable.

the tide carrying you, you need to make frequent fixes too, more than if your speed were comfortably superior to the tidal stream carrying you.

So remember, any time in tidal waters, even where there is not even a ripple from the bows, *you are not standing still* unless you are kedged, and frequent fixes are the order of the day. Never forget how often, in fine weather, a strong tidal stream can carry you faster than you can sail in a fine weather light breeze.

CURRENT SAILING

Sailing in a current such as the Gulf Stream would at first glance seem easier than sailing in a tidal stream, because the direction of the set is supposed to be always in one direction. In fact owing to wriggles in the current, which have been given the delightful name meanders, the Gulf Stream particularly and many other apparently steady currents, can cause great complication for the navigator. On the course from Newport to Bermuda the meanders of the Stream are forecast and eagerly studied by skippers and navigators in the Bermuda Race, and a technique based on water temperature has been evolved to find out whether you are in a favourable or unfavourable sector of meander, though it is beyond the scope of this book. So let us consider a simpler passage, from Bimini to the Miami area.

Gulf Stream Passage

The Florida Strait passage is shown in *Fig. 8.13* with the main strength of the Gulf Stream shown shaded (for convenience the chart used is actually far too small a scale, if making the passage you would use a much larger scale, and probably an American one, not the British Admiralty one shown here). The Coast Guard forecasts the anticipated speed of the Stream, which can be in the region of four knots in the shaded area, falling to two knots or less each side of the axis. Arrows indicate the forecast strengths. Factors affecting the strength of the current include temperatures and wind strengths and directions in the Gulf of Mexico, and there is often a counter-current close to Florida, shown by the wiggley arrow.

You have been invited to bring back a 38 foot motor sailer from Bimini to Miami. You know the boat, though not all about her equipment; your crew, though a good engine man, does not know the boat or her engine installation. Power is going to be fairly important, because the only mainsail on board has split down a seam so that it is unusable, and your first task on arrival is to get it to a sail loft. The boat has a good 52 horse diesel, though the owner has warned you that the batteries may be a bit low — a common situation in boats which have electric refrigerators. However, the boat sails well for a motor sailer on anything except a dead noser, unlikely on this passage, and will make, you are promised, six knots under a big genny and mizzen in a 15 knot wind on or aft of the beam.

The batteries sure are low. Even with both in circuit the starter won't turn the engine fast enough, and only jump leads from the express cruiser that you hitched a lift over in get the motor going, but soon a hefty charge is going into the starter battery, and later you find in a locker a portable charger motor that may be useful. By 9 a.m. you are ready to go. The forecast says wind light, variable, becoming north east 12 to 15 knots, visibility moderate. There is a nasty haze as you cross the bar, cutting visibility to little more than two miles, but you anticipate no problems. You have radio beacons both sides, the glow of Miami after dark can be seen for many miles, and you also have the convenient Omni beacon at Bimini (marked on the chart with a cross and a circle). The predicted current strengths for various positions you have drawn on the chart, and using these you expect to go all the way pretty close to the rhumb line track you have drawn in. Your True course is 274°. With only one degree of variation, you can afford to ignore it. The owner swears the compass in this boat has less than one degree of deviation on any heading. Nobody around Miami pays much attention to the magnetic anomaly reported to occur in this area, said sometimes to amount to 6 degrees, and you don't intend to either.

Ten minutes after casting off you have found she makes 6·9 knots on the clock under power even without sail, and when the north-easter gets up this will probably go up to 7·5. You are going to allow for a current set of 1·5 knots 015° for the first eight miles, then follow the predicted rates that you have written in on the chart. Sea is only slight near Bimini, but there is promise of a sharp chop later.

Your first triangle gives you 260°T as the course to steer, and your speed over the ground will be 6·4 knots. You set course at 0915, and confidently expect to be going through the Bar Cuts and Government Cut south of Miami Beach by mid-afternoon.

After less than half an hour Bimini has faded in the haze astern. It is not until 1005 (you logged it) that the motor gave a strangled snort before resuming its steady rhythm again. 'Maybe a bit of water from condensation in the fuel tank' you think. Five minutes later it does it again. Three minutes later it starts losing revs, and in a few moments it just dies with a spit. The time is 1012. 'Fuel block-age says your crew, putting down the beer can that has been like a permanent fixture in has hand since you left Miami yesterday. The wind is barely force 2, swinging about between north west and north east. Under genny and mizzen

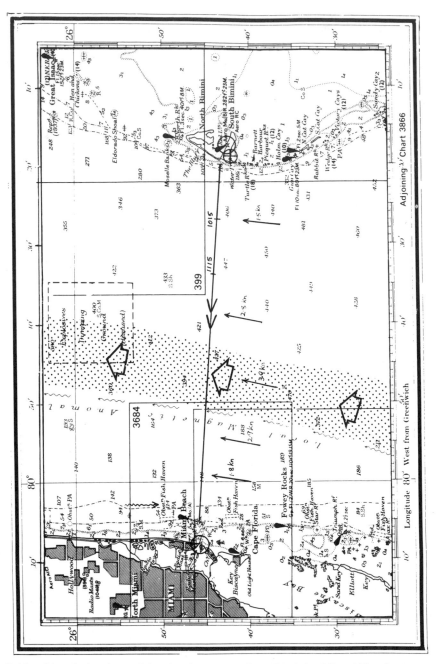

Fig. 8.13　Here is the chart of the simple passage from Bimini to Miami. The Gulf Stream main strength is shown shaded and current arrows have been drawn in, as well as a wiggly arrow as a reminder of the counter-current near the Florida shore. It was intended to be a straightforward motor-sailing trip down the track shown, until failure of the motor made things a bit different.

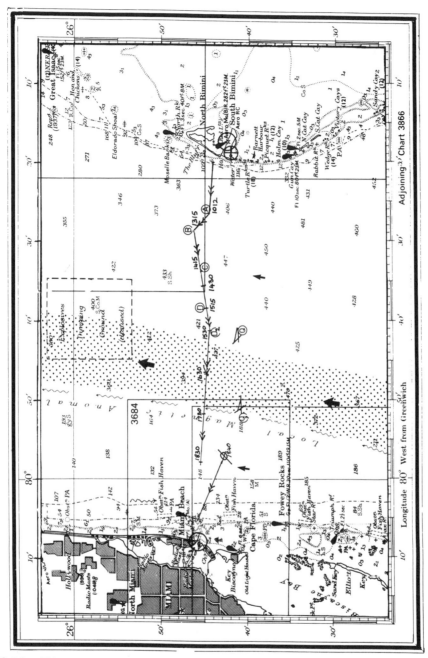

Fig. 8.14 This is the plot as it actually happened, after motor failure while the wind was light. Very careful allowance had to be made for the effect of current to avoid being carried away northward. Fortunately, after a spell of near calm, strengthening wind allowed a reasonable speed to be regained.

you are making less than 2 knots. You are really going to have to navigate, the current where you are now must be setting north east at almost two knots, the dark blue of the water shows you are well into the Stream. While your crew begins to earn his beer with wrenches and a bucket on the fuel system, you plot a bearing on Bimini Omni which puts you spot-on your rhumbline. From the distance log this gives you a reliable fix at 'A' in *Fig. 8.14*. The time is 1018. You coax her along under sail, and the wind increases until you reckon you are making 2·4 knots. Since you don't want to leave the wheel and your crew is busy clearing pipelines, cursing, bleeding the system, cursing, clearing filters and cursing some more, you work out mentally an angle off to allow for set and drift and steer 215°. At 1145 your crew has operated the starter several times without success, except for occasional bangs and puffs of smoke. He has a final go at the filters, bleeds the air out of the system again, and says 'I think that's it.' As he cleans up you press the starter button. All that gives, even with both batteries linked in, is a click and a snort. You suddenly realise that the faint noise you have been aware of since the motor stopped was the fridge, gulping down your scarce power to cool the beer.

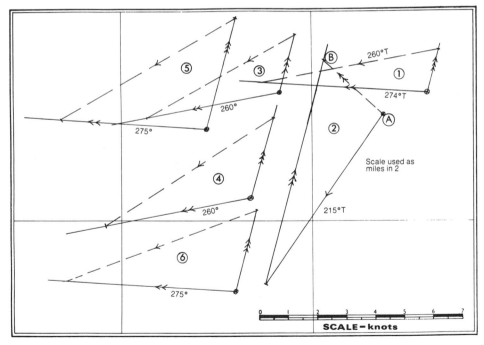

Fig. 8.15   The triangles used on the passage in *Fig. 8.14*. All are regular Class B triangles except for 2, which is Class A and uses the speed scale as a mile scale to give a direct plot of position.

Your crew is not, however, totally without virtue. He digs out the portable generator, links it in, starts it by hand and says gloomily 'It'll need two hours of that.' The situation has got beyond beer. He brings out a bottle of bourbon and two glasses, cooled with some of the ice that has swallowed your power, and restores morale somewhat. The noise and stink of the put-put are horrible but unavoidable. At 1300 the navigator's log says that since 1018 you have made 7·1 miles on 215° through the water. The current has set you in this time 015° 8·2 miles, giving you position B (Triangle 2 in *Fig. 8·15,* which has used a scale of miles): a track of 315°.

In the next five minutes you become aware that the wind has arrived. The boat begins to heel, mizzen and genny really pull, the boat's speed goes up to over five knots, and even the put-put sounds less hellish. You need it, even though you now have a good way on, because you will want to start the motor as you go through the cuts off Miami Beach, and after all this delay you will probably need navigation lights too. At 1315, you have a more satisfying plot, using a speed of 5·8 knots. For your first hour you will make the current 2·8 knots as predicted, later you will assume you are in the main current of 3·9 knots. You are nearly three miles north of the rhumb line and, with a motor you are dubious about, you would like to get back to the south of the rhumb line. You decide to aim for a track of 260°T for at least a couple of hours, and draw a triangle accordingly. This gives you a course of 240° and a ground speed of only 4·6 knots (Triangle 3). At 1415 your estimated position is at C, and both wind and sea have increased. You are making 6·1 knots on the log. Still aiming at a track of 260°T you draw another triangle, allowing 2·8 knots for current. It tells you to head 235° and your ground speed is only 4·3 knots.

At 1515 this will put you only at D, still less than halfway. At 1430 you decide to try the engine. The put-put is stopped and disconnected. Every finger crossed, you touch the button — rumble, rumble . . . she's away! Speed goes up to 7·1 knots, but she is bashing through the stiff chop that has now built up and you throttle back to give her 6·8 knots, yet keep the batteries charging at full rate.

A new triangle shows you can head up a trifle to 238° and your groundspeed has gone up to 5·1 knots. Heading this course brings you to the EP marked D_2 at 1530 (Triangle 4). At this time you take a combined Omni and radio fix that rather bafflingly puts you at Q, three and a half miles south of your rhumb line, when you reckon you are scarcely a mile south of it. Perhaps the fix is bad because of the bad cut of the position lines. You decide to treat this as a dubious fix and trust your DR, which says you can safely plan for a track of 275° now. This will bring the current of 3·9 knots dead on the beam so it will not cut your speed quite so much. Your new triangle says you must steer 240° and will have a groundspeed of only 4·9 knots (Triangle 5). Two hours of this will get you across the main set of the Gulf Stream, but as you expect it is rough and seas are choppy. Your crew, who has a cast iron stomach and believes in looking after it, has realised that dinner ashore is a diminishing possibility. Gloomily he eyes the remains of lunchtime sandwiches, and starts fossicking around in the owner's canned food lockers.

From his expression when he emerges after a few minutes with goodies, starvation is not going to be a problem. At about 1700 you take another radio fix which disturbingly puts you at Q_2 at least five miles south of your rhumb line. The unfamiliar D/F radio and Omni set and the lively motion of the boat again make you rather doubt this fix, but perhaps you are heading a bit too far south — a good fault should the wind fall light and the motor turn temperamental again.

A new triangle at 1730, using 2·9 knots for the current, says you can head up to 250°, and your groundspeed is now 5·7 knots. Between 1730 and 1830 you can see the glow of Miami Beach over to starboard, but nothing is identifiable yet. Just before 1840, as you are doing a new triangle for the weaker current, and wondering whether it isn't time to turn a bit north, your crew, who is steering, says: 'Hey, Christopher Columbus, I have Fowey Rocks fine on the port bow. Have you been at the bottle, we are miles too far south?'

Not really, a bearing of the big light flashing 2 every 20 secs shows it to be on 230°T, and you are about four miles too far south — perhaps the current predictions were too strong. But just to keep crew in place you say innocently 'Didn't I tell you we were going in the Biscayne Channel?' (south of Key Biscayne). You huff something about 'if you're really keen on Government Cut we can go in either way from where we are now, no sweat.' Suddenly everything is looming out of the haze and a few bearings tell you *exactly* where you are. Some days later your crew admits he was wondering what his wife was going to say when he telephoned and asked her to come to Fort Lauderdale (off the chart to the north) to collect you both.

You are not the first person to be fooled by a current or tidal stream that did not run as hard as predicted. The chief lesson in this passage for the beginner is the devastating effect of strong current when speed is low. In Triangle 2, the only Class A triangle in the diagram, the boat was making a track over 90 degrees different from her course, even though not yet in the main current. In Triangle 5, even when you had good speed on, a drift allowance of over 45° had to be made for the current.

EXERCISES

8.1. You are steering 160°T, making 3·2 knots in poor visibility, bound for a buoy five miles away on 140°T. The tide is said by the chart to be setting 110°T at 2·5 knots. What is (a) your track and (b) your ground speed?

8.2. You find after one hour as in 8.1 above that, instead of being hard by the mark you were making for, you are one mile to the west of it. Your course and speed have been good, so clearly the tide has not been as you thought. What has it been?

8.3. You want to make good 240°T for 18 miles starting at 0900 hrs. The tide is setting, for the first hour 100° at 1·5 knots, for the second hour 120° at 1·3 knots, and for the third hour 260° 1·2 knots. You can sail freed off at 7·4 knots on any course between 270° and 180°. What are the courses you steer (T) and the distances sailed for each hour (a), (b) and (c)? And (d) what is your estimated time of arrival?

Answers are in Appendix, page 300.

9
Electronic aids

Electronics have made such enormous strides in the past forty years that it is surprising more progress has not been achieved with them in small boats. The ravages of salt air on contacts are mainly to blame but, with the growing use of sealed integrated circuits and gold plating of contacts, greater reliability is being achieved and considerable steps forward have been made in the last few years. When, however, you consider the enormous progress ashore in electronics, the slowness of advance of boat gear is sad. Part of the problem is that the market is limited and highly competitive, so the price advantage of big production runs is not available. The other unsatisfactory field is servicing, which everywhere lags behind the quality of gear that is available. Most crack ocean racers have a display of dials that would do credit to a light aircraft, giving wind speed and direction, boat speed, a computer device working out speed made good to windward (illegal while racing, but useful for tuning), not to mention such mundane things as depth meters. Yet on any boat you race in it is quite unusual to find all the dials working properly, and getting them put right in mid-season, except with a few firms of high repute, can be difficult. Cost is also a major factor, and the higher levels of electronics are seldom found in economy cruisers.

Usually the tight-budget sailor's electronics are confined to a radio receiver for weather forecasts, probably with a direction finding aerial for obtaining radio bearings, an echo-sounder, a distance-reading and speed-reading log, perhaps an electronic self-steerer and a calculator of some kind. The owner who has to watch every penny may settle for just the radio and an echo-sounder.

I will briefly review some of the more complicated systems here as guidance when confronted by the blandishments of salesmen. Don't forget that there are few things more exasperating in a boat than a potentially useful electronic device that is not working.

RADIOTELEPHONE (R/T)

A valuable safety aid, an R/T set is not only useful in the event of disaster or injury aboard, it also enables you to keep anyone concerned informed of your progress on passage. Some of the benefits of mass production have worked through into the R/T field for boats, and sets are becoming cheaper and more compact. You can obtain weather forecasts if you have missed a broadcast, can call other vessels and also be patched in to the telephone network. Some sets have an alarm system so you can be alerted to receive a call, but personally I would prefer to avoid this . . .

The easiest and cheapest kind of R/T is on the VHF band, which has a line-of-sight range, but pressure of traffic, particularly in the United States, where regulation is less rigid, is getting very heavy. The line-of-sight range explains why results are poor if you are lying in a steep-sided estuary surrounded by high hills but, in open water, shore stations sited on high ground can be contacted at 50 miles. Inter-ship range is about 15 miles, but can be more depending on the height of the aerial. With VHF, power consumption is not so high that the average small auxiliary engine with an alternator cannot keep the battery lively enough to work it, even when the engine is not running.

R/T on lower frequencies has become much more expensive because of technical requirements which are compulsory in many countries, particularly in Europe. Medium Frequency sets are excellent for relatively long range, but the power consumption is high, and installation of the aerial is more complicated. Improvement should be on the way for this type of set, and hopefully a reduction in price. High frequency sets provide long range but are very expensive.

R/T is not cheap but, if you can afford all the other things your boat needs and still find money left over, it is a good thing to have. A licence to operate the set is necessary in most countries, and a brief test of ability must be passed — principally to see that you know the distress procedures. Initial contact is made on the calling frequency, whereupon the shore station will ask the calling yacht to shift to one of several working frequencies, depending which one is least occupied. Your set should therefore have a reasonable number of pre-tuned frequencies — anything less than half a dozen would be too few — so that you can offer as wide a choice as possible.

There are cheaper VHF sets which operate only on the distress frequency, and are for use in emergency only; they may one day make the difference between life and death for you. Locator beacons can also be obtained, which send out automatic distress signals on the emergency frequencies. Full information on yacht radio can be obtained in Britain from the General Post

Office, London, and in the USA the Government Printing Office (Superintendent of Documents), Washington DC.

SAILING INSTRUMENTS

These usually combine a team of wind indicators, electronic log (possibly with an expanded scale to give instant information on change of speed), perhaps a course computer (usually banned for racing), a speed made good to windward computer (also banned for racing), and electronic compass links, as well as the ordinary echo-sounder. The top flight racing man who wants to win at all costs seems to think that they are essential; for the cruising man, they are only a convenience — he will probably do better to buy just the D/F radio, the log and

Plate 13. Lok-Kata also make a handheld aerial D/F system linked to a fixed receiver which will drive a loudspeaker, and has digital tuning.

the echo-sounder. The full system works off internal dry batteries or the yacht electrics; the principal snags to the full set are their cost, finding a place to instal them where the dials can be read and where the electronics will not affect the magnetic compass, and the fact that you can become so hypnotised by the dials or digits that you forget how to sail a boat properly.

RADAR

The layman often thinks that a radar display will show him a sort of map of the surrounding area with every ship, buoy, shoal and pleasure craft clearly defined. It does not, except in ideal circumstances. What it shows is any area or object high enough to be within visual range, and of such a nature as to reflect the little packets of signals that the rotating transmitter sends out. This can mean, for instance that, on a low lying coast with underwater dangers off it but with high ground two or three miles inshore, you might close the coast in fog thinking that the display seen was coming from the coastline. It would in fact come from the high ground inshore and you could run into danger suddenly and unexpectedly.

Responder beacons and buoys with reflectors show up well at the appropriate range, as will large ships. Small vessels do not show up well unless they are carrying a radar reflector high enough to be effective; a reflector that cannot be raised at least 15 feet above the water level is pretty useless, and the higher the better.

Radar requires a good deal of power, involving an engine with a large capacity generator or alternator running while it is being operated, so the average auxiliary's small power unit is unlikely to be man enough. Looking at a radar screen is also one of the best ways of making those with tender tummies seasick, and it is a far from cheap way of achieving this. A relative beginner to the yachting scene, who happens to have a deep pocket, might think quite erroneously that carrying a radar set would make him safer at sea. Unless he is properly trained in how to use and maintain it, it might even lure him into danger.

One of the errors to guard against when inexperienced people are looking at a radar display is misinterpretation of the signal; it does not show the *direction* in which any vessel nearby is moving. The principle of radar is fairly well known, that a rotating time base on the screen is synchronised with the rotating aerial in both bearing and range, so that the brighter spot fed in at the point of a reflection causes a blob of light to 'paint' a small arc at the position of the target. The error that creeps in with inexperienced observers is to think that the lengthening of the echo at points away from the centre of the tube indicates the *attitude* of the target. It does not. The only way of obtaining from a radar set the *direction* in which a target is moving is by plotting a number of sweeps of the time base (the tube is internally treated to retain the glow of previous sweeps, which is a help) and then working out the target's line of movement. But it should always be remembered that movement of your own vessel, and possible alterations of course by the target, can make this deduction of the target's course very difficult. The best safety measure is to remember that, as with a visual contact with a ship, any target that stays on a steady bearing is on a collision course.

Another error to watch for is in interpreting the size of an approaching vessel. A 250,000 ton tanker approaching head-on will give no larger an echo from her bow than a local ferry beam on, though from the side the VLCC will give a huge response, especially if riding high. In certain conditions the bow and afterbody of a deep laden tanker might give two separate echoes, like a tug towing a ship. It should also be remembered that a group of small craft, such as fishing boats working at close quarters, or a power boat 'squadron', can give a misleadingly large and irregular moving response.

So if your native caution tells you that in your boat there is a suitable power source and operating site for radar, and you would like something to help in bad visibility and make crossing the shipping lanes less of a peril, fit it by all means. But don't let it become your master, and don't rely on it too much. Above all, train properly in using it, and practise with it all you can in fine weather, so in thick weather or darkness you understand it.

HYPERBOLIC NAVIGATION SYSTEMS

There are several navigational systems which rely on coded transmissions from shore stations being interpreted and then plotted on charts specially marked with the hyperbolic paths taken by the coded signals. Of these, Decca, Loran A and Omega are outside the scope of the small boat due to size, expense, high power supply requirements, or need for continuous power. Loran C is smaller than Loran A, and some details are given below. All hyperbolic systems are at present banned for IOR racing, with certain exceptions in the USA; since the 1979 Fastnet gale there is pressure to make these more widespread.

Omni

Developed originally for aircraft use, Omni, as it is known to seamen and pilots, or Visual Omnidirectional Range (VOR) to officialdom, is a directional system operating in the VHF band. It is thus restricted to line-of-sight, or some 25–30 miles, depending on the height of the beacon and the receiving boat's aerial.

A particular channel will broadcast an identification, a dial is tuned to coincide with the station concerned and the magnetic bearing is read off. Some beacons, if you have the right kind of set, can also give you a distance off.

Omni has quite a few advantages in areas where beacons are suitably sited, mainly the north east of the United States, and a few places on the Gulf and in the Caribbean. In Europe there are few beacons close enough to coasts to be of any help, though there are some in the Mediterranean. Omni requires only a light, fixed antenna. Its power requirements are low, and low-cost models intended for light aircraft can be useful in boats. You must decide yourself whether availability of beacons in the area you are concerned with justifies your fitting a set. There are reports of increasing numbers of Omni beacons being planned on the British and French coasts of the English Channel, but details have not yet been published.

Loran C

This system, based on hyperbolic plots of time measurements from shore stations, is taking over from the well known Loran A, and has advantages of greater accuracy — to within 500 yards — smaller power requirement and improved compactness. Loran C coverage, although still being extended somewhat, is far from complete, and has notable gaps. It does not cover the European west coast south of approximately Ireland, it does not cover the Caribbean, though it does go as far as Florida, and it excludes all southern hemisphere waters; most of the Mediterranean is covered. In Europe, even if you are in an area covered by Loran C, it has the great snag of picking up blanking interference from Decca Navigator stations, which are widespread. Better Loran C sets have a filter system that can reduce this, but cheaper sets do not have this facility.

Operation of the set is extremely simple. It gives two numbers digitally, which are transferred to an overprinted lattice on a chart to give two position lines providing a fix.

There is a growing feeling among navigators that the rapid improvement in satellite navigation will soon make the present hyperbolic systems obsolescent.

SATELLITE NAVIGATION

This system, using the United States Navy's Transit satellites, eight of which give world-wide coverage, has been in use for some years by naval and merchant ships, but the equipment was bulky, expensive and greedy of power.

In 1980 however a breakthrough in price, compactness and low power consumption was achieved by the British firm of Thomas Walker. Their SAT-NAV 801 is a compact set only a little bigger than a small D/F radio, using only as much 12 volt power in operation as a cabin lamp, and only 2 watts when on standby. It provides a latitude and longitude fix up to 20 times in the 24 hours, and will maintain a DR plot between fixes. Accuracy is to within 500 yards.

Operation is not difficult to learn, once one has overcome bafflement at the phrase 'geoidal height', which most people have never met. It is one of a number of simple corrections which are simply fed into the set when turned on to allow for tidal height and aerial height.

Not the least of the advantages of the SAT-NAV 801 for sailing boats is that it can be turned to standby, reducing power consumption to very little, when frequent fixes are not required, or on a long passage turned off altogether. When turned on again, it requires a 20 minute period for frequency stabilisation, but thereafter only needs a very coarse indication of present position, within 60 miles. This will be corrected at the first satellite pass, which will never be more than an hour away, and frequently is almost instantaneous. The instrument tells you, if a satellite is not at the moment in 'sight', how soon one will come over the horizon.

Information is fed into the machine by button pressing as with a pocket

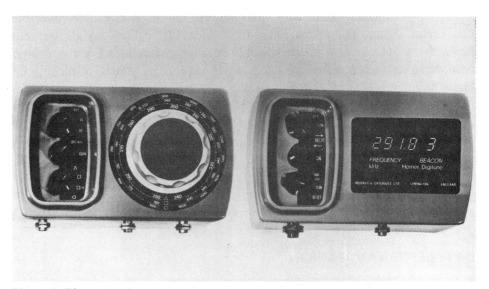

Plate 14. The world famous Brookes and Gatehouse Homer receiver with the Digitune attachment. A shortwave attachment is also available, and the Heron D/F aerial (not shown) plugs into the Homer. *(Photo: Brookes and Gatehouse)*

calculator, so care must be taken to check the information you give it for correctness — as with all computer devices, if you feed it nonsense it will give you back nonsense. Otherwise it is as nearly foolproof a device as electronics can provide.

If you are making an ocean passage, electronics being subject to failures either of the device or the satellites themselves, you must always have your sextant and tables with you. For racing, discussion is still going on about whether to permit satellite navigation systems.

It seems curmudgeonly to criticise such a miracle box, but certain minor snags for the yachtsman should be mentioned. The first is that fixes are delivered or required in latitude and longitude, not very convenient to plot in a small boat with a small chart table. The machine has the ability to work out vector triangles for you, but usually it will be quicker to draw these, because the SAT-NAV 801 requires data points to be fed in as 'way stations' defined by latitude and longitude. The coastal navigator in a small boat is much more likely to prefer his fixes as bearings and distance from landmarks or headlands.

Otherwise satellite navigation looks like being, for the well-off, the system of the future, overtaking Loran and Decca, which probably now have a limited life. The Transit satellites are expected to be effective until at least 1995, by which time a new satellite system will be in operation. The aerial required is a compact waterproof dome, the size of a kitchen plate, which can be sited almost anywhere above deck, though the higher the better.

Other models of satellite navigation devices similar to the Walker are already becoming available, and a competitive market situation is sure to bring down prices.

CONSOL/CONSOLAN

The phasing out of this system, that was used quite a lot by sailing men, has advanced so far that giving much detail is pointless. Invented by the Germans for air use in wartime, it had the great advantage that bearings or a fix could be obtained with only a simple radio receiver having a long wave band. Various transmitters broadcast a coded series of dots and dashes, in radially-coded patterns. By counting the number of dots and dashes, and allowing for those missing in the area where you passed from dots to dashes, a position line could be obtained from a special overprinted chart. A position line from another station gave a fix.

It was a long-range system, effective up to about 1000 miles, but gave very coarse fixes. It was known as Consol in Europe and Consolan in America, and two of the most important stations, at Bush Mills in Northern Ireland, and at

Nantucket, have closed down. Stations still operate in Norway and in Brittany.

In spite of its many faults Consol had a lot of advantages for the low profile, low budget navigator like the small fisherman and poor yachtsman. It will be sadly missed.

Experiments are, however, being conducted with a VHF radially-coded system in Britain, operating from North Foreland, on the Kent coast. It will be short range, but probably slightly more accurate than conventional low frequency direction finding radio.

DIRECTION FINDING RADIO (D/F)

Many lighthouses and lightships in all parts of the world carry a small radio transmitter which sends out a low-powered signal on the long wave band, suitable coded for identification purposes; special beacons are also sited inland for aircraft use. Any boat having a suitable receiver and directional aerial can align it on the transmission and then, by checking against a compass, obtain a bearing which can be plotted.

The aerial is often integral with the receiver and the whole equipment is rotated by hand for direction. Because it is easier to detect a silence, or 'null', rather than the loudest signal, the user moves round until he cannot hear the signal to which he is tuned. The direction then has to be converted to a compass bearing, and a compass is usually incorporated in the set. The system is thus not only subject to any inaccuracies which may be inherent in radio bearings, but also to those of the compass.

RADIO ERRORS. First and foremost you have to know which station you are working. A list of the morse code callsigns is given in *Reed's*, but clarity of transmission is not always as good as it might be, and the ability of your receiver (or yourself) to tune to the correct frequency of the beacon you have chosen can add to the problem. Some modern receivers have push button tuners, which help, and a digital tuning indicator is invaluable. When you have found the right station, there are errors inherent in these radio transmissions at dusk and dawn; refraction is also liable to occur where the signal crosses a coastline at a fine angle — the beam is effectively 'bent'.

COMPASS ERRORS. You should by now be aware of the compass errors you can expect. If you wave the receiver with its built-in compass around, the compass card will not settle down, and much depends on where it is pointing when you read it. Don't forget to keep it away from magnetic influences when in use. Used at long range, it is subject to the same errors as compass bearings of distant landmarks. Some receivers show the bearings as a digital read-out. This has the regrettable effect of causing the user to think that he has an exact figure — 295 on an LED display looks far more accurate than a compass card which is swinging between 285° and 300°, but is in fact just as vague.

PRACTICE.   As with all things, practice makes perfect, so may I urge you at convenient times when you are at anchor, perhaps with a glass in your hand, to become completely familiar with it. In spite of its deficiences a good D/F radio is a real friend provided you calibrate it, a process rather like swinging a compass, and learn to use it *before* you need it. Full details are given in Chapter 10. Please don't, as far too many people do, first make friends with your D/F radio in appalling conditions when its value is nullified by lack of skill, and it becomes a mere electronic aid to bewilderment.

ECHO-SOUNDER

The small echo-sounder or depth meter that has become almost universal in recent years, to the extent that even trailerboats and open day-racers use them, is probably the most valuable electronic device aboard any small craft. It is both a safety device to help stop you running aground, and an aid to navigation in thick weather because it enables you to locate a conspicuous sea bed contour line that you have noticed on the chart. Obviously it is most effective where there is a reasonably steep contour gradient, and equally obviously the user must take care, if he decides to follow a contour along a coast, that there are no dangers along it. Closing a coast in thick weather is less hazardous if you have a reliable means of telling when the depth of water is beginning to come down.

Some people use echo-sounders without knowing anything about them and, if the one they are using is in good working order and general conditions are right, they are no harder to use than a car's speedometer. But since things are not always as they should be, and someone setting out to buy a sounder may want guidance, basic facts about its principles will be useful.

Echo-sounders work by generating a small pulse of sound from a fitting in the boat's bottom called a transducer. Sound travels well through water, at a speed of 4800 feet per second. By measuring the time from the generation of the pulse of sound until a reflected echo is received, the depth of water (or indeed the horizontal distance if the transducer is set that way) can be found. This is then presented visually on a scale. Certain sounders have an audible warning system that triggers off when depth comes down to a preset level. Deciding this warning level requires delicate judgement: if set too high it will always be crying wolf unnecessarily and will tend to be ignored or switched off, if set too low you may ground almost at the instant the warning sounds. They are useful when tide-cheating or when anchored on a falling tide.

The important characteristics of any sounder should be known to the user. They are:

1. Depth below water that the transducer is mounted and its effective angle of 'vision'.

2. The maximum depth the sounder will register in good conditions, which is by no means always the same as the maximum shown on the scale.

3. Method of presentation — neon or LED flasher rotating on a circular scale, a needle pointer, or a digital readout (usually provided by light-emitting diodes). There are advantages to all three systems.

The transducer converts an electronic pulse into a pulse of sound at a high frequency far above what the human ear can hear. The sound comes from a piece of piezo-electric crystal, which is held in a suitable position with only a thin screen between it and the water. The larger the transducer face, the narrower the angle at which the sound is emitted and the further it will go so, for general use, a nice balance between ability to read to great depths, convenience of installation, and adaptability to the shape and the heeling of all sailing yachts going to windward has to be struck.

Sometimes to retain the advantages of a narrow beam two transducers are fitted, one in each bilge, with a manual or gravity-operated mercury switch to compensate for which tack the boat is on. But even with this system, some width of beam has to be retained to allow for when the boat is upright, and the beams are diverging. In simple installations, a transducer of about $1\frac{1}{2}$ ins diameter is centrally fitted somewhere around where the stem joins the keel, with a designed angle of vision of about 30 to 40 degrees.

With this system it should be remembered that sailing at a large angle of heel may cause an over-reading, and this could be tricky when operating in shallow water, such as tacking along a shore to cheat the tide.

The depth below water at which the transducer is mounted will depend on the type of boat and the installation. It is usual to leave this depth, which is added to the read-off sounding, unadjusted-for, as a safety margin. If your boat draws six feet, and has the transducer mounted two feet below the waterline, when you get a reading of seven feet, you are in fact in nine feet of water (but you only have three feet under the keel). But some people prefer to have their sounders corrected to read depth from the surface or from the keel so, if reading the sounder in a boat you are visiting, always check with the owner.

If the transducer is sited in a position where it is much affected by bubbles from the stem, close-range spurious readings will be given, because air provides a pretty solid response. For this reason the transducer should be sited away from the point where the stem cuts the water, and faired carefully so that as smooth a flow as possible passes over the transducer face — never just aft of a propeller. The face of a transducer should never be painted or scraped; any weed growth should be carefully removed, and the face polished with liquid car polish.

You sometimes meet people saying indignantly 'I was anchored in 12 feet of water on my sounder, but when I let out a few feet more chain I found I was aground on my rudder, the sounder was still reading 12 feet, and my boat only draws four feet!' The trouble was in failing to appreciate the limitations of any transducer site. It is looking down a tube, so to speak, and cannot tell you about a vertical-sided rock a rew feet outside its angle of vision. It should never be forgotten that when under way with a sounder working, such a vertical-sided and undetectable rock may lie only a few feet in front of you . . .

Depth and Scales

All but the very simplest sounders have two scales, one for operating in shallow water, and the other in deep water. Those calibrated in feet can switch to fathoms, those on the metric scale work to a multiplication of five when switched over. The important thing is that the scale should go up to a reasonable depth on the deep setting — 30 fathoms is not enough, even though the neon type of read-out goes on round the dial for the second time. On a metric reading I would expect the deep scale to read at least to 100 metres. At the same time, don't take a lavish scale as being a certain indication that a sounder will give a reading to great depths — this is as reliable as judging the speed of a car by the maximum figure on the speedometer.

The reading you get will depend on the nature of the bottom, as well as the power put out by the transducer. Hard sand or shingle, lying evenly on the bottom, gives a sharp return; rock seems to scatter and diffuse the returning signal, probably because of weed; soft mud returns a mushy echo, as you might expect. Besides the clutter caused by air bubbles which I mentioned just now, shoals of fish can cause an echo, and even a layer of water at a different temperature has been known to show up on a sensitive instrument. If the batteries are low, the effective range will drop considerably, until you can only get a reading at about twenty feet instead of a hundred or more. At greater depths than the full sweep of a rotating scale, you may get a reading on the second time round. Thus, where the full sweep covers 60 feet and you are in 70 feet, the instrument may show 10 feet — enough to cause mild panic for a few seconds.

Reading Presentation

After wide experience of all three basic types of sounder presentation, I am a little surprised to find that I still like the most basic and simple type the best, what is known as the rotating flasher. It used to be known as the neon type, because the indicator was a small neon tube, but now light emitting diodes are usually used as they are more visible in sunlight.

The principle of the rotating flasher is that a small motor drives a rotating arm holding the flasher. As a pulse is sent out, the flasher gives a flash at zero. The speed of the arm is carefully governed so that when an echo comes back from, say, 25 feet, the arm is at 25 feet on the scale, and at this point the neon or LED flashes. As the arm is rotating quite fast, repeated flashes at this point give a good reading. If the bottom is soft mud, or weed, you get a smudgy return, if it is hard sand or shingle, you get a single crisp reading.

My reason for liking this system over the far more easily-read needle or digital presentation, is that the intelligent user can get much more information out of it. The rotating flasher can, for instance, give more than one reading at a time. Suppose these is a dense shoal of fish between you and the bottom, you can see it quite clearly as a second, less determined, reading. Sometimes layers of some substance in the water such as plankton show up equally clearly. In both these cases a needle type would show you *either* the bottom *or* the intervening shoal of fish, which might give an unnerving indication.

The only snag to the rotating flasher is that it is more liable to faults from poor maintenance. It should be routine to send your sounder back for checking each winter, and not to leave it lying in the boat out of season, encouraging the ills that sea air and corrosion bring, not to mention thievery.

The needle on a dial presentation is good for those who have neither the skill nor the patience to interpret the rotating flasher. It may sometimes still make frantic efforts to give two readings at once, thus causing confusion; the needle type of reading can be illuminated for night use.

The digital reading type of sounder is likely to grow in popularity, particularly as ones with really large figures, about $1\frac{1}{2}$ inches high, are now available without slaughtering your battery. The LED type, which automatically show up in the dark, are far better than the 'numberplate' type. Either can usually be read in bright sunlight without difficulty.

My preference for the older rotating flasher to the digital reading is perhaps an old-fashioned liking for obtaining guidance from the direction in which a dial reading is moving. When you come into rapidly shoaling water, the rate at which a rotating flasher signal comes down the dial gives a much better indication of the angle of slope of the bottom than a rapidly-changing digital presentation, with its tendency to shove in the odd maverick reading every now and then.

These maverick readings are common to all echo-sounders, but tend to upset people more with digital and needle scales. The rotating flasher display will usually make it clear immediately that it is a spurious echo, because it is often weaker and in any case you can see the bottom at the same time.

LOGS

Electronic logs are an advance on the old type of rotator, trailing in the water astern and connected to a dial on the taffrail, only in their greater convenience. They are no more accurate unless properly calibrated. The kind that depends on an external rotator is subject to the same troubles with picking up weed that the old-fashioned taffrail log suffered, and there is also the possibility of spinnaker sheets or trailing lines becoming entangled with the rotator. Any log with a rotator must have easy access for clearing, and the kind in which there is no mechanical connection, only magnetic lines of force, is far superior to any system where movement of the rotator is transferred to the dial mechanically.

There are now, however, two systems whereby no external moving part is required. Each uses a transducer not unlike an echo-sounder transducer, which can be faired to the hull so that it is imperceptible, and the only worry is to stop some clot putting anti-fouling on the working surface.

The first of these two systems is the electro-magnetic type, which can be obtained at a price not beyond the pocket of a sailing man, though it may make him flinch. It compares very well with the better electronic impeller types in price, and the freedom from external moving parts is a big advantage. The system works on one of the simple basic principles of electro-magnetic theory but, like all electronic stories that begin with the word 'simple', putting the theory into force and understanding why it works is highly complicated; beyond the fact that it has something to do with the change of magnetic field as speed changes, it certainly escapes me. The only thing I can say, having sailed with one, is that the equipment works like a dream. Accurate speed and distance readings with minimal trouble can be obtained, provided the instrument is properly calibrated for the vessel in which it is installed.

The second method, already extensively in use in big ships and now coming over the small craft horizon, is the Doppler system which measures speed, and hence distance, by a comparison of sound when an object is approaching and going away. With a full Doppler system two transducers, one facing slightly forward and the other aft, generate a sound signal and then compare the echoes, receiving the answer either from the bottom or, where the bottom is too far down, from the water alone. Normal yacht types are not so complicated, and give only speed through the water, and distance.

Doppler type logs currently available protrude slightly more from the hull than electro-magnetic types, and the system at present is more expensive. Accuracy may be affected by temperature and salinity of the water, which again is in the electro-magnetic type's favour, but electronic boffins tell me they reckon the Doppler system is the thing of the future. One of its biggest advantages is the way certain Doppler systems can give speed over the ground in shallow water as well as the usual speed through the water.

Log Calibration

Whatever kind of log you fit must be properly calibrated, because the position in which the works are installed, the normal average speed of the boat, and various other factors have to be taken into consideration. The rotating spinner type trails over the stern, its rotation being connected either mechanically or electrically to a dial on the counter or taffrail. At very low speeds it will cease to read, a thing common to most logs, and at high speeds it sometimes leaps above the surface. But properly calibrated (usually a matter of adjusting the length of the line according to the instructions) it works remarkably well. The mechanical parts *must* be kept well lubricated and free from salt. If weed gathers on the line, haul in the rotator completely, remove the weed, trail the hook end of the line over the stern to free it of twists, bring it back aboard and hook on, then trail the rotator again.

STREAMING AND TAKING-IN.   The problem with streaming and taking-in a towed log of the mechanical type, is that the rotator continues to twist while the line is being paid out or taken-in. This twists the line itself because the swivel is not in operation. Thus, when streaming, the hook should be engaged with the indicator on the taffrail and, when the rotator held in one hand, the line should be doubled and paid out until it is streaming astern in a bight. The rotator should then be lowered into the water and allowed to fall astern as the line is fed rapidly through the hand; it should be braked as it nears the end. To take in the log, unhook the end from the indicator and pay it over the stern as the rotator is pulled in. This allows it to untwist as the line is eventually pulled in from the rotator end. The prudent mariner will pay the hook end out after first passing it round the backstay or an upright on the pushpit, as a precaution against losing it overboard.

The only real snags to the trailing log are that fish may take the rotator, so spares are needed, and calibration is sometimes difficult in the shallow water where it is easy to find distance markers.

When calibrating any type of log, either the tidal stream must be allowed for, or two runs, during which conditions are the same, must be made in opposite directions between transits which are charted. Most ports have such measured distances laid out for the purpose. Having discovered the error, it should then be corrected as the instructions for the instrument direct, and then another series of runs made.

It is almost impossible to correct a log completely at all speeds. The best thing is to make it correct for your boat's average good speed, and make a note of significant under-reading or over-reading at other speeds. Most logs under-read at low speeds and over-read at high speeds but the trailed rotator type sometimes under-read at high speeds if a rough sea is making the rotator break surface.

If you have been making a long passage out of sight of land, and have developed that we-ought-to-get-a-landfall-by-now sort of feeling, but the log says you still have 20 miles to go, the log, not you, is almost sure to be right.

Many logs now give a speed reading as well as distance, and a lot of beginners, being used to the speedometer of a car, think the speed reading is more important than the distance. It is not. Its value is for checking the effect of sail trimming and tuning.

ELECTRONIC CALCULATORS

The right kind of electronic calculator can, in theory, be most useful to the navigator. The best can solve almost every navigational problem, sometimes with great speed and ease. But as so often with marine equipment the key words are 'the right kind'. There are certain calculators that are so unsuitable for use in a boat that they are an active nuisance.

Any calculator for use afloat must be portable, and work off the yacht battery, internal batteries or cells that can be recharged, so they can be put away out of range of spray and accidental damage. The simplest 'kitchen' calculator will do only a little on a boat beyond speed, time and distance problems, and maybe tidal sums, but it is hardly worth the trouble of looking after it for such simple work. A good scientific model, however, can really do a lot. The answer here lies in the user. He must know all about it, and be able to work it almost with his eyes shut. There is a world of difference between pressing a series of buttons on a calculator sitting in comfort at an office desk without interruption, and trying to do the same in poor light, when cold, wet, tired, and in a tossing boat that is trying to make you seasick.

Reed's Almanac has taken enthusiastically to calculators, and its navigation section gives a number of applications. The writer of the calculator sections is, I think, a bit optimistic in his use of the word 'simple'. Many of his formulae would not seem simple to the average sailor.

WHAT THEY WILL DO.   In the mid-seventies I wrote an article for *Seahorse*, the journal of the Royal Ocean Racing Club, on two of the advanced Hewlett-Packard scientific models then available, one of which, the HP 65, had the ability to use programmes stored on magnetic cards. Although this model has been superseded by the HP 67, and other makes now have even more advanced systems of programme storage, I reproduce part of the article here because it gives a lighthearted summary of what calculators can do if properly mastered.

THE NAVIGATOR'S DREAM

Scene: Dark, blowy night, somewhere in region Casquets-Lyme Bay, wind varying between sou'west and nor'west, about force 6. Turning to windward, a well-tuned and crewed Class 2 boat, whose owner reckons she has a good chance of being in the money in this race and these conditions.

On Stage: Navigator, snug in his hutch behind his office, who crawled into his fleabag an hour ago saying to himself, 'I reckon, with luck, I might get four hours solid.'

Enter Mariner, dripping from oilskins onto sleeping bag.

Mar: 'Hey Joe, wind's backed a bit. Bill says he's making six knots on two-three-five now, and should we tack?'

Nav: (sitting up still in sleeping bag, reaching into locker for magic box and giving quick glance at chart; he presses buttons on magic box): 'No, stand on on starboard for another two hours before tacking, unless the wind frees so you can lay two-five-five, then you could ease sheets.'

Mar (shedding a few more drips): 'Okay' (lets in wave as he exits through hatch).

Nav: 'Z-Z-z-z-z-z...'

We have all had dreams like this, but now, if you can dig deep enough into your pocket, there really is gadgetry that makes life easier for offshore racing navigators, and makes them more effective navigators too. In the hot competition of the top classes the cost is insignificant when placed against the likelihood that they will save you critical minutes. My enthusiasm for the machines is that of the world's most seasick navigator, who has discovered something that means more time on deck and less at the chart table.

Since all sorts of tales, both pro and con, are going around about the gadgets, here is a summary of what they will and will not do. They will:

1. Solve any vector triangle when you press the right buttons, virtually immediately. Vectors can be added together so that a long series of courses and tides, as when beating to windward, can be produced as a single bearing and distance, which is particularly useful when planning windward strategy. A wide choice of tacking patterns can be quickly compared.

2. Resolve any problem that can be expressed as a formula, which covers most questions in navigation. For the chap who does not really understand formulae and trig (that's me), it is a matter of writing down or learning by rote the buttons to press and the order to press them. It's not true that for the chap who really understands his maths they will do a lightning headsail change, though they might give useful information as to what headsail change is desirable.

3. Calculate almost as quickly as a fullsize computer all the dreadful mathematics that have grown up round the rating rule, if you want to fight your way into that jungle. For the ordinary man they quickly give corrected time for yours and other boats. There are few mathematical calculations they will not resolve and, since they have a number of memory stores, you need a minimum of pencil and paper work.

The devices will not:

(a) Take the interest out of navigation — just the drudgery.
(b) Make a man of poor judgement into a good navigator.
(c) Go on working if immersed in bilge water, though they are moderately resistant to spray. If you want to take one into the cockpit, you would be wise to enclose it in a loose transparent plastic bag, tightly sealed with an elastic band; it can be operated or read through the bag (except for feeding the programmes into a magnetic card programmable model, which must be done in shelter).

Typical cases of the work the calculators will do are: giving course to steer to make good a given track, allowing for tide; providing actual position, allowing for tidal stream and leeway — this can be done for a long series of tacks if the navigator is snoring, provided the watch on deck has kept note of courses, times, log readings, leeway etc; establishing present rise of tide; giving, without tables, distance off a light by vertical sextant angle; or rapid working out of star sights, which is done without pre-computed tables — just a simple almanac is needed.

Finally, for a hotly contested race, either inshore or offshore, the navigator can work out, almost instantly, corrected time at a buoy against a boat on your heels, to see if it's worth snapping a luff at her. Surrounded perhaps by three or four boats that may be a menace to you, the navigator can say quickly, using the TMF formula, 'Don't bother with him or him, but a sharp luff at *that* chap might give us this race.'

I know there will be cavillers who say these calculators are nasty, new-fangled devices which no seaman should have any truck with. They make me imagine the dialogue of some hoary old admiral when Mr Hadley first introduced his octant: 'Nasty, new-fangled things, much too fussy and fragile to be any use in a ship. And not nearly as handy as my old cross-staff for livening up an idle snotty bent over a gun . . .'

It is unfortunate that a lot of people have been urging the benefits of calculators for navigation, without any sort of discrimination. The vast majority of calculators, mostly the cheap and simple ones, are *almost useless to the navigator*, certainly the small boat navigator. They may help with converting foreign currency, or for those incapable of adding and subtracting simple figures they can be used for certain tide, and speed, time and distance sums. I am aware that if you have the right formulae even a simple calculator can work out trigometric problems. The more advanced scientific ones can easily solve any problem you present it with, including complicated matters like spherical triangles, again if you know the right formulae. But, and it is a very big but, all this requires a vast amount of button-pressing; and pressing more than a minimum of buttons is just not practical when navigating a small boat. What happens is that, when you are two-thirds the way through pressing 180 buttons, the oaf on deck says 'Navigator, we have just passed out of the white sector of such-and-such a light into a red sector, what does it mean, quick?'. A calculator loses a lot of its appeal when you give it a problem of great length the second time round.

There are three key questions when considering any calculator for navigation.

1. Will it do its job with only the minimum of button pressing to feed it the facts? This means either some inbuilt programming, or a means of easily giving it a programme without having to work right through it each time, or that it will retain programmes when switched off.

2. Has it got polar to rectangular conversion? This means converting from polar information, given in the form of an angle and a distance from a point of origin, to Cartesian or rectangular co-ordinates (usually expressed as x and y) — distances from a horizontal and a vertical line. The inverse is also necessary. Without polar to rectangular conversions, usually with keys marked P→R and R→P on the keyboard, you cannot do vector triangles, except with great complication.

3. Will it accept and display information in degrees, minutes and seconds (or hours, minutes and seconds), converting quickly to and from the decimal form? If it does, it is a great advantage if it makes it quite clear which condition it is in.

The answers to these questions will almost certainly cut you down to under ten calculator models as being really desirable for navigation — a bit of a jolt when most salesmen will glibly tell you that nearly all his scores of machines are fine for navigating small boats. The list of suitable ones may grow, but since the demand is limited, probably not very fast.

I have tried at sea virtually every calculator suitable for navigation, and a number that proved highly undesirable — they made me seasick as well as furious and frustrated. I give here, in order of preference, the short roll of honour of calculators which proved useful and practical at sea. Calculators that do not help are a liability and a potential expense, and can break up friendships. Even good calculators can be a nuisance, they must be kept always in a plastic bag, cherished, shut away from people who want to play, guarded from ham-fisted and big-footed oaves, and the salt water that always splashes about the navigator's cubbyhole. They also have to be protected from plain, old-fashioned thieves. My calculator roll of honour, then, in order of preference, is as follows.

TAMAYA NC-77. Although this is a simple machine compared with the really advanced magnetic card programmable models, it is pre-programmed with nearly all that the navigator could want, both DR and astro, as well as an almanac of astro information up to beyond the year 2000. It has the enormous virtue, when you become familiar with it, of having a code-sign which shows where you are in the middle of a calculation so, if some-one demands your help in dragging a spinnaker into the cabin in the middle of a problem (a common hazard for racing navigators), you can go back and pick up where you left off. It is robust (I hope I never have to test its watertightness) and accessories to run it off the yacht battery, or recharge nickel cadmium batteries, can be obtained. I wish it had an automatic switch-off facility, four memories instead of two, and also programmed metric conversions and their inverses. Tanker officers tell me it needs to do at least cube roots as well as square roots. It will do all you ask of it in the normal DR line, like working out vector triangles, DR position by traverse, distance off by sextant angles, tide heights and speed, time and distance problems. If you are into astro it is incomparable, doing all you need quickly and simply, including the tedious little bits so often overlooked like sextant corrections for low angles. The instruction book is excellent. Although it has an equals sign for simple problems, which go quite normally, it works on what is known as Reverse Polish Notation logic for its programmed problems.

This alarming phrase need not worry any one, it is merely the way certain calculators like to receive their information. The alternative method is Algebraic Logic, which most people find simpler to understand. With RPN, if you want to add 2 to 7, you press 2, then a key usually marked 'Enter', but on the Tamaya is a blob inside a circle, then 7, then +. With algebraic logic (which the Tamaya uses when doing a simple problem), you merely key in $2 + 7 =$ and get the answer 9. It is important to know which system your machine works on, because you can get the wrong answer if you give the information the wrong way. The Texas Instruments machines mentioned below have an even more advanced algebraic system, that will sort out a formula with lots of different signs into their correct order. For advanced mathematics RPN is better, but the ordinary man will prefer algebraic logic. The Tamaya's mixture of the two systems works well.

TEXAS SR 59. This is an advanced scientific calculator that accepts programmes from magnetic cards, including programmes you have written yourself, and also takes programmes from modules that you insert to cover the subject you are interested in. Quite a good navigational module is available, but it lacks a few things the small boat navigator would like. These you can work out for yourself, or Texas will send you a programme, that you write on a magnetic card. I have myself given Texas a programme for tide levels in an area of straight-forward tides. Since it can be set to have 100 memories, it is not difficult to write a programme that will give you a Solent tide table which would be of considerable benefit when racing. The Nav module does not contain an astro almanac, but I expect one could be obtained or created — the mathematics required to create an almanac, starting from last year's *Reed's Nautical Almanac*, while tedious, are well within the machine's capabilities.

If you were, for instance, a merchant banker who was a keen offshore sailor, you might find the Texas 59 a better bet than the Tamaya, because you could feed it a financial module when working, switching to a navigation module at sea. The navigation module provides all you need for DR, including vector triangles, speed, time and distance problems, some useful conversions (the module deals in US, not Imperial gallons), and most things that are needed for astro. At present the Texas 59 does not have the valuable attribute of the Texas 58C (below) of remembering programmes when turned off, but I would not be surprised if this were not incorporated in later models. The instruction book is good. A transformer to enable it to run off the yacht battery is available.

TEXAS SR 58C.   This accepts the same programme modules as the Texas 59, but has fewer memories and programme steps, and lacks the magnetic card programme facility of the 59. It does, however, have the valuable asset of retaining a programme when turned off, which for the small boat navigator is of great importance. The Texas SR 58 (without the C) lacks this facility. Except that it will not accept such long programmes the 58C does everything that the 59 does, other than having the magnetic card facility. The same power connection for a yacht battery is available. Both Texas models work on alternating current, so the correct adaptor is essential. The Texas 58C is, at the time of writing, the cheapest calculator that has all the facilities the navigator needs. It is about half the price of the Tamaya or Texas 59.

CASIO FX 502P and FX 501P.   These are two similar models, the only difference being that the 502 has more programme steps and memory registers. They are remarkable machines, potentially of great value to the navigator, except that their instruction books are inadequate and printed in such small type as to be almost illegible without a magnifier. Programmes can be stored, through a compact attachment, onto a tape recorder, and a large number of programmes can be stored in a single cassette of the type used in office pocket recorders. Programmes provided with the machines include three for navigation, but the man who wrote the book of programmes suffered from the same inability to communicate as the writer of the instruction book, and makes things unnecessarily hard to understand. Nevertheless the qualities of these two machines are such that I persisted with the 502 and eventually found it excellent. It has the same valuable attribute as the Texas 58C of retaining its programmes and memories when switched off. For coastal work it will happily memorise indefinitely all you need for DR. The calculator switches itself off if left idle, to save battery life. It will give 1000 hours of use off two tiny silver oxide watch batteries. The display is liquid crystal, rather easier to see in a boat than the red illuminated digits of the Texas and Hewlett-Packard models. If useful and intelligible instruction books were available these Casios would be highly recommended. As it is, even though reasonably well-educated in calculators, it took me weeks to get the hang of making the 502p do what I wanted it to do.

HEWLETT-PACKARD HP 67.   This is the successor to the HP 65, which was the first magnetic card programme pocket calculator to be marketed. Although it lacks the Texas 59's splendid ability to use programmes from a compact internal module, it is an outstanding machine, and the Nav-Pack and its instructions are better than those for the Texas. It also contains various almanac cards. The *Seahorse* article quoted above gives an indication of its abilities. All Hewlett-Packards work on RPN logic, and several models — not the 67 at present — will retain their programmes when turned off.

The cards for all magnetic card programmable calculators should always be carefully guarded against magnetic influences like loudspeakers, echo-sounders, most electronic instruments generally, and the slightest trace of grease or saltwater. Placing a magnetic card on a bridgedeck over an engine that has an alternator churning out 20 amps will do the oddest things to the programme on the card. For this reason, if you have a magnetic card type, carry in a safe place duplicates of all your programmes. Any trace of salt crystals on a card will do irreparable damage to the reading head in the calculator, but rinsing a card gently in fresh water, and drying without energetic rubbing will do no harm.

CBM N 60. This calculator is designed for aircraft navigation, with a number of very useful pre-programmed facilities, but without the ability to take a programme created by the user. If you feed in the *reciprocal* of your tide direction it will do all tidal vector triangles quickly and easily, being designed for wind triangles. It has a number of useful conversions, and a particularly valuable ability to distinguish in use between degrees, minutes and seconds and decimalised degrees. It has no astro facilities, but celestial navigation is simplified when operating manually, by this easy decimalisation distinction. It is particularly handy for summing vectors. Not the least of its advantages is that it is the cheapest calculator that is useful for the navigator, though it lacks some of the facilities of the Texas 58C, which costs about one third more. You must decide yourself whether the programme module facility, which includes astro, is worth the extra money. The N 60 works off internal rechargeable batteries, and at present there is no accessory charger for working off yacht batteries, though an electronics expert could easily make one up for you.

OTHER TYPES.   In the event that you already have a calculator, and want to know if it is suitable for use afloat, look back at the three key questions above, and also consider your own mastery of the device. If you are a mathematician or engineer who can use it almost without thinking, it may be of help to you. A good scientific calculator will, in theory, do all that you need, if it has the facilities referred to. All it lacks is the ability to be seagoing in a small boat, and a tolerance of seawater to the extent that it must always be doubly protected. Thinking these snags over, it is up to you whether you want to take that so-useful office servant into such a hostile environment. . . .

If a salesman has somehow convinced you that a calculator is essential to happy navigation in your boat, and you cannot afford one of the models recommended above, sit down in the shop for at least half an hour and try working out on the model that takes your fancy what you want to do on it. Only buy if you *can* do it, surrounded by other customers, anxious salesmen, cashtills buzzing and other interference. These will be nothing to the interference you will get at sea.

Getting the best use out of a calculator requires knowing the right formulae, and being able to transpose into a form to suit the particular machine you are using. *Reed's Almanac* is helpful here, and a book called *Navigation by Pocket Calculator* by Conrad Dixon, published by Adlard Coles Ltd, has many useful formulae and programmes for calculators in a compact form.

POCKET COMPUTERS.   Computers scarcely any bigger than a calculator, but with much more extensive capabilities, are now available. They will perform all navigational and many other tasks, while working off small internal batteries, and have sufficient memory and programme capacity to run a small warship. They are available for the cost of a genoa for a small cruiser.

I have been much impressed by the TRS-80 pocket computer from Tandy, which has 1600 programme steps and can put programmes and data onto tape cassettes. Sharp make a similar model, and others can be expected. I am not going into them further because I feel not many sailors will be bothered to learn the somewhat intricate details of programming them. When ready-written navigational programmes become available, they may become more popular. Computers are specifically banned at present from RORC racing, but this situation may change.

SIMPLE EXAMPLES

Virtually all the useful things a scientific calculator can do can be found in the book mentioned above, but some of the very simplest are mentioned here for those who are frightened by formulae.

You have travelled at 6·2 knots for 4 hours 22 minutes. How far have you gone?

First you need to decimalise the 4 hours 22 minutes. If your calculator has a decimalise button, it will tell you straight away that this is 4·3666 hours; otherwise you obtain it by dividing the minutes by 60.

The formula for distance is simple: speed×time=distance, so the answer to your question is (rounded off) 27·07 miles.

If you want to know when you are going to arrive at a port 42 miles away, making a steady 8·2 knots, you use the time formula: distance÷speed=time. Both distance and speed will already be decimalised, but you will want to unscramble the calculator's answer of 5·1219512 hours into hours and minutes. The five hours are correct, simply multiply the figures to the right of the decimal point by 60: the time taken is 5 hours 32 minutes.

The third of the speed/time/distance problems is when you know how far you have gone (say 36 miles) and how long it has taken you (say 7 hours 50 minutes). Distance÷time=speed. All you have to do is again to decimalise the minutes part of the time by dividing by 60, giving 7·833333. Your answer is 4·59 knots.

This will immediately show you what a valuable feature in a calculator for navigation is the interchangeability between decimalised hours, and hours minutes and seconds. There is also an angular equivalent. Some calculators also operate other angular measures besides degrees, usually radians. A radian is a length round the arc of a circle equivalent to the radius. You will find such a calculator will have a control enabling you to set either degrees or radians, and if it gives funny answers, you have probably forgotten to set it to degrees.

Another virtue of a scientific calculator is that it enables somebody who does not understand trigonometry, to use it with great effectiveness and no fiddling with often incomprehensible tables, rather as you can tell the time from a watch without any idea of what goes on inside it. The trig functions of the sine, cosine and tangent, normally shortened to sin, cos and tan, with their inverses, are the basis of nearly all navigational and surveying theoretical work, because they make the solution of triangles simple. They are obtained just by pressing the correct button on a calculator. But you don't have to worry about this if you don't want to.

Although most calculators come with a case or box, these are seldom practical for use afloat where the greatest risk to the instrument is of being dropped, sliding off a chart table, or being doused in spray that often finds its way below. I have even heard of one spoiled by drips off the oilskins of a crew member coming through the hatch and passing the chart table.

The best thing to do if you take a calculator afloat is to make it a *box in which it can be used*, yet is waterproof, provides some degree of shock protection and can be fastened to a short lanyard, so if it is dropped or slides off a surface it does not hit the cabin sole.

This is not as difficult as it sounds. Using scraps of marine ply and solid mahogany, make a tray a quarter of an inch or so bigger all round than the calculator. The lid is a flat sheet of ply, with cut-outs for the keyboard and display, and so it can be turned on and off; it must have a reliable fastening. Varnish or paint to suit your fancy, and line the whole thing, including lid with foam rubber or plastic at least a quarter inch thick. Screw to one of the more solid pieces a good eye to which a lanyard can be permanently spliced. All you have to do now is make sure the lanyard is always attached to something. The foam is essential, because the shock of stopping short at the end of the lanyard is considerable.

To protect from spray, wrap the calculator in one of those thin plastic bags sold in supermarkets for holding sandwiches, with a metal strip that makes an almost waterproof seal. The calculator can be worked and read *through* the bag, which can occasionally be renewed, and bag and all go inside the box. All you have to do now is protect the device from thieves.

Plate 22 shows the box I knocked up in an evening for my Tamaya NC 77. The hardest part of making it was finding a shop that sold foam rubber. When not in use, calculator and box together go inside a leather case found in the junk box of a camera shop.

10
D/F Radio

At this stage I must, as the politicians say, declare an interest. I deliberately expanded this D/F radio section to contradict an opinion expressed in a book by an electronics expert, who said that small D/F radios incorporating a ferrite rod aerial and a bearing compass close together gave poor results and were not worth what they cost. He urged the benefits of large loop aerials and massive, well-corrected master compasses, by which the helmsman knows exactly, at any time, what his course is, and when he deviates from it he is flogged at the gratings.

I don't think that this particular author cares a lot about the problems of small boats of the kind that you and I go to sea in, nor has he noticed that the majority of offshore racing boats uses exactly the system he dislikes. He appeared to be thinking in terms of large power cruisers or trawlers, that do not heel much and don't have to worry about sensitive devices which get grabbed by stumbling crews (or owners) in the dark, and are also likely to become snarled in genoa and spinnaker sheets. If he went to sea in our sort of boat, he would quickly discover that the largest of the admittedly large errors which D/F radio is heir to comes when the navigator, twiddling his loop, says 'Steer 180° exactly, I am just getting a fix', only to be checkmated by the helmsman replying 'It's impossible in this head sea.'

There is in fact a better way — to brief the helmsman to note his course when the navigator says 'Now!'. But the net result is almost always that, on top of all the other sources of error, there is a helmsman-to-navigator error of uncalibrated size, which with some helmsman may amount to 15 degrees or more. The virtue of the compass-on-the-aerial system is that it cuts out this major source of error. Other errors which the system may introduce can reasonably be assessed and allowed for.

There would have been more point in the criticism of this technical expert if he had concentrated on stressing how the errors of the hand held compass-plus-aerial system are magnified by unskilful use, particularly through being operated in unsuitable positions, and how these troubles can be reduced. It is an odd thing how few people read the handbooks given with D/F sets. I have sailed with scores of people who own the excellent Brookes and Gatehouse Homer-Heron system, and only a few had ever read the instruction manual right through.

MINIMISING ERROR

People who make and sell D/F radios naturally do not want to put buyers off by emphasizing faults in the system, so they tend to be brief about problems and built-in error, or perhaps to camouflage it with jargon baffling to the layman. My aim, as well as explaining things to beginners, is to help you, in as untechnical a way as possible, to choose and instal your set to minimise the errors inherent in the system; to improve your radio fixes from poor to medium (in a small bouncing sailing boat you cannot expect much more); and to recognise when and why radio fixes are so bad that they must be disregarded altogether.

RADIO BEACONS

Bearings of transmitters which broadcast radio entertainment programmes are quite possible, but they are not always sited most conveniently for the mariner, nor do they identify themselves at frequent enough intervals for the stranger. So something more specialist is required, and this need is met on most coastlines frequented by shipping through a network of marine radio beacons. Details of them are given in *Reed's* and various yachtsmen's guides.

They operate in the frequency band 190–420 kHz (1600–700 m long wave). In Europe they seldom operate below 260 kHz; in the USA many also cover the medium wave band and parts of the VHF and UHF bands. They are marked on charts by a magenta or purple circle; those used for air navigation (which operate on similar frequencies up to 410 kHz), and likely to be useful to the mariner, are usually marked on the chart with the word 'aero' added.

Should you find yourself operating a very old-fashioned set calibrated in metres instead of kilohertz, conversion is not difficult: divide the one you know into 300,000 to get the other.

$$\frac{300,000}{\text{kHz}} = \text{metres, and } \frac{300,000}{\text{metres}} = \text{kilohertz}$$

Marine beacons are usually linked in groups up to six in number, using a common frequency (which will be well-spaced from any adjacent group). Each beacon transmits in turn a signal which contains its callsign and a long dash, variously arranged depending on location, but which lasts precisely one minute, and the complete sequence of any particular group takes six minutes. Thus a particular beacon in a group of six will transmit once every six minutes; one in a group of three will transmit every three minutes; and so on. If there are six stations in a group and you are only interested in one of them, you will have to wait five minutes for the one you want to transmit again. This is not as tiresome as it sounds, since the groups are carefully arranged, and you are almost certain to want bearings also from some of the others on the same frequency. Remember that it is not unknown for beacons to go silent, either through breakdown or for maintenance.

DIRECTIONAL BEACONS.   Some beacons indicate a safe line of approach, by transmitting complementary morse code letters such as A ($\cdot$ –) and N (– $\cdot$). These overlap on the safe line, to give a steady signal; to port you would only get A signals and to starboard it would be N. You must switch off any automatic gain control while using these beacons or the signal will distort.

DISTANCE FINDING.   Some beacons transmit their radio signal at exactly the same time as their fog signal when the weather is thick. By comparing the time difference between hearing the two signals, it is possible to work out the distance of the beacon.

TYPES OF SET

Direction finding radios for small boats come in a variety of shapes and sizes, and range in price from about a week's wages up to three month's salary for a white collar worker. The big expensive set will give you full duplex radio telephone on both MF and VHF, but is liable to be too big for the average small boat and will require too much power. The average man wants a set which will work off his boat circuit without the need to run a generator, or perhaps even off its own internal batteries. Most of them incorporate a beat frequency oscillator (BFO) which helps with reception of certain beacons, though it must often be switched off for identification. A switch to cut out automatic gain control, which is normally working on broadcast bands, is valuable.

RESERVE BATTERIES.   If your set will only work off its own internal dry batteries, you must have an ample stock of reserves. I once did an offshore race in light winds and a lot of fog, with practically still water. The boat was equipped with the very latest hand-held D/F set, so recent that the owner did not know the characteristic of the then newly-introduced mercury cell batteries in that they give virtually full power almost up to the moment they die, suddenly. We were getting quite good fixes in ideal conditions, so much so that the owner spent some time teaching stray members of the crew how to work his latest toy. Then, fairly abruptly, it began losing urge, so that there was not enough to last until we got home.

'No I haven't got any spare batteries,' snapped the owner testily. 'They were new only three weeks ago, so there should be plenty in them still.'

What he didn't know was that, while the boatyard was attending to various jobs in the previous two weeks, the shipwrights had made good use of the spanking new set to pick up their pet radio entertainment — and if it helped them do a good job, who begrudges it? But the lesson is:

ALWAYS HAVE PLENTY OF SPARE BATTERIES UNLESS YOU CAN CONNECT TO THE CHARGEABLE YACHT BATTERY CIRCUIT.

Choosing a Set

Most people will have their choice of radio dictated for them by the depth of their pocket. For the man of deep pocket, who wants the best regardless of cost, there is little problem. His boat is probably large, and with adequate power (even racing you are allowed to run a generator). He will probably choose some system of automatic direction finder, which will be used in conjunction with a repeater compass which is free from all deviation. The aerial of an automatic direction finder can often be mounted so that it is free from everything except propagation error, that is, error arising at the transmitter. The man of deep pocket will have plenty of people to help him choose the best installation and system for his boat, but he must remember that automatic D/F is not at present allowed under the IOR. The rest of us will choose from one of the following:

PORTABLE RECEIVER WITH ROTATING FERRITE AERIAL, POINTER AND SCALE, DERIVING THE BEARING FROM THE STEERING COMPASS. This system, though quite a number of them are sold, gives the worst of every world. The portability of the instrument reduces the likelihood of it ever being calibrated for one particular site, and at the same time it usually suffers from the operator-to-helmsman error I have spoken about. As normally used, the only thing to be said is that it is better than nothing, and will get the weather forecasts. Even skilfully used, the fixes are likely to be low grade.

With this type of set I have seen a home-made lashup that can be a slight improvement. If the set has its aerial locked in a fixed position, and is then mounted endways at one end of a piece of wood at least two feet long, and a compass capable of taking bearings mounted at the other end — the two feet

Plate 15. Recently Brookes and Gatehouse have added to their outstanding series of D/F sets the multiple-band Heron 5, which is used in conjunction with the standard Homer aerial/compass. The Homer 5 incorporates digital frequency display, digital and crystal-controlled frequency selection, and a memory for retaining chosen beacons. It also has an alarm system for putting the weather forecast on a separate tape-recorder when you are ashore. It is singularly easy to use for such an advanced device, but it is pricey. The unit shown on the right is the mounting panel. *(Photo: Brookes and Gatehouse)*

separation is to avoid the loudspeaker of the set affecting the compass — at least the operator-to-helmsman error can be reduced. But this is an awkward arrangement to stow and to use in a small boat. The separation of compass and set needs to be *at least* two feet, because the magnetic affect of even a small loudspeaker is quite large.

PORTABLE SET WITH ATTACHED COMPASS. Intelligently used these can be excellent, and the best ones incorporate digital tuning, like the Lok-Kata 5 in Plate 13. But they must be used in a place where deviation is nil, or else deviation must be carefully allowed for. The theory that they can be used at the chart table or down below out of reach of spray, takes a severe knock when you get a couple of miles away from a station that is transmitting continuously for calibration purposes, and the position line you plot is visibly 15 degrees different from what those on deck can see by eye. Nevertheless good versions of this system are some of the best. The Aptel is notable for its excellent digital tuning system, but unfortunately spoils the ship for a ha'porth of tar by having an undamped compass that locks with a trigger effect. This compass can introduce a lot of error unless skilfully used, and if I had one I would change the compass for a liquid-damped one, and forget about the trigger.

There are several cheap portable direction finders and they work well if carefully looked after. The Seafix has built up a good reputation as a poor man's D/F, and the latest models have been improved by raising the compass on a small pedestal to get it away from the batteries, which can now be obtained only steel-cased. If you possess an earlier model you will find the performance notably improved by putting a two-inch pedestal of wood or light alloy between compass and body.

HAND-HELD COMPASS AND AERIAL, FIXED SET.   This system, made world-famous by the British firm of Brookes and Gatehouse with their Homer-Heron, is one of the best for small craft, and is fitted to multitudes of offshore racers equipped regardless of price. Part of the Homer-Heron system's high reputation is because of its very high-grade circuitry, sturdiness, reliability and waterproofness, including such details as specially plated contacts which keep the sets going in sea air. They are expensive, but worth every penny if you learn to operate them properly. It is unfortunate that Brookes and Gatehouse put out a publicity brochure showing a navigator using a Homer-Heron on a chart table, in close proximity to other electronic devices, and off the centreline of the boat. All these factors reduce the effectiveness of the D/F radio.

Although the basic idea has been in use for about a quarter of a century, and is much copied, the Homer-Heron has evolved and improved steadily. A digital tuning attachment is available which is particularly useful, it allows the required beacon to be picked up instantly with the minimum of searching.

The idea of a separate D/F aerial, with compass, linked by remote wire to a fixed set has been adopted by other makers, with varying degrees of expense and success. The Danish made Sailor version is the only one that is an improvement on the Homer-Heron, and it is bulkier and more expensive.

ROTATING LOOP.   This system is slightly more accurate in its null than any ferrite rod, but is too bulky for convenience in small boats. Small loops are little use. Ideally the loop should be on deck, and even with a fold-down loop it is likely to get lassoed by odd lines. On big boats such as motor yachts, where a large loop can be fixed above the deckhouse and rotated by the operator inside, it makes a good system. But boats in this price range have mostly gone over to automatic direction finders, which cannot be used in IOR races (at present), so are not much fitted in small sailing craft.

Some really big yachts have a fixed double loop (I have vague recollections of an RAF lecturer, who tried vainly to teach me the rudiments of electronic theory when I was learning to fly, saying it was called a Bellini-Tosi loop; everyone thought this was a manoeuvre performed by Italian fighter pilots) which, in conjunction with an electronic control called a goniometer, can give very accurate results. The goniometer must be close to a well-adjusted compass.

TUNING AND IDENTIFICATION

Unless you have a digitally tuned set, with the digits controlled electronically by the circuit, a radio beacon is often like Mrs Beeton's hare — first you must catch it. Few ordinary receivers are accurate in the calibration of their tuning dial, so hunting for a particular station, which may be so spaced in time from the rest of its group that you get periods of silence before the one you want comes up, can be tedious. But even the beginner can do it. The morse identification signals are sent out very slowly, so you do not even need to know morse well: just remember the particular signal you have heard, and then look it up on a card or in *Reed's*. Once you have got a single station in your group, all you have to do is wait for the ones you are interested in to come up. A few minutes listening on the beacon band quickly attunes the ear to the very slow morse code signals. It helps if you say to yourself 'dit' for a dot and 'dah' for a dash. 'Dit-dit-dah' (letter U, single letter code, you are standing into danger) is much quicker to think, say and identify than 'Dot-dot-dash'.

Many receivers have a switch labelled 'identify' which cuts out the directional aerial and uses an all round one, while you are searching for your call-sign. Having caught your beacon you then switch to D/F to take the bearing. But the more economical sets do not have this facility so, when hunting for a particular beacon, you must rotate the aerial to a suitable line so it is in a position to receive the signal.

There are D/F sets which have a preset crystal-tuned facility, in which you previously insert the crystals for the frequencies you are going to want, and just press a button to tune. This is a most valuable ability, but they are not cheap and the crystals themselves are expensive. If you are on a cruise in a wide area, you will perhaps need a lot of crystals.

Certain beacons transmit on their own wavelength continuously. These are particularly useful for calibration and practice purposes.

Most air beacons also transmit continuously. Sometimes, if the tuning dial of your receiver has become displaced, a continuously transmitting beacon is easier to find, and you can then note how far your dial is off-set. This facilitates later beacon finding.

Finding your Beacon

When you come for the first time to the business of tuning in one particular beacon, you will be horrified at the great number there are bleeping away, and this applies particularly when the one you want is perhaps faint and distant. At Boat Shows, demonstrators usually insist that they cannot let you listen to their receivers inside the hall 'because of the interference.' This may indeed be true, but many people might refuse to buy sets if they discovered the jungles they have to thread their way through in order to pick up their desired beacon. There always seems to be one powerful transmitter drowning out everything else, and it never seems to be in your list of call signs; the drowning effect applies especially when practising at home. The offender is almost certainly a nearby air beacon, which are not all given in lists for sailors. Things get better at sea, and particularly when within the operational range of any beacon. As you approach a beacon, perhaps close beside your destination, it is most heartwarming as the call gets gradually louder and gives a sharper null while you close in.

As I have already said, you can never get too much practice; don't wait until a stormy night, when you are in force 7 and considerable doubt as to your location, before you learn the particular sound and rhythm produced by radio beacons. But be careful if you are tied alongside some commercial wharf which has giant steel cranes all over the place, or if you are nestling in a snug marina surrounded either by tall hills or tall metal masts, or if there are overhead power lines running close by; the signals you receive will be distorted or even completely nullified. So do your practising at an open anchorage or at sea.

Direction Finding

Once you have begun receiving and identifying beacons with reasonable certainty, you will soon acquire the knack of finding the null. Sometimes there

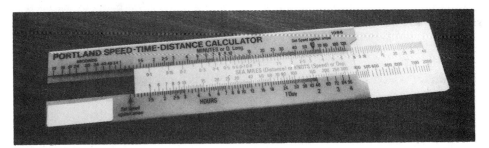

Plate 16: The Portland calculator, a handy device for working out speed, time and distance problems.

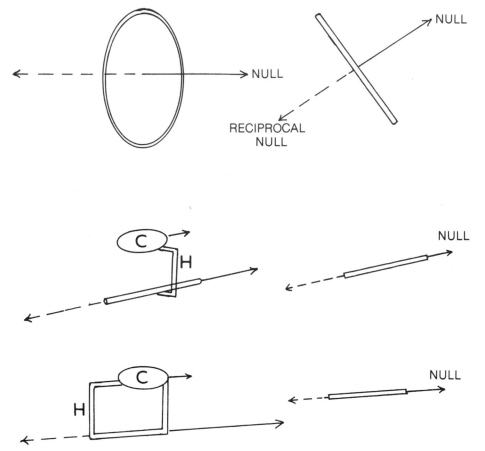

Fig. 10.1　A direction-finding aerial or antenna is designed to have a line relative to the bearing of the transmitting station along which the signal received drops to nothing. This is called a null. Equally it has a null on the reciprocal of this line. With a loop, the null line goes through the centre of the loop. With a ferrite rod antenna, the null line is on the axis of the length of the rod. Some portable aerials attached to a compass have the handle at the side, as in the centre drawing, others have the handle at the back. The compass sighting prism will usually make it clear which kind you have got. The best D/F aerials have a system of sensing, so that you can tell which is the true line and which is the reciprocal.

is a meter which helps you get the correct direction, but more often you will have to judge by ear.

Whichever type of aerial you have, you point the equipment to and fro around the null point (*Fig. 10.1*). To the uninitiated this often looks like some pagan religious dance, as the headphoned navigator bobs and weaves in his search for an interference-free spot. Meanwhile he twists the black box from side to side and holds up a hand in an imperious gesture for silence, as he appears gradually to select one luckless part of the cabin furniture for what surely must be a forthcoming bloody sacrifice.

If the beacon is within about 15 miles, a reasonable null can usually be found by swinging through it several times. This bearing is of course open to the usual compass errors, and no D/F fix of three or more distant bearings will ever be as good as one derived from closer visual sightings. It should be remembered that you are often using a compass bearing of an object maybe 20–30 miles away, so the bearing cannot be very accurate.

Having satisfied yourself that you have as good a bearing as circumstances will allow, you have to convert it to a True reading before plotting it on the chart. Correct from Compass to Magnetic by applying deviation where applicable, and then turn the Magnetic bearing into True by applying variation. Remember? Anything West, Compass Best, so *subtract* westerly deviation and variation, *add* easterly.

Snag to Portability

The very portability conferred by use of the ferrite rod aerial brings with it a disadvantage which almost outweighs the enormous advantage of giving a direct compass reading: if it is used in a position unsuitable for a compass, its deviation is large, hard to calculate and worst of all, changeable.

One of the most unsuitable positions for this type of ferrite aerial is down below on the chart table, probably off the centre line, usually surrounded by other electronic instruments, all of which affect both the compass and the radio signal giving the null point, as well as often generating interference.

At this stage I think I should move to the interesting moment when you first plot three radio beacon bearings. Let us be charitable and assume that none is further away than about 20 miles, so some sort of accuracy may be hoped for. Consternation! The cocked hat is enormous, with each side about ten miles long if not more.

Well, if you absorbed my words in Chapter 5 about the inaccuracy of compass bearings of objects many miles away, you should not be surprised. What sort of cocked hat did you expect from objects 20 miles off?

There is a second factor which has helped turn to dust and ashes your new and expensive aid to the forlorn navigator. Various characteristics of radio waves may have deflected the transmissions from each radio beacon, so that the bearing given by your aerial may sometimes be more than 15° (yes, fifteen degrees) out before even considering any inaccuracy of the compass used. These are the results of ground effect and refraction.

It is at this stage that unkind thoughts are often nourished about the man who persuaded you to buy the outfit. But do not despair. You have absorbed the first lesson towards getting better results out of it. It can be summed up in the words:

Never forget that a D/F bearing is subject to the total error of the radio and aerial system, of the natural conditions existing at the time, of the surroundings of the beacon, its distance away, and the error of the compass too.

There are some basic rules for reducing and eliminating at least some of these errors. Tackle things in this order:

1. Make sure that a loop or non-portable ferrite aerial is always used on the fore and aft centre-line of the boat, not offset to one side or the other, and that the lubber-line if you use a bearing is *exactly* fore and aft.

2. Eliminate as much as possible all sources of compass deviation as described for compasses generally. With a compass mounted on a ferrite aerial this means using it away from any steel or magnetic object such as engines, instruments, other compasses, winch handles or steel parts of winches, metal objects in your pockets, loudspeakers, cameras and frequently the headphones you use to hear the radio signal. It may even be an improvement on some makes to raise the compass further away from the ferrite rod itself. With the most suitable grade of ferrite and the compass mounted absolutely centrally above it, a little over four inches should be enough.

3. Use the D/F aerial in *exactly the same place* in the boat each time. Experiment to find the best place, then stick to it.

4. Find a beacon that is transmitting continuously, and calibrate the error found in the bearings of a visible beacon; make out an error card for every 20 or 30 degrees of heading, as you slowly rotate your boat approximately in one spot. Draw this out in graph form as you would for your steering compass if you found deviation excessive. Certain beacon stations put out special low power continuous transmissions as a calibration service. Remember that D/F error changes as the boat's heading relative to a beacon changes.

5. When taking a radio bearing, make sure that all machinery likely to cause interference is switched off. This includes the engine (even diesel if it has a generator or alternator), a radio telephone, fluorescent lamps, radar sets and even tape recorders; if you have taken a TV set to sea you are not my sort of sailor, but switch if off when using D/F radio. If you have an R/T transmitter this *must* be switched off, or the D/F radio can be damaged.

6. Any length of wire (or railing) longer than about 36 feet should be

interrupted by insulation. This particularly applies to main shrouds, fore and back stays and lifelines, which often form a continuous circuit round a boat. Breaking the circuit at bow and stern each side with an insulator — a Terylene or Dacron lanyard does well — often has a dramatic effect on errors in radio bearings, as does fitting insulation where wires go through stanchions. On large racers, where the fashion of having extruded perforated alloy toe rails is spreading, there should be breaks so that there is no continuous length of more than 35 or 36 feet. Navigation lights leaking current into lifelines can cause irritating interference if the lifelines have any slackness in the stanchions, and a bulb loose in its socket can be infuriating.

RADIO BEARING ERRORS

Errors in the bearing received from the D/F aerial come from two sources:
1. Adverse influences on the transmitter, known as propagation error.
2. Ill effects on the receiving aerial, generally classified as reception error, which is further broken down by the boffins into other error titles. The only one the average user needs to know the name of is quadrantal error, because it changes polarity every 90 degress.

Propagation Error

Chief culprit here is what is known as **skywave effect** or **night effect**. Changes in the reflecting capacity of layers surrounding the earth as day changes to night do drastic things to the apparent direction of a radio bearing. It may not be possible to obtain a true null at all when they are at their worst (an hour either side of dusk and dawn), and the effect will persist for distant beacons all night. At the periods near dusk and dawn, beacons less than 15 miles away should be possible to use, but distant beacons should always be distrusted if it is hard to get a good null, or if there appears to be a surging in the strength of the signal.

The second aspect of propagation error that has to be watched for is caused by high ground over which the radio signal passes on its way to you, or land near which it passes at such a fine angle that it has a reflective effect. As a general rule, bearings should be rejected if the signal passes more than a minimal distance over land.

Another error arises if the signal makes an angle of less than 20 degrees with any length of coastline, especially cliffs; *Fig. 10.2* demonstrates this. No bearing of station A should be regarded as reliable if you are anywhere inside the broken line. The tendency to go on using this station after its bearings become unreliable would be particularly strong if you were standing in to the

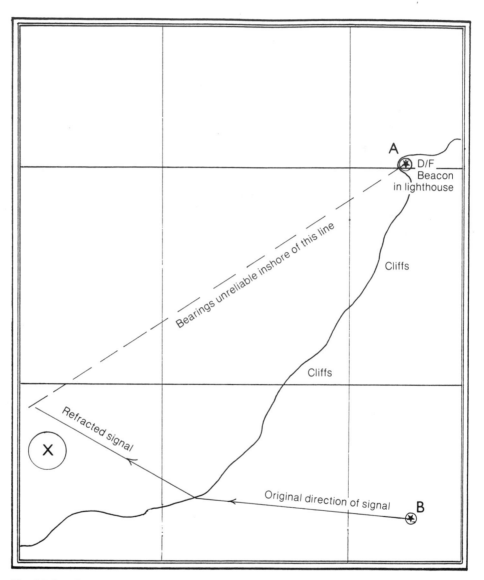

Fig. 10.2   Coastlines, particularly those, with cliffs, can 'bend' the radio signal coming from a station inshore, to give a false reading; it can also deflect them if the waves you receive travel at a narrow angle to the cliffline. Any boat inshore of the broken line would get unreliable fixes from beacon A. Any boat heading towards the coast in the region X could receive dangerously misleading signals from beacon B too, perhaps saying she is further offshore than she really is. This is why beacons are sited on isolated lighthouses or lightships whenever possible.

base of the bay to the west of the station. The danger of refraction or reflective effect is increased when there are high cliffs close to the line along which the signal comes to you.

Reception Error

The basic cause of this is reception and retransmission of the radio signal by various metal parts of your boat, particularly things like lifelines, rigging and metal spars. The effect is to make the null less well-defined because it has several little weak signals eroding its edges. An almost exact parallel is when someone erects a steel-framed high-rise building not far from the television aerial at your home. The steel framing, especially in the construction stage, bounces back an additional signal which produces a ghost image on your screen. The effect on a D/F radio is often to make the signal appear to come from a different angle.

The error becomes alternately positive and negative as you rotate your boat, and the greatest swings will usually be found to occur at every 90 degrees of rotation. This is quadrantal error. There may also be additional errors changing every 180 degrees which alter the smooth pattern of swing, so the total as shown in a graph can be like any of those in *Fig. 10.3*.

CALIBRATION

For calibration you have to take your boat, in her normal cruising or racing trim, to a position in sight of and less than five miles from a transmitting station, and rotate her a few times, while an experienced D/F operator takes a series of bearings not more than 30 degrees apart. It will probably be necessary to do this under engine even in a sailing boat, and the engine should be stopped as each bearing is taken if there is the slightest trace of interference from it. It is no bad idea to do one swing under power and another under reduced sail, say a mainsail only, though obviously you will not be able to hold the boat steady through the sector when she is pointing too close to the wind to hold a tack. This will give you an opportunity to find out whether running the engine has an adverse effect on the accuracy of the steering compass, or D/F aerial compass. If you are calibrating a loop or automatic direction finder this is all you need, but you will find a pelorus useful. If you are calibrating a combined ferrite rod/compass aerial you must, before you even begin to think about the aerial error, find out the deviation of the compass attached to it when in the operating position. This you can do in conjunction with the main compass, provided this has been properly adjusted. It is a good thing to do it for two positions of the D/F aerial compass, one either on deck or in the cockpit, and the other in the

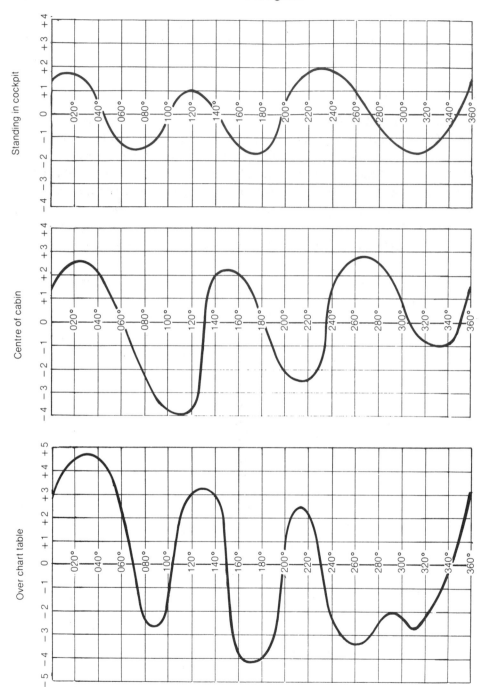

Fig. 10.3   D/F error graphs drawn up for three different positions in the same boat during the same calibrating session. Note that the worst one is over the chart table, and the best in the cockpit.

cabin for those occasions when it is blowing so hard that taking a bearing anywhere except below could be hazardous. Both positions should be on the central fore and aft line of the boat, as free from magnetic influences as possible.

It is an eye-opener to see how different the results are. *Fig. 10.3* shows three deviation cards I drew up in a 32-footer using three positions: in the middle of the cockpit, on the centreline of the cabin, and over the chart table on the starboard side. The job was made easier by the fact that the boat had a repeater compass, with its master unit carefully installed and adjusted so that it had no deviation on any heading. Note that over the chart table the deviation is not only much larger, but much more irregular (the boat had an iron keel). I think that the situation on the fore and aft line of the cabin was probably affected by a large cooker on the port side, and moving forward would have been better. I was being lazy and standing in the position where I could most easily see the compass repeater over the chart table.

Having found the optimum position for your aerial/compass, draw up a proper deviation card for it — doing this will often make you realise the position you had planned to use it in was not, in fact, the optimum, thus making you think again.

The problem now arises of combining your deviation with your D/F error; combining the product of two graphs is not that easy in a boat. One way is to draw up both your deviation graph and your D/F error graph, or at least one of them, so it goes twice round the 360°, and do one of them on tracing paper or transparent plastic (I believe it is possible to get squared tracing paper, but I have never found any and you will probably have to draw it yourself). You can then overlay the transparent graph so the heading of the boat by compass comes at the appropriate point on the D/F error graph. Provided you have drawn your graphs with the + and − signs the right side (if a D/F bearing over-reads it should be given a − sign, as should West on the deviation graph) and then sum them algebraically. This merely means happily going either side of the ' zero point: to sum −7 and +2? the answer is −5. Similarly +3 summed with −6 = −3. It is convenient when you superimpose the two graphs to have a card or scrap of paper handy to jot down the total error for the bearing you have taken. If the boat is on a reasonably steady course, and the direction of the D/F station or stations is fairly well known, this can even be done in advance. It should be remembered that the correction will not, like variation, be a fixed correction for several bearings. It will almost certainly be different for each one.

Fig. 10.4 shows the effect of the two graphs superimposed, and the total error extracted at three points. But many people are allergic to graphs, and the same result can be obtained by drawing up a table.

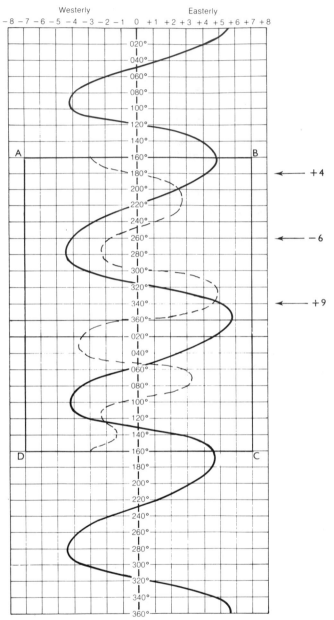

Fig. 10.4 By making an oversize deviation card going twice through the 360° mark, and also a D/F error graph on tracing paper or transparent plastic, an immediate figure for the total error can be quickly extracted. Here the vessel's course is 160°T, so the zero point of the D/F error graph ABCD is placed here. Then the total error on any bearing (magnetic) can be extracted from the algebraic sum of the two graphs, e.g. the top arrow on a bearing around 180° is nil D/F error, 4°E deviation, total +4°. The next one has 4°W deviation and −2° D/F error, total −6°.

HERON CALIBRATION FORM

YACHT	LOCATION OF HERON DURING CALIBRATION		DATE

BEACON USED kHz	APPROXIMATE DISTANCE FROM BEACON	LOCATION OF YACHT DURING CALIBRATION

1	2	3	4	5	6	7	8	9
SHIP'S HEAD BY MAIN COMPASS (CORRECTED FOR DEVIATION)	SHIP'S HEAD BY HERON COMPASS	MAGNETIC ERROR OF HERON COMPASS 2-1	OBSERVED DF BEARING	DF BEARING CORRECTED FOR MAG. ERROR 4-3	CORRECT BEARING OF BEACON (OR AVERAGE OF 5)	RADIO ERROR 5-6 OR 4-9	RELATIVE BEARING 5-1 (IF NEGATIVE ADD 360°)	OVSERVED VISUAL BEARING (MAGNETIC)

REFER TO NOTES OVERLEAF BEFORE USING THIS FORM

TOTAL

AVERAGE

PLOT 7 AGAINST 8 TO ENABLE THE RESULTS TO BE EASILY INTERPOLATED

Fig. 10.5   The calibration form provided with the excellent Homer-Heron D/F outfit. It is reproduced here by permission of the makers, Brookes and Gatehouse Ltd. This can be as deep (vertically) as necessary, and is shown in cut-down form here for convenience only.

Calibrating a Loop

A table for entering your error as you detect it can easily be drawn up. For a rotating loop in a fixed position the headings you need are:

(1)	(2)	(3)	(4)
True heading (by main compass after correction)	Relative bearing of beacon by pelorus	Angle by D/F aerial	Error

It will simplify your task if before starting, assuming your compass has a fair amount of deviation, you draw up the actual headings on the steering compass that you want to steady the boat on. The error is given a + or − sign in the same way as deviation.

Combined Compass/Ferrite Rod

Fig. 10.5 shows the D/F error form provided with the Brookes and Gatehouse Homer-Heron. It does the job most effectively all on one sheet. If you have not got this form, but you have rigged yourself up a simple pelorus, you can simplify things by utilising your already drawn-up deviation graph for your aerial/compass and using the following column headings:

(1)	(2)	(3)	(4)
True heading (by main compass, corrected for var'n & dev'n)	True bearing of beacon by aer/compass (corrected for var'n, and dev'n for ship's head)	Relative angle of beacon by pelorus	Error

APPLYING CORRECTION

The possibility of making a mistake in applying correction for error in D/F bearings will be much reduced if you make yourself out a small notebook, again divided into columns (with two headings filled in), as follows:

(1)	(2)	(3)	(4)	(5)	(6)	(7)	(8)
Ship's head (T)	Dev'n	Aerial/compass Bearing (Var 10° W)			Relative angle	D/F error	True D/F bearing
		(C)	(M)	(T)			
360°	5° E	225°	230°	220°	140°	−3°	217°
030°	3° E	217°	220°	210°	180°	+3°	213°

This method first corrects for deviation and then for D/F error, rather than combining them. It may seem a bit cumbersome, but the purpose will quickly become apparent. The columns should stop you falling into the two common errors of applying deviation for the bearing instead of for the boat's heading; and applying D/F correction for the compass bearing instead of for the angle relative to the boat's head. The relative angle can be obtained from Columns (1) and (5) by adding or subtracting as appropriate, but usually the act of using the aerial gives you a fair idea. You have first to obtain the compass deviation for the boat's course. Having done so, you regard the boat's heading as 360° and find what the angle of the corrected bearing is relative to this to find the D/F error to apply.

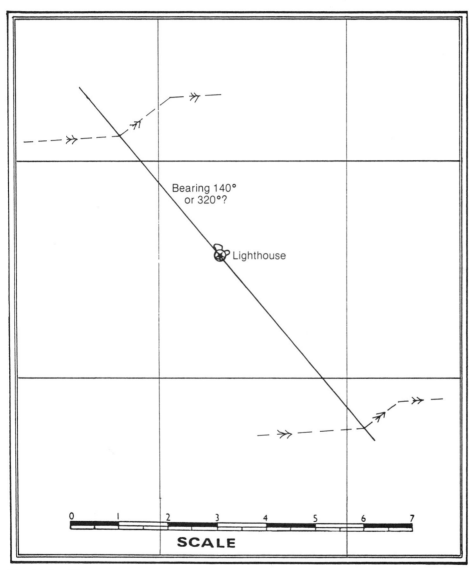

Fig. 10.6   How to check which is the reciprocal bearing when your D/F set has no sensing switch. Turn the boat until the bearing is on the beam and hold a steady course. The station lies on the side where the bearing begins to draw aft.

I have entered in the columns two cases, using a variation of 10° W, that demonstrate how the two corrections interact. If you made both mistakes I mention above, the total error could be large and, when added to the human error implicit in taking any compass bearing, could account for those enormous cocked hats you have been getting.

In case you are the sort of person who becomes benumbed by columns of figures (I know the feeling) you can state things more simply:

Correct compass reading for deviation and variation — use the *Can Dead Men Vote Twice* mnemonic because you are going from compass to true.

Correct the true reading for D/F error, from your D/F error graph, for relative angle of beacon from ship's head.

You will often find that the errors cancel each other out, all but a degree or two, but there will always be some cases when the errors add up, as in the one in *Fig. 10.4* giving a total error of +9°, giving you very bad fixes.

PLOTTING RADIO BEARINGS

The radio bearings are plotted on the chart just like compass bearings. The only complication is when perhaps you have a bearing of only a single station, and are so uncertain of your position that it might be thataway or the reciprocal of thataway. Many sets have a sensing system which overcomes this difficulty, but if yours does not there is a fairly simple way of finding out. Alter course temporarily onto a heading so that the radio signal comes from abeam, and then monitor the bearings. The transmitter lies on the side where the bearing begins to draw aft. *Fig. 10.6* shows this more clearly than it is possible to describe in words. If you are racing it can be tiresome doing this, so any other possible means of checking position should be called in — even a sounding might help.

11
More accurate tidework

If your normal sailing area is one of modest tidal range, less than 6 metres or about 20 feet at the highest springs, you will probably sail for years happily working out your depths by the Rule of Thumb given in Chapter 3. But one day you may find yourself somewhere like Dinard, in Brittany, or the tricky part of the Bay of Fundy, where 10–12 metre (35–40) feet tides are commonplace. You may have just missed the lock for St Malo and have anchored off Dinard opposite until it opens again. Suddenly someone raises a cry of alarm.

'How much water have we got? I've been watching that rock while you were getting lunch and it's gone down nearly six feet in less than an hour...'

Depending on where you put your hook down, you may be all right, though taking in a bit of scope until the level rises again would be a good thing. This is one of those occasions when you urgently need to work out your tidal levels with more accuracy. It can be tedious, but it makes for peace of mind.

You must remember that even the more accurate methods given in this chapter are still subject to the effects of unusual weather, and a *large safety margin* must be allowed, however precise your working.

This safety margin should never be less than one metre in sheltered water, perhaps crossing a well-charted and marked mudbank; where the danger is rock, in open water where there is some sea, the safety margin should be over two metres — more if much sea is running, when the range of tide is large, or if there is any doubt about datum as mentioned later. Throughout this chapter refer back frequently to *Fig. 3.1* on page 33 and note certain datum ambiguities.

GENERATION OF TIDES

Before looking at the nuts and bolts of finding your tide level here and now, let us consider the forces which make the level of water on the earth rise and fall as it does, in two long waves going round the globe. These travel in a westerly direction, though the interference of land masses often changes, even reverses, the direction of these wave-crests.

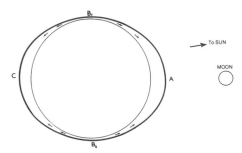

Fig. 11.1   Generation of tides. This sketch of the earth looking from above the North Pole shows how the gravitational attraction of the sun and the moon causes the sea to heap up towards the sun and the moon; it also piles up on the opposite side of the earth. The hump on the opposite side arises because the attraction of the moon (the main source of gravity because it is so much closer) is strongest at A, less strong at B 1 and B2, and least of all at C. This causes a horizontal flow towards C as well as A, which is shown by the arrows. The two humps of water move round the earth once every twenty-four hours, plus about fifty minutes.

Most people can understand that the sun and the moon have a gravitational attraction for the water on the earth, and tend to make it rise up in a hump, as at A in *Fig. 11.1*. They often remain baffled by the fact that a second hump develops at C, even when the moon, the main gravitational influence, and the sun, which has less effect because of its much greater distance, are the other side of the earth. The reason is mainly centrifugal force, which acts equally on all parts of the earth regardless of position of sun or moon. The moon's attraction (disregarding the sun for the moment) combines with centrifugal force at A, causing a high hump. Because B_1 and B_2 are further away, the moon's attraction is less; at C the moon's attraction is a lot less, but centrifugal force is still the same. This causes a difference of force between B_1 and B_2 and C, which creates a horizontal force towards C as shown by the arrows. The same horizontal force also acts towards A, where there is already a hump, causing low tides at B_1 and B_2, followed by the further high water at C. This accounts for the fact that succeeding high waters during a day are never the same height.

So a 'normal' tidal pattern is **semi-diurnal**, with two high water and two low waters during just over 24 hours — 24 hours and 50 minutes usually, though land masses sometimes cause a variation. This pattern is broken up in certain parts of the world by the effect of gulfs, basins, large islands or land masses, or straits, and there may be only one high and low water in the 24 hour 50 minutes period, these being known as **diurnal** tides, as occur in the Gulf of Mexico and in the Caribbean, where there are freak tides, disguised by the fact that the rise and fall is small.

Other freak patterns caused by obstructions are kinks in the curve of the tide, giving long high water stands like that in the Solent, or at monthly intervals in the Gulf of Mexico, or the stand at low water in the Firth of Forth in Scotland. There are many places, all over the world, that have unusual tide patterns, but nearly all have been observed and plotted. Between some of the Caribbean islands, for instance, a flood tide sometimes runs eastward, overcoming the normal tradewind-induced westward current.

In the open ocean tides are usually small, and tidal streams flow only near land. Horizontal movement of water in open oceans is mainly generated by wind and differences in water temperature. These ocean currents are far from constant in strength and direction.

Certain bodies of water of limited size, with only restricted access to large water masses, are almost tideless because there is not enough water in them to allow the generation of a proper tide, which can be thought of as a low wave of enormous length. The best known examples are the Baltic, the Black Sea and the Mediterranean. An arm of the Mediterranean, the Adriatic, develops a measurable tide at its northern end near Venice, and slight tides are recorded in certain Greek waters and the Black Sea. The tide levels are so slight that they are usually disguised by wind and pressure-induced changes in sea-level, but sometimes they can cause strong tidal streams.

Springs and neaps

When the sun and moon are approximately the same or opposite sides of the earth, their attraction magnifies the tidal humps, and high tides occur known as

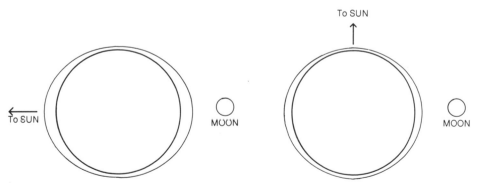

Fig. 11.2   When the moon and sun are either opposite to each other or on the same side of the earth, they exert a stronger combined influence, so a greater depth of water is pulled by them, causing a spring tide (left). When they are at right angles to each other, looking from the top of the earth, they work against each other and a smaller hump appears, so there is a neap tide.

Spring tides (nothing to do with the season of spring). Owing to a lag in the effect of the generating forces because of the drag of the water, these occur just *after* full moon and new moon. When sun and moon have about 90 degrees between them they tend to reduce the tide-generating force, and a **Neap tide** occurs, with a lower level at high water, and a higher low water than at springs (*Fig. 11.2*). In areas of large tides, anchorages that cannot be entered at springs because they dry can often be used throughout the 24 hours at neaps.

As one would expect, the force of tidal streams is greatly enhanced during spring tides. The change from springs to neaps operates in a fairly steady curve, as can be seen by plotting high water levels thoughout the two week cycle on a piece of squared paper. From the seaman's point of view, the vital thing is not to run aground just at high water on the peak of a spring tide — the tide may not reach that level again for a fortnight, or if it was a specially high springs, perhaps even longer. The appealing word for being caught in this unhappy situation is 'beneaped'.

Surge effect

The wide difference in tidal heights in areas quite close to each other is often due to a rhythmic oscillation of the water, such as develops when you sit up

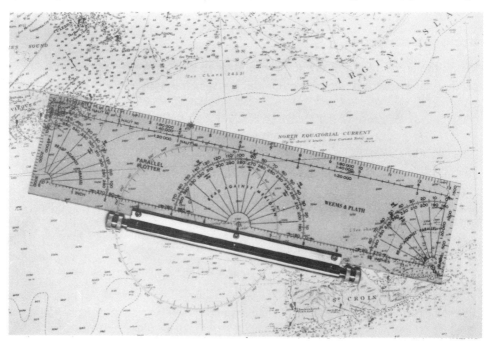

Plate 17. The Parallel Plotter, from Weems and Plath of Annapolis (USA), the only parallel rule that is any use in a small boat.

suddenly in the bath. The water level in the middle remains almost steady, but the level each end swoops up and down, bringing reproaches from those who have to mop it up. One of the best-known examples is the Bay of Fundy, on the Atlantic coast of the USA and Canada.

Similar surges can be caused in areas where the land is of suitable shape, by wind either impelling extra water into a restricted area, or more often holding back what should have escaped during previous outflow periods. The effect can be even more devastating when accompanied by an intense depression, which also encourages the water level to rise. The effect of storm surges is often disguised by their not coinciding with high water but, since the North Sea virtually overflowed its shore with great loss of life in January 1953, much more notice of the effect has been taken, and it was remembered that much the same thing happened twice during the nineteenth century. A similar raising of the water level in tropical revolving storms is one of their most damaging features. In American roofed marinas, boats that have escaped damage from wind are often wrecked against the roofs by a sudden rise of sea level.

Seiches

An almost equally unpleasant freak effect is a **seiche**, a rapid change in water level caused by meteorological conditions like a line squall. A sharp rise in water level, perhaps as much as a metre and a half within 15 minutes, is followed by an equally sharp drop. If a seiche coincides with high or low water springs it can cause great damage to moored craft and shore installations. Luckily they are rare.

Tidal Waves

This title is often given wrongly to **tsunamis**, or earthquake waves, caused by seismic disturbances in the seabed. They have nothing to do with tides. Often starting as a series of fairly low waves travelling at high speed, they tend to get higher and steeper as they move into shallow water. In open water they are usually low and pass almost unnoticed (though what it is like to be exactly over a sub-sea earthquake I would not like to speculate), but on shelving shores of the Pacific and Indian oceans have burst onto the land at heights of over 150 feet. They can travel for vast distances. The wave from the Krakatoa eruption and earthquake near Java went right round the world, and a recent Alaskan earthquake's wave caused heavy damage in the Hawaian islands. I mention them here only because certain popular yachting areas, the Caribbean and the Greek Islands, not to mention California and the American north-west, are in volcanic and active earthquake areas. Should you be anchored in such an area and an earthquake takes place, perhaps with its centre some way off, you might save your boat or your life by moving from a shallow shelving-bottom anchorage into deep water quickly. There is usually a time delay between the earth shock and the arrival of a tsunami, which is often signalled by a lowering of water level just before it arrives. Frequently there is more than one wave.

Bores

Of greater importance to yachtsmen, since they occur in rivers used as sailing centres, are bores, where at certain high tides the shape of the estuary holds back the incoming flood until it eventually advances as a steep-fronted wave, sometimes of dangerous height. Engineering progress and greater knowledge of their causes have tamed some of the best-known bores. The technique for meeting a bore at anchor is to pay out the longest possible scope of anchor line, with weights hung on it if possible. The wave of a bore should be little problem to a good seagoing boat, it is being tied to posts or a pontoon when it arrives that can be damaging.

I am fortunate to have seen in the thirties the most dramatic bore in the world, at Hangchow Bay in China, which was over 20 feet high and steep-fronted when I saw it, and is said sometimes to have reached 30 feet. The Chinese, many centuries ago, built cunningly shaped junk harbours on the shore of the bay, where grounded cargo junks suddenly sprang afloat in safety. and the crews yu-lohed them hastily out so that they were swept up the bay on the crest of the bore at over 30 knots. Various civil wars having damaged the ancient harbours, I was not able to see this fascinating regatta, but it was still to be seen in the early nineteen twenties.

WHAT THE YACHTSMAN NEEDS

Tidal streams are adequately covered in Chapter 3, unless you are sailing in certain specialised areas like the straits between Malaysia and Indonesia, when ATT give special tables. In this chapter it is tidal rise and fall we are mainly interested in

Let us suppose that a small boat owner, who has perhaps sailed for years in his home waters of two feet maximum rise and fall, has borrowed a boat in an area where it is over 25 feet. Coming into a strange anchorage with only the chart and pilot book to guide him, he urgently needs to know the answer to several tidal questions:

1. What is the present rise of tide above chart datum?

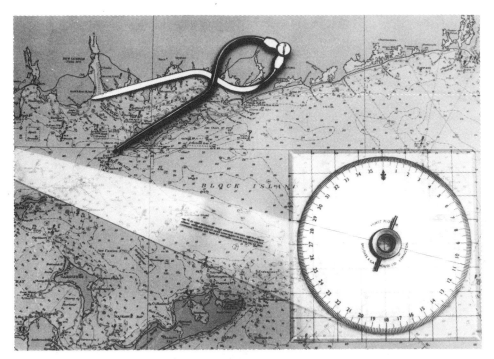

Plate 18. Dividers and a Hurst Plotter. Variation can be set and locked with a centre screw.

2. Is the level rising or falling? If the first, what time will it reach the top of its rise and what will the depth be then? If the second, what time is low water, and how high, if anything, is that above datum?

3. If there are drying heights to be negotiated, such as the sill of a lock or rocks, what time will there be adequate depth of water?

4. If a suitable rise has not yet been reached, what time will it occur?

All these questions can be answered with the right books of tidal information. They must be up to date and cover the right areas. The relevant editions of *Reed's* cover from the St Lawrence to the Caribbean, and from Denmark to Gibraltar, including Britain and Ireland. *British Admiralty Tide Tables* cover the whole world in three volumes, Vol 1 for European waters and Vol 2 for America, north and south, Africa and the Indian Ocean. Vol 3 covers the American West Coast, Australasia and the Far East. *American Tide Tables*, published by the Department of Commerce and the National Oceanic and Atmospheric Administration, cover the whole world in four volumes. Vol 1 covers Europe and western Africa, Vol 2 the eastern seaboard of the American continent, Vol 3 the western seaboard and Hawaii, and Vol 4 the Pacific and

Indian Oceans. All three systems work on a table of standard ports, known in the USA as reference stations, with 'differences' given for minor ports in a second table.

All three systems have their advantages and disadvantages. I would advise any American going outside his local waters, where he will be used to his own tables, *not* to use American tables. The reason is their amazing inconsistency over datum. In 1980 an additional datum for the Gulf of Mexico became effective, but the tide tables do not even mention it. Sometimes the American Mean Low Water is used, sometimes the datum of a foreign hydrographic service, and not enough attention is drawn to which one is being used. Sometimes soundings are in feet, sometimes in metres, sometimes in both. Owing to the high datums a lot of negative values are given.

The British ATT have inconsistencies too, but not so many (most are in Vol 2, where the figures are based sometimes on American surveys and datum) and

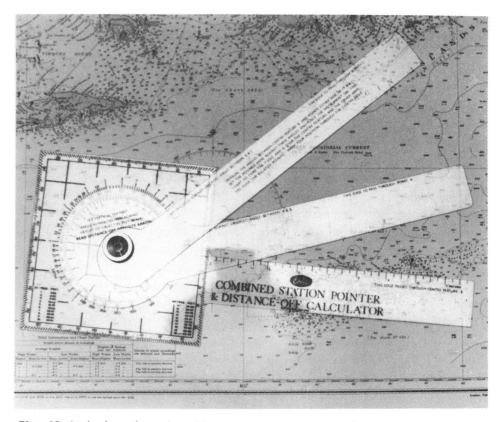

Plate 19. A plastic station pointer (three-arm plotter to Americans) made by the East Berks Boat Co., who make the Ebbco plastic sextant, is well worth its stowage space if you carry a sextant.

CHANNEL ISLANDS - ST. HELIER

LAT 49°11'N   LONG 2°07'W

TIME ZONE GMT   TIMES AND HEIGHTS OF HIGH AND LOW WATERS   YEAR 1980

HEIGHTS IN METRES

MAY

Day	Time M	Time M	Time M	Time M		Day	Time M	Time M	Time M	Time M
1 TH	0124 1.6	0700 10.6	1344 1.7	1919 10.7		16 F	0159 0.8	0733 11.4	1420 1.0	1951 11.2
2 F	0159 1.6	0733 10.5	1416 1.8	1948 10.6		17 SA	0242 1.1	0815 10.9	1500 1.5	2030 10.7
3 SA	0233 1.8	0804 10.4	1447 2.1	2019 10.4		18 SU	0321 1.7	0854 10.3	1536 2.2	2107 10.1
4 SU	0305 2.1	0834 10.1	1518 2.5	2051 10.1		19 M	0356 2.3	0934 9.6	1609 2.9	2146 9.4
5 M	0336 2.5	0910 9.7	1549 2.9	2128 9.7		20 TU	0431 3.0	1016 8.9	1644 3.5	2230 8.8
6 TU	0413 3.0	0950 9.3	1627 3.4	2214 9.2		21 W	0509 3.6	1106 8.3	1727 4.1	2327 8.3
7 W	0458 3.4	1045 8.8	1720 3.9	2319 8.7		22 TH	0603 4.0	1217 7.9	1831 4.4	
8 TH	0604 3.7	1204 8.4	1842 4.1			23 F	0045 8.1	0719 4.2	1337 8.0	1954 4.3
9 F	0050 8.6	0731 3.7	1338 8.6	2016 3.7		24 SA	0201 8.2	0837 4.0	1443 8.3	2105 3.9
10 SA	0216 9.0	0856 3.1	1456 9.3	2134 3.0		25 SU	0303 8.6	0939 3.5	1536 8.8	2200 3.3
11 SU	0324 9.8	1004 2.3	1556 10.1	2235 2.2		26 M	0353 9.1	1028 3.0	1621 9.4	2248 2.8
12 M	0421 10.6	1104 1.6	1649 10.9	2330 1.4		27 TU	0438 9.5	1113 2.6	1702 9.8	2332 2.4
13 TU	0513 11.2	1157 1.0	1737 11.4			28 W	0519 9.8	1156 2.2	1742 10.1	
14 W	0022 0.9	0603 11.5	1248 0.7	1825 11.6		29 TH	0015 2.0	0558 10.1	1236 2.0	1818 10.4
15 TH	0113 0.7	0649 11.6	1335 0.7	1909 11.6		30 F	0056 1.8	0635 10.3	1317 1.9	1853 10.5
						31 SA	0137 1.7	0712 10.4	1355 1.9	1930 10.6

JUNE

Day	Time M	Time M	Time M	Time M		Day	Time M	Time M	Time M	Time M
1 SU	0216 1.8	0747 10.4	1433 2.0	2005 10.5		16 M	0305 1.8	0840 10.1	1518 2.2	2051 10.1
2 M	0254 1.9	0825 10.2	1510 2.3	2042 10.3		17 TU	0339 2.2	0917 9.7	1549 2.7	2128 9.7
3 TU	0331 2.2	0903 10.0	1546 2.6	2122 10.0		18 W	0410 2.7	0955 9.2	1619 3.1	2206 9.3
4 W	0410 2.5	0948 9.6	1627 3.0	2210 9.6		19 TH	0442 3.1	1035 8.8	1655 3.5	2251 8.8
5 TH	0457 2.9	1040 9.2	1719 3.4	2311 9.2		20 F	0523 3.5	1126 8.4	1743 3.9	2349 8.5
6 F	0556 3.2	1149 9.0	1828 3.6			21 SA	0618 3.8	1231 8.2	1848 4.0	
7 SA	0025 9.0	0710 3.3	1309 8.9	1951 3.6		22 SU	0056 8.3	0727 3.9	1341 8.2	2001 4.0
8 SU	0145 9.1	0829 3.0	1425 9.3	2107 3.0		23 M	0205 8.4	0837 3.8	1444 8.5	2107 3.6
9 M	0256 9.6	0938 2.5	1529 9.8	2210 2.4		24 TU	0305 8.6	0938 3.4	1538 8.9	2203 3.2
10 TU	0357 10.1	1040 1.9	1626 10.4	2308 1.8		25 W	0357 9.0	1030 3.1	1626 9.3	2254 2.8
11 W	0454 10.6	1136 1.4	1719 10.8	2343 2.4		26 TH	0445 9.3	1119 2.7	1711 9.8	
12 TH	0004 1.4	0546 10.8	1228 1.3	1807 11.0		27 F	0530 9.7	1207 2.3	1751 10.1	
13 F	0055 1.2	0634 10.9	1317 1.3	1853 11.0		28 SA	0031 2.1	0612 10.1	1253 2.1	1834 10.5
14 SA	0144 1.2	0720 10.8	1402 1.5	1935 10.8		29 SU	0117 1.8	0653 10.4	1337 1.8	1913 10.7
15 SU	0227 1.4	0801 10.6	1443 1.8	2015 10.5		30 M	0201 1.6	0734 10.6	1420 1.7	1954 10.8

JULY

Day	Time M	Time M	Time M	Time M		Day	Time M	Time M	Time M	Time M
1 TU	0243 1.5	0815 10.6	1501 1.8	2034 10.8		16 W	0318 2.0	0856 9.9	1525 2.3	2105 10.1
2 W	0324 1.6	0856 10.5	1541 2.0	2115 10.6		17 TH	0346 2.3	0928 9.6	1555 2.6	2139 9.8
3 TH	0404 1.9	0939 10.2	1623 2.4	2202 10.2		18 F	0414 2.6	1002 9.3	1626 3.0	2216 9.4
4 F	0449 2.3	1028 9.8	1711 2.8	2254 9.7		19 SA	0447 3.0	1041 8.9	1704 3.3	2258 8.9
5 SA	0542 2.7	1126 9.4	1810 3.2	2357 9.3		20 SU	0529 3.5	1127 8.5	1753 3.7	2350 8.4
6 SU	0646 3.0	1236 9.0	1923 3.4			21 M	0622 3.8	1229 8.2	1857 4.0	
7 M	0113 9.1	0801 3.1	1354 9.0	2039 3.2		22 TU	0057 8.1	0733 4.0	1342 8.1	2011 4.0
8 TU	0229 9.2	0914 2.9	1505 9.3	2148 2.8		23 W	0211 8.1	0844 3.9	1453 8.4	2118 3.7
9 W	0338 9.5	1019 2.5	1609 9.7	2251 2.4		24 TH	0318 8.4	0949 3.6	1552 8.9	2219 3.2
10 TH	0438 9.9	1118 2.2	1704 10.1	2349 2.0		25 F	0416 8.9	1045 3.1	1642 9.4	2313 2.7
11 F	0533 10.2	1212 1.9	1754 10.4			26 SA	0506 9.5	1140 2.6	1729 10.0	
12 SA	0042 1.7	0622 10.3	1302 1.8	1839 10.5		27 SU	0007 2.2	0553 10.1	1231 2.0	1814 10.6
13 SU	0130 1.6	0706 10.4	1347 1.6	1920 10.6		28 M	0057 1.6	0638 10.6	1319 1.6	1857 11.1
14 M	0211 1.6	0745 10.3	1425 1.9	1958 10.5		29 TU	0145 1.2	0720 11.0	1405 1.3	1940 11.4
15 TU	0247 1.7	0822 10.2	1457 2.1	2032 10.3		30 W	0229 0.9	0802 11.2	1447 1.2	2020 11.4
						31 TH	0311 0.9	0843 11.2	1529 1.3	2103 11.2

AUGUST

Day	Time M	Time M	Time M	Time M		Day	Time M	Time M	Time M	Time M
1 F	0352 1.2	0925 10.9	1610 1.7	2145 10.8		16 SA	0345 2.3	0927 9.8	1556 2.5	2139 9.8
2 SA	0434 1.7	1009 10.3	1655 2.3	2233 10.1		17 SU	0413 2.7	0959 9.4	1628 3.0	2213 9.2
3 SU	0522 2.4	1059 9.6	1747 2.9	2327 9.4		18 M	0445 3.2	1034 8.9	1708 3.5	2254 8.7
4 M	0619 3.0	1201 9.0	1853 3.4			19 TU	0527 3.8	1122 8.4	1800 4.0	2347 8.1
5 TU	0039 8.8	0731 3.4	1321 8.6	2012 3.6		20 W	0628 4.2	1231 8.0	1913 4.2	
6 W	0206 8.6	0850 3.5	1446 8.7	2131 3.4		21 TH	0109 7.8	0749 4.3	1404 8.0	2034 4.1
7 TH	0327 8.8	1003 3.2	1556 9.1	2238 2.9		22 F	0240 8.0	0911 4.0	1.19 8.5	2146 3.6
8 F	0430 9.3	1105 2.8	1652 9.6	2337 2.4		23 SA	0349 8.7	1019 3.4	1617 9.3	2248 2.9
9 SA	0523 9.7	1158 2.4	1742 10.0			24 SU	0444 9.5	1116 2.6	1708 10.1	2344 2.1
10 SU	0028 2.0	0610 10.1	1246 2.1	1824 10.3		25 M	0533 10.3	1210 1.9	1754 10.9	
11 M	0113 1.7	0649 10.3	1326 1.9	1902 10.5		26 TU	0036 1.3	0618 11.1	1259 1.2	1839 11.6
12 TU	0151 1.6	0726 10.4	1401 1.8	1937 10.6		27 W	0124 0.8	0702 11.6	1345 0.8	1921 11.9
13 W	0223 1.6	0758 10.4	1432 1.8	2009 10.6		28 TH	0211 0.4	0744 11.9	1430 0.6	2004 12.0
14 TH	0253 1.7	0829 10.3	1500 1.9	2039 10.5		29 F	0253 0.4	0825 11.8	1512 0.8	2044 11.7
15 F	0319 1.9	0858 10.1	1528 2.2	2108 10.2		30 SA	0335 0.8	0905 11.4	1553 1.3	2125 11.2
						31 SU	0416 1.4	0946 10.6	1635 2.0	2209 10.3

Fig. 11.3   A page from British *Admiralty Tide Tables Vol I* for St Helier in the Channel Islands.

FRANCE, NORTH COAST

Sailing men can ignore this section.

No.	PLACE	Lat. N.	Long. W.	HW 0800 and 2000	HW 0100 and 1300	LW 0200 and 1400	LW 0700 and 1900	MHWS	MHWN	MLWN	MLWS	M.L. Z₀ m.	M₂ g°	M₂ H.m.	S₂ g°	S₂ H.m.	K₁ g°	K₁ H.m.	O₁ g°	O₁ H.m.	f₄	F₄	f₆	F₆	
1605	**ST. HELIER**	(see page 222)						**11·1**	**8·1**	**4·1**	**1·3**														
1609	Iles Chausey	48 52	1 49	+0048	+0044	+0104	+0058	+1·8	+1·7	+0·8	+0·6	7·50	218	3·94	238	1·46	111	0·09	355	0·09	266	0·035	177	0·002	i
1610	Dielette	49 33	1 52	+0119	+0116	+0115	+0110	−1·6	−0·9	−0·5	−0·1	5·51	223	3·07	263	1·13	111	0·09	355	0·09	300	0·026	214	0·002	i
1611	Carteret	49 22	1 47	+0103	+0109	+0108	+0111	−0·1	−0·3	0·0	+0·1	6·30	223	3·50	263	1·30	111	0·09	355	0·09	293	0·020	073	0·001	i
1612	Granville	48 50	1 36	+0049	+0040	+0115	+0053	+1·7	+1·5	+0·5	+0·1	7·21	218	4·16	258	1·54	111	0·09	355	0·09	323	0·025	347	0·003	i
1613	Cancale	48 40	1 51	+0048	+0043	+0101	+0050	+2·2	+2·0	+1·0	+0·7	7·76	216	4·12	256	1·53	111	0·09	355	0·09	326	0·024	345	0·003	ix
1614	St. Malo (F)	48 38	2 02	+0044	+0034	+0052	+0046	+1·0	+1·0	+0·3	+0·1	6·85	207	3·69	257	1·44	111	0·09	355	0·09	286	0·020			ix
1615	Erquy	48 38	2 28	+0049	+0039	+0035	+0032	+0·1	+0·4	+0·2	−0·1	6·40	204	3·58	244	1·32	111	0·09	355	0·09	302	0·016	041	0·001	i
1616	Dahouet	48 35	2 34	+0038	+0031	+0027	+0036	+0·1	+0·4	−0·2	−0·1		⊙	⊙	⊙	⊙	⊙	⊙	355	0·09	⊙	⊙	004	0·001	i
1617	Le Légué	48 32	2 44	+0033	+0026	+0022	+0031	+0·1	+0·4	0·0	0·0	5·6	205	3·61	245	1·34	111	0·09	355	0·09	345	0·027	004	0·004	i
1618	Binic	48 36	2 49	+0033	+0026	+0022	+0031	+0·1	+0·4	0·0	0·0	5·6	205	3·61	245	1·34	111	0·09	355	0·09	345	0·027	004	0·004	i
1619	Portrieux	48 38	2 49	+0033	+0026	+0022	+0031	+0·1	+0·4	−0·3	−0·1	6·38	203	3·61	243	1·34	111	0·09	355	0·09	298	0·017	043	0·001	i
1620	Paimpol	48 47	3 02	+0038	+0025	+0025	+0021	−0·8	−0·3	−0·9	−0·8	5·52	202	3·58	242	1·32	102	0·10	009	0·08	295	0·013	180	0·001	i
1621	Ile de Bréhat	48 51	3 00	+0045	+0030	+0014	+0019	−0·7	−0·1	−0·5	−0·2	5·85	198	3·36	238	1·24	102	0·10	009	0·08	321	0·008	072	0·001	ix
1622	Les Heaux de Bréhat (F)	48 55	3 05	+0055	+0031	−0011	+0042	−1·3	−0·6	−0·7	−0·3	5·51	195	3·25	244	1·15	097	0·10	346	0·08	060	0·003	060	0·003	i
1623	Lezardrieux	48 47	3 06	+0038	+0026	+0004	+0012	−1·1	−0·6	−0·7	−0·4	5·57	193	3·15	241	1·22	102	0·10	⊙	⊙	290	0·006	290	0·006	i
1624	Plougrescant	48 51	3 13	+0004	−0005	−0017	−0013	−1·5	−0·7	−0·8	0·0	5·55	⊙	⊙	⊙	⊙	⊙	⊙	⊙	⊙	⊙	⊙	⊙	⊙	i
1625	Tréguier	48 47	3 13	+0012	+0012	−0018	−0007	−1·4	−0·7	−0·8	−0·4	5·46	185	3·14	225	1·16	090	0·06	346	0·06	318	0·018	166	0·001	i
1626	Ploumanac'h	48 50	3 29	+0002	−0009	−0026	−0024	−2·2	−1·1	−0·7	−0·4	5·15	181	2·85	221	1·05	090	0·06	346	0·06	194	0·017	140	0·003	i
1638	**BREST**	(see page 226)						**7·4**	**5·8**	**3·0**	**1·3**														
1628	Trebeurden	48 46	3 35	+0111	+0107	+0122	+0105	+1·6	+1·2	+0·5	−0·1	5·28	175	2·81	215	1·04	090	0·06	346	0·06	259	0·025	158	0·005	i
1629	Rade de Morlaix / Morlaix (Chateau du Taureau) (F)	48 41	3 53	+0114	+0056	+0014	+0046	+1·5	+1·1	+0·5	−0·1	5·20	173	2·77	213	1·03	090	0·06	346	0·06	⊙	⊙	⊙	⊙	i
1630	Roscoff	48 43	3 58	+0103	+0049	+0110	+0055	+1·4	+1·0	0·0	−0·1	5·17	172	2·77	212	1·03	090	0·06	346	0·06	264	0·017	173	0·002	i
1631	Ile de Batz	48 44	4 00	+0105	+0105	+0105	+0045	+1·4	+1·0	+0·5	0·0		⊙	⊙	⊙	⊙	⊙	⊙	346	0·06	⊙	⊙	⊙	⊙	i
1632	L'Aberwrac'h / Fort Cézon	48 37	4 36	+0035	+0020	+0040	+0035	+0·5	+0·2	−0·1	−0·3	4·52	194	2·45	194	0·90	090	0·06	346	0·06	254	0·016	199	0·003	i
1633	L'Aberbenoit	48 35	4 38	+0020	+0025	+0035	+0035	+0·6	+0·5	+0·1	−0·2	4·70	⊙	⊙	⊙	⊙	⊙	⊙	346	0·06	⊙	⊙	⊙	⊙	i

Column group headings: TIME DIFFERENCES (High Water / Low Water, Zone −0100); HEIGHT DIFFERENCES (IN METRES) MHWS MHWN MLWN MLWS; M.L. Z₀ m.; HARMONIC CONSTANTS (Zone −0100) M₂ S₂ K₁ O₁; S.W. CORRECTIONS ½ diurnal f₄ F₄ / ¼ diurnal f₆ F₆.

Fig. 11.4   A page from Part 2 of *Admiralty Tide Tables* for secondary ports on St Helier. The whole section referring to harmonic constants on the right may be ignored, unless you want to go into the very complicated new Admiralty method.

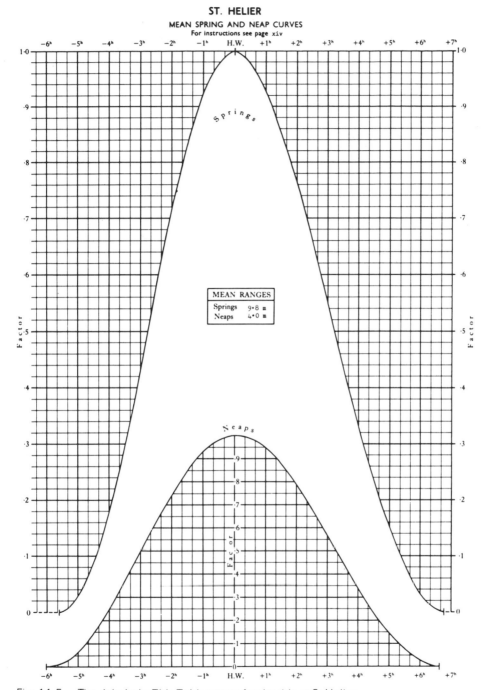

Fig. 11.5 The *Admiralty Tide Table* curves for the tide at St Helier.

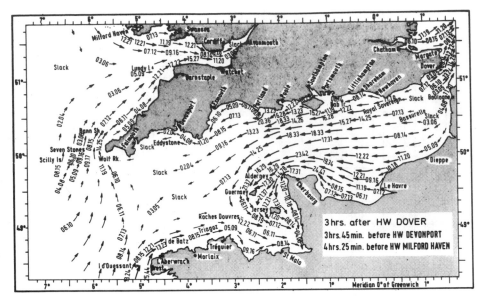

Fig. 11.6   Tidal chart from *Reed's*.

TIDAL COEFFICIENTS BASED ON CHERBOURG

D of M	JAN am	JAN pm	FEB am	FEB pm	MAR am	MAR pm	APR am	APR pm	MAY am	MAY pm	JUNE am	JUNE pm	JULY am	JULY pm	AUG am	AUG pm	SEPT am	SEPT pm	OCT am	OCT pm	NOV am	NOV pm	DEC am	DEC pm
1	81	83	82	84	80	83	87	88	86	86	84	82	87	86	91	86	70	62	51	45	41		42	44
2	85	85	85	85	88	87	88	84	86	84	80	78	84	82	81	76	56	51	42		44	48	46	50
3	87	86	85	84	88	88	86	84	83	80	75	71	79	76	71	66	47		42	43	52	57	53	57
4	85	84	83	80	87	86	82	78	77	73	68	65	73	70	61	58	47	48	47	51	61	66	61	65
5	82	79	78	75	84	81	75	70	69	64	62	60	67	64	56		51	55	56	62	70	74	68	71
6	76	73	71	67	78	75	65	60	60	56	59	59	63	62	55	56	60	65	61	71	77	80	74	77
7	69	65	63	59	71	66	55	50	52	50	59		63		59	62	70	74	75	79	82	84	79	81
8	61	57	55	50	61	56	46	43	49	51	63	66	64	66	66	70	78	81	82	85	85	85	82	83
9	53	50	46	43	51	47	42	44	54		70	75	69	72	73	77	84	86	86	88	85	84	83	82
10	46	44	41	40	43	40	48		59	65	79	83	75	78	80	83	87	88	88	88	83	81	81	79
11	42	42	41		39		54	61	71	78	87	90	81	83	85	86	88	87	87	85	78	75	77	75
12	42		44	48	41	45	69	78	85	91	92	94	85	86	86	86	85	83	83	80	71	67	71	68
13	44	47	54	61	51	59	87	95	97	101	94	94	87	87	85	84	81	77	76	72	63	58	65	62
14	51	56	68	76	67	76	102	108	104	106	93	91	86	84	82	79	73	69	68	63	54	50	59	57
15	61	67	84	91	85	94	112	114	106	105	88	85	82	79	76	72	65	60	58	53	48	46	56	56
16	73	78	97	103	101	108	115	114	102	98	81	76	76	73	68	64	54	49	48	44	47	49	58	
17	84	89	108	111	113	116	111	107	94	88	72	67	69	65	60	55	45	41	41	39	53		60	64
18	94	97	113	112	118	117	101	94	82	76	62	58	61	57	51	47	38	37	40		59	66	69	74
19	100	102	111	107	115	111	86	78	69	63	54	50	53	50	43	40	39		44	49	73	81	79	83
20	102	101	102	96	105	98	70	62	57	52	47	45	47	44	39		42	48	57	65	88	94	88	92
21	99	96	89	81	89	81	54	48	47	44	44	43	43	42	39	41	55	63	74	82	100	104	95	97
22	92	87	72	64	71	63	43	40	42	41	44	43	44	47	45	50	72	80	91	99	107	108	98	98
23	82	76	57	51	54	48	39		42		46	48	44	47	56	63	89	97	105	111	108	107	97	95
24	70	64	46		42	40	40	43	44	47	51	55	51	55	70	77	104	109	114	116	104	99	92	88
25	60	56	44	44	39		46	51	51	54	58	62	60	65	84	91	114	116	116	114	94	88	84	79
26	53		46	50	41	45	55	60	58	62	66	70	71	76	97	102	117	116	110	105	81	75	74	69
27	53	54	54	59	49	55	65	69	66	70	74	78	81	86	106	109	112	107	98	90	68	61	64	59
28	56	59	64	69	60	65	73	77	73	77	81	83	90	93	110	109	101	93	82	74	55	50	53	50
29	63	67	73	77	70	74	80	82	79	81	86	87	96	98	107	104	85	76	65	57	46	43	46	44
30	70	74			78	81	84	86	83	84	88	88	98	98	99	92	67	58	50	45	42		42	
31	77	80			84	86			85	85			97	94	85	78			42	41			42	42

Extracted from Annuaire des Marées, Vol. 1, by kind permission of Service Hydrographique et Oceanographique de la Marine

Fig. 11.7   Tidal coefficients from *Reed's*, for use with the graph on page 233.

TIDAL COEFFICIENTS

The opposite page gives tidal coefficients for the year, based on Cherbourg, as presented in Reed's. They are designed principally to assist in the more accurate calculation of tidal stream velocities.

Explanation

The figures in the list of coefficients are based on the scale where:

45 is the coefficient for mean neap tides

90 is the coefficient for mean spring tides

Therefore, if on a particular day the coefficient given is 67, the tide is halfway between springs and neaps. If a figure in excess of 90 is given, then the range of that day's tide will be greater than mean springs and streams will run that much faster. If a number less than 45 is given, then a tidal range less than mean neaps is predicted.

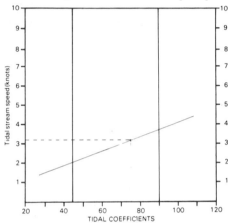

Fig. 11.8

Method of use

On the graph, tidal stream speeds are set against tidal coefficients. The vertical lines pick out the neap and spring coefficients, i.e., 45 and 90.

The neap and spring tidal stream rates for the tide in question are taken from the appropriate tidal stream chart and plotted on the 45 and 90 lines, and a straight line drawn across the two points, extending either side of them.

The coefficient of the day is noted and its position along the botton of the graph pinpointed. Moving vertically upwards from this point, the line drawn earlier will be met and at this level the tidal stream speed can be read off.

Example

On the opposite page it can be seen that the rate between Alderney and Guernsey is 2.1, 3.7. On the graph these points have been plotted on the 45 and 90 lines and a line drawn across.

The tidal coefficient of the tide in question is found against its date in the table and seen to be 75. On the graph this is seen to cut your line at the level where the stream rate is 3.2 knots. It can be seen that an extra high range tide (say coefficient 97) will result in tidal streams faster than for normal springs.

In the same way the figures up the left-hand side can be used to express depths of water (multiplying the scale by ten or perhaps two, as necessary). If the depths at neaps and springs are plotted on the 45 and 90 lines, a line joining can be drawn in the same way and the depth read off against the coefficient for the day.

any margin is likely to be on the safe side, i.e. they will tell you that you have *less* water than in fact there is. The print is large and very legible.

The chief disadvantage to the British ATT is that their Table 2, the differences for secondary ports, have recently had added a lot of harmonic influences used for a very complicated new system, using books of two kinds of graphs. The system is unsuitable for sailing boats, and unnecessary, and means that Table 2 is more awkward to use. You must refer to your standard port, turn the book sideways to find the differences in Table 2, then turn back to a graph of the tidal curve for the standard port. Vol 2 has a single tidal curve, but Vol 1 has tidal curves for all standard ports, and a series of curves based on Low Water for the Solent area, which are only marginally better, and a lot more complicated than *Fig. 3.2*. One of the biggest advantages of ATT is their proforma (*Fig. 11.12*) which simplifies everything.

TIDES BY REED'S

Reed's for Europe gives the sailor a choice of three systems: the twelfths method mentioned in Chapter 3, for which a table is given to make it even simpler; a method based on Mean Tide Level and Duration of Mean Rise; and in 1980, for the first time, a method based on the excellent French coefficient system. This is easier than it sounds — coefficient is a word that drives people away in droves — and can be understood easily from *Figs. 11.6–11.8*. For the ordinary Duration of Mean Rise system I have evolved a work form, printed in *Fig. 11.9*, which will be found to make things simpler and avoid errors — or at least if you make an error, will show you where it is.

Reed's for the US East Coast is much simpler over tides, because the rise and fall is so much less. Tidal atlases are given only for the most popular yachting areas.

Examples with Reed's

I am giving several examples, all based on a similar situation and area, that of a boat which is in the region of the Channel Islands and Brittany, where tides of 14 metres (46 feet) are far from uncommon, and naturally in this area they are important. If your foreign plans are confined to a bareboat charter in the Virgin Islands, with their trivial rise and fall of just over a foot (though tidal streams can run hard) the exercise is less vital. I am using the standard port of St Helier, with further examples for secondary ports. Sailors regularly in this area will find the new publication, *Channel West and Solent* which gives an actual table for St Malo, based on French information, of great help. So that an exact

WORK FORM FOR FINDING HEIGHT OF TIDE USING REED'S ALMANAC

DATE: Year **1980** Month **JULY** Day **22**   Time zone **BST** TIME: Hours **16** Mins **50**

REQUIRED HEIGHT _____

STANDARD PORT **ST. HELIER** _____   SECONDARY PORT **—** _____

A

Time of nearest HW (a)	1442
Height of HW (b)	8·1m
Duration of Mean Rise (c)	5·45
Mean Tide Level (d)	6·1
Time LW (e) — — (a) minus (c) +12 10	2107
Height LW (f) (b) minus twice difference between (b) and (d)	4·1
Range	4·0

B

Time difference (g)	
Time HW (h)	
Height difference (j)	
Height HW (k)	
Duration Mean Rise (l)	
Mean Tide Level (m)	
Time LW (n) — — (h) minus (l)	
Height LW (k) minus twice difference between (m) and (k)	
Range	

C

BEFORE HW	
DMR used to suit table (q)	
Interval before HW (r)	
Height HW minus ML (s)	
Correction in metres to be subtracted from HW level	
Rise in Tide	

D

AFTER HW	
DMR used to suit table (t)	5·40
Interval after HW (u)	2·00
Height HW minus ML (v)	2·0m
Correction in metres to be subtracted from HW level	0·8m
Rise in Tide	7·3

E

TO FIND TIME FOR GIVEN RISE	
Height of HW (b) or (k)	
Height required (subtract from above)	
Correction figure	
HW (b) or (k) minus ML (d) or (m)	
Interval to add or subtract from HW	
Time for required height	

REQUIRED RISE _____

Fig. 11.9   Here is a work form for making tidal problems using *Reed's* very clear; it helps if you need to pick up an error. Here it is used to find the tide height at 1650 BST. The result is minutely different from ATT.

Lat. 49°11'N.   Long. 2°07'W.   **ST. HELIER, JERSEY**

HIGH WATER

TIDAL DIFFERENCES PAGE 585   **1980**

Day of Month	D of W	JULY Time h.min	Ht. m.	Time h.min	Ht. m.	D of W	AUGUST Time h.min	Ht. m.	Time h.min	Ht. m.	D of W	SEPTEMBER Time h.min	Ht. m.	Time h.min	Ht. m.
1	Tu	0815	10.6	2034	10.8	F	0925	10.9	2145	10.8	M	1033	9.8	2259	9.4
2	W	0856	10.5	2115	10.6	Sa	1009	10.3	2233	10.1	Tu	1129	8.9	—	—
3	Th	0939	10.2	2202	10.2	Su	1059	9.6	2327	9.4	W	0008	8.5	1249	8.2
4	F	1028	9.8	2254	9.7	M	—	—	1201	9.0	Th	0147	8.1	1429	8.2
5	Sa	1126	9.4	2357	9.3	Tu	0039	8.8	1321	8.6	F	0317	8.4	1543	8.7
6	Su	—	—	1236	9.0	W	0206	8.6	1446	8.7	Sa	0420	8.9	1638	9.3
7	M	0113	9.1	1354	9.0	Th	0327	8.8	1556	9.1	Su	0509	9.5	1723	9.9
8	Tu	0229	9.2	1505	9.3	F	0430	9.3	1652	9.6	M	0550	10.0	1803	10.3
9	W	0338	9.5	1609	9.7	Sa	0523	9.7	1742	10.0	Tu	0625	10.3	1838	10.6
10	Th	0438	9.9	1704	10.1	Su	0610	10.1	1824	10.3	W	0659	10.6	1912	10.8
11	F	0533	10.2	1754	10.4	M	0649	10.3	1902	10.5	Th	0730	10.7	1942	10.8
12	Sa	0622	10.3	1839	10.5	Tu	0726	10.4	1937	10.6	F	0759	10.6	2011	10.7
13	Su	0706	10.4	1920	10.6	W	0758	10.4	2009	10.6	Sa	0827	10.5	2039	10.4
14	M	0745	10.3	1958	10.6	Th	0829	10.3	2039	10.5	Su	0854	10.2	2107	10.0
15	Tu	0822	10.2	2032	10.3	F	0858	10.1	2108	10.2	M	0922	9.7	2136	9.5
16	W	0856	9.9	2105	10.1	Sa	0927	9.8	2139	9.8	Tu	0953	9.2	2210	8.9
17	Th	0928	9.6	2139	9.8	Su	0959	9.4	2213	9.2	W	1033	8.6	2257	8.3
18	F	1002	9.3	2216	9.4	M	1034	8.9	2254	8.7	Th	1132	8.1	—	—
19	Sa	1041	8.9	2258	8.9	Tu	1122	8.4	2347	8.1	F	0012	7.8	1314	7.9
20	Su	1127	8.5	2350	8.4	W	—	—	1231	8.0	Sa	0205	7.9	1449	8.4
21	M	—	—	1229	8.2	Th	0109	7.8	1404	8.0	Su	0324	8.7	1552	9.3
22	Tu	0057	8.1	1342	8.1	F	0240	8.0	1519	8.5	M	0420	9.7	1644	10.3
23	W	0211	8.1	1453	8.4	Sa	0349	8.7	1617	9.3	Tu	0509	10.7	1732	11.2
24	Th	0318	8.4	1552	8.9	Su	0444	9.5	1708	10.1	W	0556	11.5	1817	11.9
25	F	0416	8.9	1642	9.4	M	0533	10.3	1754	10.9	Th	0639	12.0	1900	12.3
26	Sa	0506	9.5	1729	10.0	Tu	0618	11.1	1839	11.6	F	0723	12.2	1944	12.3
27	Su	0553	10.1	1814	10.6	W	0702	11.6	1921	11.9	Sa	0804	12.1	2025	11.9
28	M	0638	10.6	1857	11.1	Th	0744	11.9	2004	12.0	Su	0844	11.5	2105	11.2
29	Tu	0720	11.0	1940	11.4	F	0825	11.8	2044	11.7	M	0924	10.7	2148	10.3
30	W	0802	11.2	2020	11.4	Sa	0905	11.4	2125	11.2	Tu	1007	9.8	2235	9.2
31	Th	0843	11.2	2103	11.2	Su	0946	10.6	2209	10.3					

Day of Month	D of W	OCTOBER Time h.min	Ht. m.	Time h.min	Ht. m.	D of W	NOVEMBER Time h.min	Ht. m.	Time h.min	Ht. m.	D of W	DECEMBER Time h.min	Ht. m.	Time h.min	Ht. m.
1	W	1059	8.8	2342	8.3	Sa	0046	7.8	1319	7.9	M	0113	7.9	1338	8.2
2	Th	—	—	1217	8.0	Su	0218	7.9	1440	8.3	Tu	0225	8.2	1444	8.5
3	F	0124	7.8	1404	7.9	M	0319	8.5	1536	8.8	W	0321	8.7	1539	9.0
4	Sa	0258	8.1	1521	8.4	Tu	0407	9.1	1621	9.4	Th	0407	9.3	1626	9.4
5	Su	0359	8.7	1614	9.1	W	0447	9.7	1701	10.0	F	0449	9.7	1706	9.8
6	M	0444	9.3	1657	9.7	Th	0523	10.2	1739	10.3	Sa	0529	10.1	1746	10.1
7	Tu	0522	9.9	1734	10.2	F	0558	10.5	1814	10.5	Su	0605	10.4	1824	10.2
8	W	0557	10.3	1810	10.6	Sa	0632	10.7	1848	10.6	M	0642	10.5	1859	10.3
9	Th	0629	10.6	1842	10.8	Su	0704	10.7	1919	10.5	Tu	0716	10.6	1934	10.3
10	F	0700	10.8	1913	10.8	M	0735	10.6	1949	10.4	W	0751	10.5	2008	10.2
11	Sa	0730	10.8	1944	10.7	Tu	0805	10.4	2020	10.1	Th	0825	10.4	2044	10.0
12	Su	0759	10.6	2012	10.5	W	0836	10.1	2053	9.7	F	0901	10.1	2124	9.8
13	M	0826	10.4	2040	10.1	Th	0908	9.7	2129	9.3	Sa	0943	9.8	2209	9.4
14	Tu	0854	10.0	2108	9.6	F	0949	9.2	2216	8.8	Su	1034	9.4	2306	9.0
15	W	0925	9.5	2142	9.1	Sa	1044	8.7	2323	8.4	M	1139	9.0	—	—
16	Th	1003	8.9	2228	8.5	Su	—	—	1205	8.5	Tu	0021	8.8	1259	9.0
17	F	1059	8.3	2340	8.0	M	0056	8.4	1338	8.7	W	0142	9.0	1418	9.3
18	Sa	—	—	1235	8.1	Tu	0220	9.0	1451	9.4	Th	0254	9.5	1525	9.8
19	Su	0131	8.1	1416	8.5	W	0325	9.8	1550	10.3	F	0356	10.1	1624	10.4
20	M	0254	8.8	1524	9.4	Th	0420	10.7	1644	11.0	Sa	0452	10.7	1720	10.8
21	Tu	0355	9.8	1619	10.4	F	0511	11.3	1734	11.5	Su	0543	11.1	1811	11.1
22	W	0445	10.8	1708	11.3	Sa	0558	11.7	1824	11.8	M	0632	11.2	1859	11.1
23	Th	0532	11.6	1754	11.8	Su	0645	11.8	1910	11.7	Tu	0717	11.2	1944	10.9
24	F	0618	12.1	1841	12.2	M	0728	11.6	1954	11.3	W	0759	10.9	2025	10.6
25	Sa	0702	12.2	1924	12.2	Tu	0811	11.2	2036	10.7	Th	0837	10.6	2103	10.1
26	Su	0744	12.0	2008	11.7	W	0851	10.5	2118	10.0	F	0914	10.1	2139	9.6
27	M	0826	11.4	2049	11.0	Th	0931	9.8	2200	9.2	Sa	0952	9.6	2219	9.0
28	Tu	0905	10.6	2131	10.1	F	1014	9.1	2249	8.6	Su	1033	9.1	2304	8.6
29	W	0948	9.7	2217	9.1	Sa	1108	8.5	2354	8.1	M	1123	8.6	—	—
30	Th	1035	8.8	2316	8.3	Su	—	—	1219	8.2	Tu	0001	8.2	1227	8.3
31	F	1143	8.1	—	—						W	0113	8.1	1340	8.2

RACE OF ALDERNEY— Between Alderney and coast of France. Streams SW. and NE. SW. begins –0050 Dover max. rate +0200 Dover. NE. begins +0520 Dover max. rate –0420 Dover. Little slack water in Race. **Max. Spring rate 7-9½ kn. Neap rate 5½ kn.** With wind and tide in opposition — seas break heavily. Heavy overfalls over submerged rocks and banks.

DEPTHS— St. Helier: In channel . . . 8.5 m.; in anchorage . . . 2.4 m.-3.4 m. Spring rise . . . 11.1 m.; Neap rise . . . 8.1 m.

TIMES OF H.W. are suitable for: ROZEL, GOREY, LES ECREHOUX, LES MINQUIERS, CARTERET.

Fig. 11.10   A page from the tide tables in *Reed's Almanac* for St Helier, Jersey in the Channel Islands.

comparison can be made between the *Reed's* method and the British ATT, some of the same examples are worked by ATT below. You will see the *Reed's* and ATT differences on St Helier for French ports are not the same, because *Reed's* keeps to British time while ATT tells you to convert to French time.

It would be inadvisable to use American tide tables in these waters. If you speak and understand French well, the French tidal methods are excellent. But whatever system you use, with any rise of tide above six metres (about 20 feet) always *use a safe margin*.

TIDAL DIFFERENCES ON ST. HELIER

PLACE	MHW		ML	DMR	RULING DEPTH AT			
	Tm Diff. h. min.	Ht Diff. m.	m.	h. min.	HWS m.	HWN m.	CD m.	POSITION
Channel Islands								
The Casquets	+0 22	—	—	—	—	—	27.4	Anchorage S.E.
Alderney (Braye)	+0 45	-4.8S -3.4N	3.6	5 45	15.4	13.8	9.1	Anchorage off
Guernsey								
St. Peter Port	+0 05	-1.7	5.0	5 50	10.8 18.8	8.5 16.5	1.8 9.8	Grand Havre (Anche.) Anchorage off
St. Sampson's	—	—	—	—	—	—	Dries	
Jersey								
St. Helier	0 00	0.0	6.1	5 45	13.8	10.8	2.7	Entcc. and S. part new Hr.
Rozel	-0 09	-0.1	6.1	5 45	—	—	Dries	Harbour
Gorey	-0 05	—	6.1	5 45	16.9	15.4	9.1	Outer Road. Harb. dries
Les Ecrehoux	+0 10	0.0	6.1	5 55	13.9	11.4	3.0	Anche. close Marmotier
Les Minquiers	+0 05	+0.6	6.4	5 45	—	—	—	
Iles Chausey	-0 15	+1.5	7.0	5 30	—	—	—	
France, North Coast								
Diélette	+0 15	-1.2	5.3	5 50	4.6	2.3	-4.9	Jetty
Carteret	+0 05	0.0	6.1	5 45	1.8	0.2	-9.1	Alongside Quay
Granville	-0 15	+1.5	7.0	5 25	5.8	2.5	-7.0	Avant-port
Cancale	-0 15	+2.0	7.5	5 35	7.5	4.3	-5.8	Hd. J'etee de la Houle
St. Malo	-0 20	+0.9	6.6	5 35	12.9	9.9	0.9	Chenal des Vedettes
Erquy	-0 20	+0.2	6.1	5 50	7.2	4.5	-4.0	Alongside jetty
Dahouet	-0 25	+0.2	6.1	5 50	4.7	2.1	-6.4	Entrance channel
Le Légué	-0 30	+0.2	6.2	5 50	5.7	2.9	-5.5	Channel
Binic	-0 30	+0.2	6.2	5 50	5.1	2.3	-6.1	Avant-port
Portrieux	-0 30	+0.2	6.2	5 50	4.8	2.0	-6.4	Alongside
Paimpol	-0 30	-0.5	5.4	6 00	5.5 16.2	2.8 13.5	-4.9 5.8	Chan. to Harbour Rade de
Ile de Bréhat	-0 25	-0.4	5.7	6 05	15.3	12.9	5.5	Rade de
Heaux de Brehat	-0 30	-1.0	5.4	6 00	10.1	7.7	0.3	Passe de la Gaine
Lesardrieux	-0 30	-0.6	5.5	6 10	13.2	10.7	3.0	Channel to
Plougrescant	-1 00	-1.1	5.4	6 00	—	—	—	
Treguier	-0 55	-1.0	5.3	6 00	9.8	7.4	0.0	Chan. to Treguier
Ploumanach	-1 05	-1.7	5.0	6 05	—	—	Dries	Harbour

Time differences are relative to the standard port. For secondary ports not in the same time zone, adjustment should be made when local time is required.

Refer to predictions on pages 586-587   **Tidal streams on pages 588-591**

Fig. 11.11   Tidal difference page from *Reed's* for St Helier secondary ports.

INSTRUCTIONS

Box No.

Complete Heading.

1 to 4	Enter daily prediction data from ATT Part I.
5 and 6	Enter data from ATT Part II (not required for Standard Port or Vol. 1).
7 to 10	Enter Differences from ATT Part II (interpolation necessary for Vol. 1) (not required for Standard Port).
11	Enter sum of 1 and 7 (for Standard Port enter 1).
12	Enter sum of 2 and 8 (for Standard Port enter 2).
13	Enter sum of 3, 5, 6 and 9 (for Standard Port enter 3).
14	Enter sum of 4, 5, 6 and 10 (for Standard Port enter 4).
15	Enter Duration. Difference of times in 11 and 12 (not required for Vol. 1).
16(a)	Enter Range at Standard Port. Difference of heights in 3 and 4.
16(b)	Enter Range at Secondary Port. Difference of heights in 13 and 14.

*Delete Springs, Neaps, Interpolate as appropriate to Standard Port Range 16(a) (Vol. 1 only).

TO FIND HEIGHT AT GIVEN TIME

17	Enter required time.
18	Enter HW time from 11.
19	Enter Interval. Difference of 17 and 18.
20	*Enter Factor obtained from interpolation of appropriate curve entered with Interval 19.
21	Enter Rise = Factor 20 × Range 16(b) (for Standard Port use 16(a)).
22	Enter LW Height from 14.
23	Enter sum of Rise 21 and LW Height 22.

TO FIND TIME FOR A GIVEN HEIGHT (Start at bottom of column)

23	Enter required height.
22	Enter LW Height from 14.
21	Enter Rise = Height 23 − LW Height 22.
20	Enter Factor = Rise 21/Range 16(b) (for Standard Ports use 16(a)).
19	*Enter Interval obtained from interpolation of appropriate curve entered with Factor 20.
18	Enter HW Time 11.
17	Enter Interval 19 applied to HW Time 18.

*NOTE Do not attempt to extrapolate additional curves. In ATT Vol. 1 use the Spring curve for Spring Ranges and greater, and the Neap curve for Neap Ranges and less. For intermediate ranges interpolate between curves using the Range at the Standard Port (Box 16(a)) as argument. In ATT Vols. 2 and 3 if duration is outside those shown in Table II use NP 159.

STANDARD PORT ...ST. HELIER... TIME or HEIGHT REQUIRED...1650.....

SECONDARY PORT ....—........ DATE JULY 22/80 TIME ZONE ...BST.....

	TIME		HEIGHT	
	HW	LW	HW	LW
STANDARD PORT	1 1442 0311 (23)	2 2111 0944 (23)	3 8.1 8.1	4 4.0 3.9
Seasonal Changes in ML	− Standard Port		5 —	
	+ Secondary Port		6 —	
DIFFERENCES	7 —	8 —	9 —	10 —
SECONDARY PORT	11 —	12 —	13 —	14 —
DURATION	15 —	RANGE(a)St (b)Sec	16(a) 4.1 4.2	16(b)

*Springs/Neaps/Interpolate

START— Height at Given Time ⤵

REQUIRED TIME	17 1650
TIME HW	18 1442
INTERVAL	19 + 2.08 (after)

| FACTOR | 20 .77 | x Range 4.1
|---|---|

RISE	21 3.2
HEIGHT LW	22 4.0
HEIGHT REQUIRED	23 7.2

START— Time for Given Height

*Delete as necessary

Fig. 11.12   The *Admiralty Tide Table* prediction form which makes using the tables much simpler. Here it is worked to find the height of tide at 1650 at St Helier. The instructions on the left are clear and self-explanatory.

EXAMPLE 1.   You are close to St Helier, Jersey, at 1650 hrs on July 22, 1980 (pages from St Helier tide tables from both *Reed's* and Admiralty Tide Tables and the auxiliary tables required are in *Figs. 11.3–11.5* and also *Figs. 11.10–11.13*).

When is low water and what height is it above datum?

Next St Helier HW: 0211 GMT = 0311 BST on July 23: Rise 8·1 metres

Last St Helier HS: 1342 GMT = 1442 BST July 22: Rise 8·1 metres

Mean level St Helier: 6·1 metres

Duration of Mean Rise: 5 hrs 45 min.

A glance at the table generally comparing heights shows that this day is almost exactly at neaps, and a very modest neaps at that, high water being only 8·1; this is only 2 m above mean level of 6·1 metres.

LW level will therefore be 6·1−2·0 = 4·1 metres, answering part of the question above.

At low water you will have 4·1 metres more water than any charted depth. A rock that dries 1·5 metres will still have 2·6 metres of water over it.

Turning to present rise of tide you require:

Range for today — 2·0 multiplied by 2 = 4·0 metres.

Duration of Mean Rise — 5 hrs 45 min. To obtain the time of low water, subtract this from the time of next high water, giving 2126 BST. This is the answer to the rest of the question above.

To find the present rise of tide, you need *Reed's* table for finding the height of tide before and after HW, which is reproduced in *Fig. 11–13*.

Present time after HW: 1650 −1442 = 2 hrs 8 min.

Note that both the time figures were BST — the 2 hrs 8 min is purely an interval.

The *Reed's* table recommends using the nearest approximate time, it tabulates times four times in the hour, none will ever be far away. Doing this you take Duration of Mean Rise as 5 hrs 40 mins, instead of 5 hrs 45 mins, and the interval from HW as 2 hrs instead of 2 hrs 8 mins. This avoids unnecessary and complicated interpolation by eye.

The table is used for height of tide by starting in the top left hand corner, moving down the column found under the relevant duration of mean rise, going to the top right hand corner to choose the column under the height of HW minus mean level, and then following that column down till you reach the horizontal line you were at with your interval from high water, and you then read off a correction to be subtracted from the height of high water. I strongly recommend people to photocopy this table and make a small pad of the copies. Then using the copies as expendable (they can be used at least twice each) mark out with a pencil and straight edge as I have done in *Fig. 11.13*. Make a practice of drawing the lines so the figure you want is above and to the right of the line

HEIGHT OF TIDE TABLE

TABLE FOR FINDING THE HEIGHT OF TIDE BEFORE AND AFTER HIGH WATER

Enter Duration of Mean Rise as appropriate — follow column down to interval between HW and time of height required — follow line across to column Height of HW minus ML = height to be subtracted from Height at HW to give height of tide at time required.

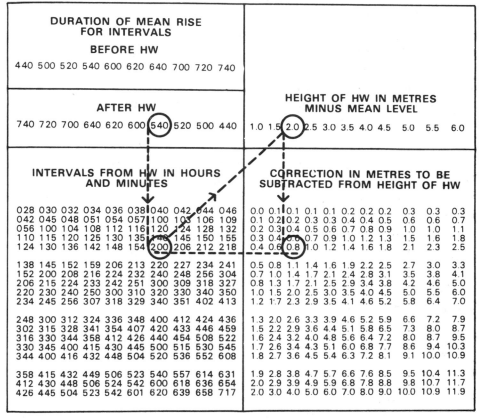

DURATION OF MEAN RISE FOR INTERVALS																				
BEFORE HW																				
440 500 520 540 600 620 640 700 720 740																				

HEIGHT OF HW IN METRES MINUS MEAN LEVEL

AFTER HW											HEIGHT OF HW IN METRES MINUS MEAN LEVEL									
740 720 700 640 620 600 (540) 520 500 440											1.0 1.5 2.0 2.5 3.0 3.5 4.0 4.5 5.0 5.5 6.0										

INTERVALS FROM HW IN HOURS AND MINUTES											CORRECTION IN METRES TO BE SUBTRACTED FROM HEIGHT OF HW									
028 030 032 034 036 038 040 042 044 046											0.0 0.1 0.1 0.1 0.1 0.2 0.2 0.2 0.3 0.3 0.3										
042 045 048 051 054 057 100 103 106 109											0.1 0.2 0.2 0.3 0.3 0.4 0.4 0.5 0.6 0.6 0.7										
056 100 104 108 112 116 120 124 128 132											0.2 0.3 0.4 0.5 0.6 0.7 0.8 0.9 1.0 1.0 1.1										
110 115 120 125 130 135 140 145 150 155											0.3 0.4 0.6 0.7 0.9 1.0 1.2 1.3 1.5 1.6 1.8										
124 130 136 142 148 154 (200) 206 212 218											0.4 0.6 (0.8) 1.0 1.2 1.4 1.6 1.8 2.1 2.3 2.5										
138 145 152 159 206 213 220 227 234 241											0.5 0.8 1.1 1.4 1.6 1.9 2.2 2.5 2.7 3.0 3.3										
152 200 208 216 224 232 240 248 256 304											0.7 1.0 1.4 1.7 2.1 2.4 2.8 3.1 3.5 3.8 4.1										
206 215 224 233 242 251 300 309 318 327											0.8 1.3 1.7 2.1 2.5 2.9 3.4 3.8 4.2 4.6 5.0										
220 230 240 250 300 310 320 330 340 350											1.0 1.5 2.0 2.5 3.0 3.5 4.0 4.5 5.0 5.5 6.0										
234 245 256 307 318 329 340 351 402 413											1.2 1.7 2.3 2.9 3.5 4.1 4.6 5.2 5.8 6.4 7.0										
248 300 312 324 336 348 400 412 424 436											1.3 2.0 2.6 3.3 3.9 4.6 5.2 5.9 6.6 7.2 7.9										
302 315 328 341 354 407 420 433 446 459											1.5 2.2 2.9 3.6 4.4 5.1 5.8 6.5 7.3 8.0 8.7										
316 330 344 358 412 426 440 454 508 522											1.6 2.4 3.2 4.0 4.8 5.6 6.4 7.2 8.0 8.7 9.5										
330 345 400 415 430 445 500 515 530 545											1.7 2.6 3.4 4.3 5.1 6.0 6.8 7.7 8.6 9.4 10.3										
344 400 416 432 448 504 520 536 552 608											1.8 2.7 3.6 4.5 5.4 6.3 7.2 8.1 9.1 10.0 10.9										
358 415 432 449 506 523 540 557 614 631											1.9 2.8 3.8 4.7 5.7 6.6 7.6 8.5 9.5 10.4 11.3										
412 430 448 506 524 542 600 618 636 654											2.0 2.9 3.9 4.9 5.9 6.8 7.8 8.8 9.8 10.7 11.7										
426 445 504 523 542 601 620 639 658 717											2.0 3.0 4.0 5.0 6.0 7.0 8.0 9.0 10.0 10.9 11.9										

Fig. 11.13   *Reed's* table for finding the height of tide before and after high water. Enter the table with your time before or after high water, on the left hand side (the drawing on the diagram shows a point 5 hours 40 minutes after high water). Follow down to the required interval from high water, and then go up to the top right, to the high water in metres minus mean level. You then follow down to the point in the correction section below, level with the time interval you have found shown by the dotted line. It sounds complicated, but it's simple as soon as you have the knack.

drawn, which is the normal orienting principle used in all maps and in mathematics. Then we can lay things out systematically, and you would be wise to write it out neatly so it is easy to check back. I find it convenient to make out a form as in *Fig. 11.9* and photocopy it.

Wanted: Height of tide, St Helier, 1650 BST

Time of nearest HW: 1442 BST

Height of HW: 8·1 metres

Duration of mean rise: 5 h 45 m (to suit the table call it 5 h 40 m)

Mean level: 6·1 metres

Time interval from HW: 2 h 8 m (to suit table call it 2 hrs)

Height of HW minus mean level: 8·1 − 6·1 = 2 metres

Correction to be subtracted from HW: 0·8 metres

$$8·1 − 0·8 = +7·3 \text{ metres}$$

Rise of tide at 1650 is 7·3 metres

This, I can hear you saying, is all very well but, having read the charts and pilot books about St Helier, with its depressing facilities for yachts and discouraging approach, you have no intention of wasting any time there; it is the fleshpots of Brittany you hanker after. So now we will tackle one of the commonest problems for a boat visiting Brittany.

EXAMPLE 2.   You are approaching St Malo and you know the lock there is open for one and a half hours each side of local high water. It is now 1730 hrs BST, the wind is light and you are wondering whether you need to motor to catch the lock. Under power it will take you an estimated one and a half hours to get to the lock approaches; under sail, more like three hours

(a) What time is St Malo high water, and when is the lock open?

(b) What is the height of tide above datum at low water if you miss the lock?

HW St Helier is 1927 (GMT) = 2027 BST, height 11·5 metres. From tidal difference table, St Malo time difference is −20 minutes, and height difference +0·9 metres. Thus for answer (a) HW St Malo is 2007 BST, height 12·4 metres, 5·8 metres above mean level, and the lock will be open from 1837 BST to 2137 BST.

Mean tide level for St Malo is 6·6 metres, so low water rise is 6·6 − 5·8 = 0·8 metres (answer (b)).

You should make it under sail but, being a prudent man and hoping you may clear customs in time for dinner ashore, you start your engine. You will, however, find the lock-keepers at St Malo are charitable, hard-working souls, who often keep going longer than their scheduled times. (Timing the lock at St Malo is much easier since *Channel West and Solent* gives tables for several French ports, including St Malo.)

WORK FORM FOR FINDING HEIGHT OF TIDE USING REED'S ALMANAC

DATE: Year ____ Month ____ Day ____   Time zone ____ TIME: Hours **17** Mins **30**

REQUIRED HEIGHT ____ **12·8** ____

STANDARD PORT ____ **ST. HELIER** ____   SECONDARY PORT ____ **CANCALE** ____

A

Time of nearest HW (a)	**1641**
Height of HW (b)	**8·7m**
Duration of Mean Rise (c)	**5–45**
Mean Tide Level (d)	**6·1**
Time LW (e) — — (a) minus (c)	**2258**
Height LW (f) (b) minus twice difference between (b) and (d)	**3·5** *
Range	**5·2**

B

Time difference (g)	**−0·15**
Time HW (h)	**1626**
Height difference (j)	**+2·0**
Height HW (k)	**10·7**
Duration Mean Rise (l)	**5·35**
Mean Tide Level (m)	**7·5**
Time LW (n) — — (h) minus (l) **+12**	**2243**
Height LW (k) minus twice difference between (m) and (k)	**4·3**
Range	**6·4**

C

BEFORE HW	
DMR used to suit table (q)	
Interval before HW (r)	
Height HW minus ML (s)	
Correction in metres to be subtracted from HW level	
Rise in Tide	

D

AFTER HW		
DMR used to suit table (t)		**5–40**
Interval after HW (u)		**1–00**
Height HW minus ML (v)	**3·2**	**3·0m35**
Correction in metres to be subtracted from HW level		**0·3** OR **0·4**
Rise in Tide		**10·4** OR **10·3**

E

TO FIND TIME FOR GIVEN RISE	
Height of HW (b) or (k)	
Height required (subtract from above)	
Correction figure	
HW (b) or (k) minus ML (d) or (m)	
Interval to add or subtract from HW	
Time for required height	

REQUIRED RISE ____

Fig. 11.14   Work form completed for finding the rise of tide at Cancale, using *Reed's*.

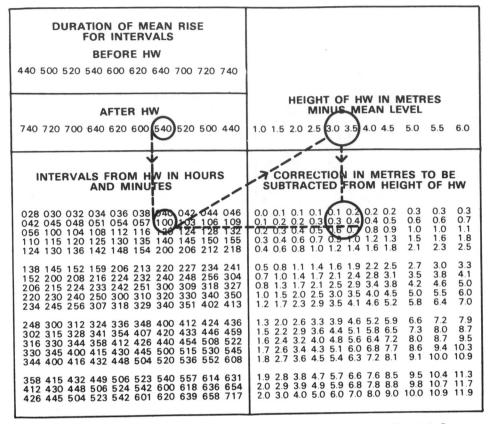

Fig. 11.15   Using the *Reed's* table to find the rise of tide at Cancale. See Example 3.

EXAMPLE 3.   Now let us take things to extremes. You are approaching Cancale, east of St Malo, and at 1730 BST you obtain a sounding of just over 11 metres (corrected for transducer depth) in what looks a convenient position to anchor. You draw 4 ft 6 ins (1·4 m).

(a) How much water will you have under your keel at low water?

(b) What is the shallowest sounding now for a position to anchor that gives you at least one metre under your keel at low water? Let us take it that on this particular day the tides are: Last HW St Helier, 1541 GMT = 1641 BST, height 8·7 metres.

Next HW St Helier, 0413 GMT = 0513 BST, height 8·7 metres.

Mean level Cancale, 7·5 m; duration of mean rise, 5 hrs 35 min.

Time difference, −0·15; height difference 2 metres.

Afternoon HW Cancale = 1641 −15 mins = 1626 BST.

Height 8·7 (St Helier) +2·0 = 10·7.

Next high water is at 0513 −15, = 0458; height also 10·7 metres.

Next low water will be at 0458, minus duration of mean rise.

So LW Cancale is 2243 BST, height 4·3 metres.

Range for this tide is 10·7 −4·3 = 6·4 metres.

This example shown on my work form is in *Fig. 11.14.*

You need the rise for one hour and four minutes after high water — calling it one hour will do. With the working shown in *Fig. 11.14* and table in *Fig. 11.15,* this will be high water level minus between ·3 and ·4 of a metre. Take the safer level by using the larger figure, then present rise is 10·7 −·4 = 10·3 metres.

You have a sounding of 11 metres, so at low water you will have only ·7 of a metre — not nearly enough (answer (a)). You require your draft plus at least one metre, call it 2·5 metres altogether.

What you need is 11 metres, plus 2·5 metres minus ·7 of a metre — 12·8 metres. So you look around for a suitable spot with between 12·5 and 13 metres of water, and there it is safe to put down your anchor. Cancale having a large rise of tide even at neaps, and wide shallow mud flats off shore, the spot found is probably inconvenient for going ashore by dinghy. It is a place really suitable only for boats that can take the ground fairly close to high water mark.

EXAMPLE 4.   You are lying in the Tréguier river before dawn, and want to go through the narrow inshore channel, the Passe de la Gaine, to Ile Bréhat, passing just south of the great lighthouse known as Héaux de Bréhat. There are several drying rocks in this channel, and one of them dries six feet. You decide you want at least five metres above datum in case you should cross it. What time will you have this amount?

Today's tidal situation is:

HW St Helier 0604 GMT = 0704 BST; height 10·9 metres

HW St Helier 1827 GMT = 1927 BST; height 11·2 metres

Time Difference Héaux de Bréhat −00 30 mins

Height difference Héaux de Bréhat −1·0 metres

So HW Héaux = 9·9 metres at 0634 BST and 10·2 metres at 1858 BST

Mean Tide Level: 5·4 m

At this stage you have to rephrase your question. The tide will be falling and, since you don't want to wait till the evening when the setting sun will make the leading marks for the channel hard to see, how late can you afford to go through the channel?

Mean level Héaux = 5·4 metres, which gives us a chance to cheat by saying 'This is a fraction over what I want so, if I go through exactly halfway between high and low water, I will be all right.' But let us ignore this bit of cheating and

WORK FORM FOR FINDING HEIGHT OF TIDE USING REED'S ALMANAC

DATE: Year ____—____ Month ____—____ Day ____—____   Time zone ____—____ TIME: Hours ____—____ Mins ____—____

REQUIRED HEIGHT **5·0 metres**

STANDARD PORT _**ST. HELIER**_   SECONDARY PORT _**HÉAUX de BRÉHAT**_

A

Time of nearest HW (a)	**0704**
Height of HW (b)	**10·9**
Duration of Mean Rise (c)	**5-45**
Mean Tide Level (d)	**6·1**
Time LW (e) — — (a) minus (c)	**01-19**
Height LW (f) (b) minus twice difference between (b) and (d)	**1·3**
Range	**9·6**

B

Time difference (g) ✱	**−30**
Time HW (h)	**0634**
Height difference (j)	**−1m**
Height HW (k)	**9·9**
Duration Mean Rise (l)	**6-00**
Mean Tide Level (m)	**5·4**
Time LW (n) — — (h) minus (l) **+12·10**	**1244**✱
Height LW (k) minus twice difference between (m) and (k)	**·9**
Range	**9m**

C

BEFORE HW	
DMR used to suit table (q)	
Interval before HW (r)	
Height HW minus ML (s)	
Correction in metres to be subtracted from HW level	
Rise in Tide	

D

AFTER HW	
DMR used to suit table (t)	
Interval after HW (u)	
Height HW minus ML (v)	
Correction in metres to be subtracted from HW level	
Rise in Tide	

E

TO FIND TIME FOR GIVEN RISE	
Height of HW (b) or (k)	**9·9**
Height required (subtract from above)	**5·0**
Correction figure	**4·9**
HW (b) or (k) minus ML (d) or (m)	**4·5**
Interval to add or subtract from HW	**3-10** ✱
Time for required height	**0944**

REQUIRED RISE _____**5·0 metres**_____

At E here, normal use of the table in Reed's is reversed as shown in Fig 11.17. Select column on right hand side given by HW—ML and follow down until correction figure is reached. Take a line over to left of table. At top on left select column for DMR and follow down until it meets line from right. This gives time interval to subtract from time of HW.

Fig. 11.16   Work form for *Reed's* completed to find the time for a required tide height of 5 metres at Héaux de Bréhat.

Opposite

Fig. 11.17   The *Reed's* form used for working out time for required height at Héaux de Bréhat. See Example 4.

work it out in full. From *Fig. 11.16*:

LW Héaux = ·9 m

So range Héaux = 9·9 −0·9 = 9 m

Duration of mean rise is 6·00 exactly

LW Héaux = 1258

You now need to obtain from *Fig. 11.17* what *Reed's* calls the **correction figure**, which is HW minus required rise

= 9·9 −5·0

= 4·9

Looking at *Figs. 11.16* and *11.17*:

So 3 hrs 10 minutes after HW Héaux is the latest time you have the 5 metres you want:

= 0634 +0310

= 0944 BST

You would be wise, however, to allow plenty of time, and arrange to be at the shallow part not later than 0915.

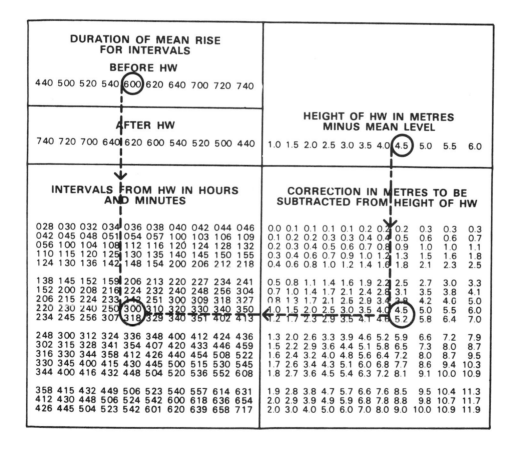

STANDARD PORT .....ST. HELIER.....TIME or HEIGHT REQUIRED...5 METRES

SECONDARY PORT HÉAUX DE BRÉHAT DATE........—........TIME ZONE ..BST....

	TIME		HEIGHT	
	HW	LW	HW	LW
STANDARD PORT	1 0704	2 0119	3 10.9	4 1.3
Seasonal Changes in ML	− Standard Port		5	
	+ Secondary Port		6	
DIFFERENCES	7 +0030 ✱ BST −0030	8 −0011 −0111 BST	9 −1.3	10 −0.3
SECONDARY PORT	11 0634	12 0008	13 9.6	14 1.0
DURATION	15 —	RANGE(a)St (b)Sec	16(a) 9.6	16(b) 8.6

*Springs/Neaps/Interpolate

START— Height at Given Time ⤵

REQUIRED TIME	17 0954
TIME HW	18 0634
INTERVAL	19 +3.20

FACTOR	20 .46

RISE	21 4.0
HEIGHT LW	22 1.0
HEIGHT REQUIRED	23 5m

↑ START— Time for Given Height

*Delete as necessary

✱ Watch out for zone time differences

Fig. 11.18   The Admiralty tidal prediction form completed for working out time for required height of 5 metres at Héaux de Bréhat.

Suppose we had followed our cheating method, and halved the time between high and low water, what would it have given us?

HW (at 0634) to LW (at 1258) is 6 hrs 24 mins. Half of this is 3 hrs 12 mins, making the answer to the question: 0946, only about two minutes different. This kind of problem emphasises an old and well-tested principle when going near drying heights:

On a falling tide, go early

On a rising tide, leave it late

TIDE LEVELS BY US EDITION OF REED'S

Tide levels are treated more casually in the American East Coast edition of *Reed's Almanac*, which is understandable since it is only in Maine and Canada that levels even approach those in Europe, and over much of the American eastern seaboard and the Caribbean a rise and fall of two feet is uncommon. Many yachtsmen totally ignore tide levels, finding sea level more affected by meteorological conditions.

Tidal streams, however, are another matter, and *Fig. 11.9*, showing a page of the *Reed's* tidal atlas for Long Island Sound, demonstrates that they must be taken seriously. This atlas is unusual because instead of giving the directions relative to a time at a reference station, they are given relative to 'ebb' and 'flow'. The key to ebb and flow is a special table for The Race, giving the times of slack water.

Other tidal atlases in *Reed's* for popular American sailing areas are given in the normal way, relative to high water at a reference station.

Another specialist feature of the American East Coast *Reed's* is the table for the new Gulf Coast Low Water Datum (GCLWD) which has been introduced between a point close south of Miami to match a new chart series. An extensive series of correction figures, some amounting to as much as 2·9 feet, is given for a large number of tidal points in the form of a ratio. Until these new charts are in general use, the tables are academic, but will become of increasing importance.

ADMIRALTY TIDE TABLES

It is an unfortunate fact that *British Admiralty Tide Tables* have become in recent years slightly less convenient than they used to be for the small boat owner. Although three volumes cover the whole world, they are all larger than they used to be — the inconvenient-for-small-boats international A4 size, which in a soft-covered book is also very floppy. They have also recently been

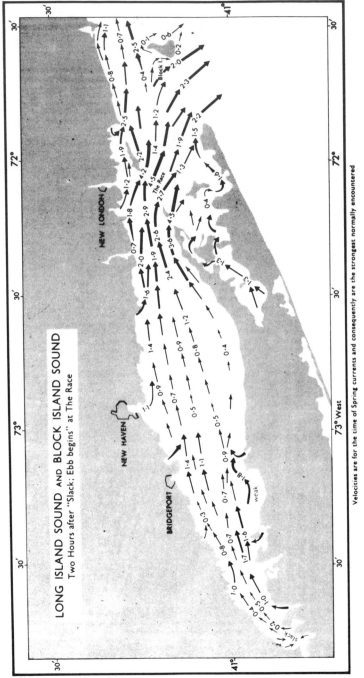

Fig. 11.19   A page from the American edition of *Reed's* showing tidal streams for Long Island Sound.

CURRENT TABLE—THE RACE

LONG ISLAND SOUND   **1980**

F—FLOOD, DIR. 295° TRUE   E—EBB, DIR. 100° TRUE

JULY

Day	Slack Water (h.min.)	Maximum Current (h.min.)	knots
1 Tu	0102	0429	3.9E
	0743	1029	3.4F
	1338	1658	3.5E
	1959	2251	3.3F
2 W	0153	0520	3.9E
	0831	1121	3.4F
	1429	1749	3.5E
	2055	2344	3.3F
3 Th	0247	0615	3.7E
	0923	1214	3.4F
	1523	1847	3.6E
	2155	—	—
4 F	—	0042	3.2F
	0345	0710	3.6E
	1019	1311	3.4F
	1621	1948	3.7E
	2300	—	—
5 Sa	—	0141	3.1F
	0446	0812	3.5E
	1119	1410	3.4F
	1720	2048	3.8E
6 Su	0006	0244	3.1F
	0550	0914	3.5E
	1221	1510	3.4F
	1821	2149	4.0E
7 M	0110	0351	3.1F
	0654	1015	3.6E
	1322	1612	3.5F
	1921	2249	4.2E
8 Tu	0211	0456	3.2F
	0756	1113	3.6E
	1422	1715	3.5F
	2019	2345	4.3E
9 W	0309	0557	3.3F
	0855	1210	3.7E
	1518	1814	3.6F
	2114	—	—
10 Th	—	0039	4.4E
	0403	0656	3.4F
	0951	1303	3.8E
	1612	1905	3.6F
	2205	—	—
11 F	—	0129	4.4E
	0453	0745	3.5F
	1042	1354	3.8E
	1703	1956	3.5F
	2254	—	—
12 Sa	—	0218	4.4E
	0541	0833	3.4F
	1130	1443	3.7E
	1752	2040	3.4F
	2340	—	—
13 Su	—	0305	4.2E
	0626	0915	3.3F
	1215	1529	3.5E
	1839	2123	3.2F
14 M	0024	0350	3.9F
	0710	0956	3.2F
	1259	1616	3.4E
	1925	2206	2.9F
15 Tu	0107	0436	3.6E
	0752	1034	3.0F
	1341	1701	3.2E
	2011	2248	2.7F
16 W	0149	0520	3.3E
	0835	1115	2.8F
	1423	1746	3.0E
	2058	2330	2.4F
17 Th	0233	0605	3.0E
	0917	1156	2.6F
	1507	1833	2.8E
	2148	—	—
18 F	—	0017	2.2F
	0319	0653	2.8E
	1002	1242	2.4F
	1553	1924	2.7E
	2241	—	—
19 Sa	—	0106	2.0F
	0409	0742	2.5E
	1050	1330	2.3F
	1641	2015	2.6E
	2336	—	—
20 Su	—	0159	1.9F
	0502	0834	2.4E
	1140	1421	2.2F
	1732	2109	2.7E
21 M	0031	0254	1.9F
	0558	0930	2.3E
	1233	1514	2.2F
	1823	2202	2.8E
22 Tu	0125	0350	2.0F
	0654	1021	2.4E
	1324	1605	2.3F
	1914	2253	3.0E
23 W	0216	0443	2.2F
	0748	1113	2.5E
	1414	1656	2.5F
	2004	2341	3.2E
24 Th	0302	0535	2.4F
	0839	1201	2.7E
	1501	1745	2.8F
	2052	—	—
25 F	—	0027	3.5E
	0346	0623	2.7F
	0926	1247	3.0E
	1546	1833	3.0F
	2138	—	—
26 Sa	—	0112	3.8E
	0428	0706	3.0F
	1012	1331	3.3E
	1630	1918	3.3F
	2224	—	—
27 Su	—	0154	4.0E
	0509	0752	3.3F
	1057	1417	3.5E
	1715	2005	3.5F
	2310	—	—
28 M	—	0240	4.2E
	0551	0836	3.6F
	1142	1502	3.6E
	1802	2054	3.7F
	2357	—	—
29 Tu	—	0323	4.3E
	0634	0922	3.8F
	1229	1548	4.0E
	1850	2141	3.8F
30 W	0045	0411	4.3E
	0720	1010	3.9F
	1317	1636	4.0E
	1942	2233	3.7F
31 Th	0136	0501	4.2E
	0808	1100	3.8F
	1408	1731	4.1E
	2038	2324	3.6F

AUGUST

Day	Slack Water (h.min.)	Maximum Current (h.min.)	knots
1 F	0230	0553	4.0E
	0901	1153	3.7F
	1502	1826	4.0E
	2138	—	—
2 Sa	—	0021	3.4F
	0327	0652	3.8E
	0958	1249	3.6F
	1559	1927	3.9E
	2242	—	—
3 Su	—	0122	3.2F
	0429	0753	3.6E
	1059	1348	3.4F
	1700	2029	3.9E
	2349	—	—
4 M	—	0229	3.0F
	0533	0855	3.5E
	1204	1454	3.3F
	1803	2131	3.9E
5 Tu	0055	0338	3.0F
	0639	0959	3.4E
	1309	1602	3.2F
	1905	2232	4.0E
6 W	0158	0447	3.0F
	0743	1100	3.4E
	1410	1707	3.3F
	2005	2330	4.0E
7 Th	0256	0551	3.1F
	0843	1155	3.5E
	1508	1806	3.3F
	2101	—	—
8 F	—	0023	4.1E
	0349	0646	3.2F
	0938	1249	3.6E
	1601	1859	3.3F
	2152	—	—
9 Sa	—	0114	4.1E
	0438	0737	3.3F
	1026	1336	3.6E
	1650	1946	3.3F
	2238	—	—
10 Su	—	0159	4.1E
	0522	0818	3.3F
	1110	1423	3.6E
	1735	2026	3.2F
	2321	—	—
11 M	—	0244	3.9E
	0604	0854	3.2F
	1151	1506	3.5E
	1818	2102	3.0F
12 Tu	0001	0326	3.7E
	0643	0928	3.0F
	1229	1547	3.4F
	1900	2138	2.9F
13 W	0040	0407	3.5E
	0720	1001	2.9F
	1307	1630	3.2E
	1940	2210	2.7F
14 Th	0118	0448	3.2E
	0757	1035	2.8F
	1345	1711	3.0E
	2021	2255	2.5F
15 F	0158	0527	2.9E
	0834	1114	2.6F
	1424	1753	2.9E
	2105	2336	2.3F
16 Sa	0240	0609	2.7E
	0914	1200	2.4F
	1507	1839	2.7E
	2153	—	—
17 Su	—	0025	2.1F
	0326	0657	2.4E
	0958	1247	2.3F
	1553	1930	2.6E
	2246	—	—
18 M	—	0116	1.9F
	0418	0751	2.2E
	1049	1336	2.2F
	1643	2024	2.6E
	2343	—	—
19 Tu	—	0210	1.9F
	0514	0847	2.2E
	1144	1429	2.2F
	1737	2120	2.7E
20 W	0040	0307	1.9F
	0612	0943	2.3E
	1241	1526	2.3F
	1833	2215	2.9E
21 Th	0135	0405	2.1F
	0710	1039	2.5E
	1337	1622	2.5F
	1928	2306	3.1E
22 F	0225	0457	2.4F
	0804	1129	2.8E
	1429	1715	2.8F
	2021	2355	3.5E
23 Sa	0312	0551	2.8F
	0855	1216	3.2E
	1519	1807	3.2F
	2112	—	—
24 Su	—	0043	3.9E
	0356	0638	3.2F
	0943	1304	3.6E
	1606	1855	3.6F
	2201	—	—
25 M	—	0130	4.2E
	0440	0724	3.6F
	1030	1350	4.0E
	1654	1944	3.9F
	2249	—	—
26 Tu	—	0215	4.4E
	0524	0810	4.0F
	1117	1439	4.3E
	1742	2032	4.1F
	2338	—	—
27 W	—	0302	4.6E
	0609	0859	4.2F
	1205	1525	4.5E
	1832	2121	4.2F
28 Th	0027	0348	4.6E
	0656	0948	4.2F
	1254	1616	4.6E
	1924	2212	4.1F
29 F	0119	0439	4.4E
	0746	1038	4.1F
	1345	1707	4.5E
	2019	2307	3.9F
30 Sa	0212	0533	4.2E
	0839	1131	3.9F
	1439	1805	4.3E
	2119	—	—
31 Su	—	0002	3.6F
	0310	0632	3.8E
	0938	1228	3.6F
	1537	1906	4.1E
	2223	—	—

TIME MERIDIAN 75°W.   0000 IS MIDNIGHT   1200 IS NOON   ADD 1 HOUR FOR DAYLIGHT SAVING TIME

Fig. 11.20   The table to use with *Fig. 11.19* for calculating present tidal streams in Long Island Sound, again from *Reed's* US edition.

replanned to contain information needed in the new Admiralty Method of Tidal Prediction, a complicated system involving a lot of mathematics, including logarithms, graphs and polar diagrams. I think this is part of the paper-dominated navigator's outlook mentioned at the start of this book, because the method seems to have few advantages, and a lot of disadvantages. You end up with a graph of tidal levels for 12 hours, which gives an impression of great accuracy. But the depths taken off the graph are likely to be quite as much in error from meteorological conditions as any other system. One suspects the method was evolved by old salts to find something for young watch-keeping officers to do in preference to keeping an eye out ahead for other ships, or even sailing boats.

The ordinary British Admiralty Tide Tables system uses graphs, which for those who like a pictorial display is simple and effective. A graph of the tidal pattern is given for each standard port, and a glance at it tells you immediately the tidal pattern, whether it has a dramatic rate of rise and fall or just a modest one, whether there are irregularities, like a stand at high or low water, and how the duration of rise compares with the duration of ebb.

BASIC SYSTEM.　The basis of the Admiralty system is to refer to the standard port in Part One, which will give you the time and height of high and low water directly for the date concerned. If you want height at an intermediate time, you use a **factor** obtained from the graph for the standard port for the relevant time, and then multiply the range by the factor. Add to the result the depth at LW and you have the depth.

SECONDARY PORTS.　After obtaining times of high and low water for the standard port, and height of high and low water, you then turn to Part Two at the back of the book and obtain time and height differences for the secondary port you are interested in. Great care must be observed if the standard port is in a different time zone from the secondary port. Having worked out the relative time and height for your secondary port, you turn back to the graph for the standard port and again obtain the **factor**. Applying this will give you your height at any given time or, working the opposite way, the time for any given height.

The system sounds complicated but really is not, and it is made much simpler by using a pro-forma printed at the back of the Tables. This can be photocopied, or a booklet of forms can be purchased. The instructions are very clear, and the whole thing, with examples to compare with *Reed's*, is printed as *Figs. 11.12* and *11.18*.

The only real complication in *Admiralty Tide Tables* is when your standard port is in a different time zone from a secondary port, so that times must be checked most carefully. But a difficulty hits the eye immediately on turning to Part Two — the right hand half of each page is covered with a series of mysterious symbols under the heading Harmonic Constants. These are all to do with the Admiralty method mentioned earlier, which need not concern us. But they take up nearly half of each page, and make it harder to follow down from the column headings to the secondary port you are working on. I recommend photocopying column headings, pasting them to a piece of card, and paper-clipping this to the page just above where you are working, otherwise you will waste time constantly finding and refinding which column you are in.

Solent Tides

The Admiralty tables and *Reed's* have dropped the simple and effective Portland to Nab Tower table which covered the whole area of double high water around the Solent. It has been replaced by a series of graphs, based on *low water*, not high water as are the rest of the graphs in the Admiralty tables. These low water graphs are used otherwise in just the same way as the ordinary system, with Portsmouth as the standard port. They take longer to use than the single table, and the increase in accuracy is so small I would recommend anybody to use the old Solent height of tide table in *Fig. 3.2*. The only virtue of the ATT graphs for the ordinary user is that they emphasize the very wide change of tidal pattern over a limited area, and how when the level starts to fall, it goes down with great speed.

Datum

British Admiralty Tide Tables are now nearly all to a datum of Lowest Astronomical Tide, so you will seldom get a negative figure, which is common in American Tide Tables, due to their higher datum. But, for American ports the datum of US charts is used, so again negative figures may occur. Application of negative figure is obvious: where you have a drying height of 3 metres, and the tide tables give a low water figure of −0·2 m, your sounding of 3 metres will be drying 3·2 metres at low water that day.

TABLE 2.—TIDAL DIFFERENCES AND OTHER CONSTANTS

No.	PLACE	POSITION		DIFFERENCES				RANGES		MEAN TIDE LEVEL
		Lat.	Long.	Time		Height		Mean	Spring	
				High water	Low water	High water	Low water			
		°N.′	°W.′	h. m.	h. m.	feet	feet	feet	feet	feet
	Vineyard Sound Time meridian, 75°W.			on, NEWPORT, p.40						
	Quicks Hole									
1099	South side	41 26	70 51	−0 07	+0 14	−1.0	0.0	2.5	3.1	1.2
1101	Middle	41 27	70 51	+0 03	+0 15	−0.5	0.0	3.0	3.7	1.5
1103	North side	41 27	70 51	−0 05	−0 03	0.0	0.0	3.5	4.4	1.7
	Buzzards Bay									
1105	Cuttyhunk Pond entrance	41 25	70 55	+0 04	+0 06	−0.1	0.0	3.4	4.2	1.7
1107	Penikese Island	41 27	70 55	−0 14	−0 11	−0.1	0.0	3.4	4.2	1.7
1109	Kettle Cove	41 29	70 47	+0 12	+0 07	+0.3	0.0	3.8	4.7	1.9
1111	West Falmouth Harbor	41 36	70 39	+0 24	+0 23	+0.5	0.0	4.0	5.0	2.0
1113	Barlows Landing, Pocasset Harbor	41 41	70 38	+0 27	+0 23	+0.5	0.0	4.0	5.0	2.0
1115	Abiels Ledge	41 42	70 40	+0 14	+0 21	+0.4	0.0	3.9	4.9	2.0
1117	Monument Beach	41 43	70 37	+0 26	+0 23	+0.5	0.0	4.0	5.0	2.0
1119	Cape Cod Canal, RR. bridge (6)	41 44	70 37	+1 18	− −	0.0	0.0	3.5	4.1	1.8
1121	Great Hill	41 43	70 43	+0 20	+0 20	+0.6	0.0	4.1	5.1	2.0
1123	Wareham, Wareham River	41 45	70 43	+0 25	+0 21	+0.6	0.0	4.1	5.1	2.0
1125	Bird Island	41 40	70 43	+0 08	+0 03	+0.7	0.0	4.2	5.2	2.1
1127	Marion	41 42	70 46	+0 12	+0 15	+0.5	0.0	4.0	5.0	2.0
1129	Mattapoisett	41 39	70 49	+0 13	+0 10	+0.4	0.0	3.9	4.9	2.0
1131	West Island (west side)	41 36	70 50	+0 12	+0 13	+0.2	0.0	3.7	4.6	1.8
1133	Clarks Point	41 36	70 54	+0 06	+0 08	+0.2	0.0	3.7	4.6	1.8
1135	New Bedford	41 38	70 55	+0 10	+0 12	+0.2	0.0	3.7	4.6	1.8
1137	Belleville, Acushnet River	41 40	70 55	+0 10	+0 14	+0.3	0.0	3.8	4.7	1.9
1139	South Dartmouth, Apponagansett Bay	41 35	70 57	+0 28	+0 38	+0.2	0.0	3.7	4.6	1.8
1141	Dumpling Rocks	41 32	70 55	+0 04	+0 03	+0.2	0.0	3.7	4.6	1.8
	Westport River									
1143	Westport Harbor	41 30	71 06	+0 12	+0 38	−0.5	0.0	3.0	3.7	1.5
1145	Hix Bridge, East Branch	41 34	71 04	+1 43	+2 35	−0.8	0.0	2.7	3.4	1.3
	RHODE ISLAND, Narragansett Bay									
1147	Sakonnet	41 28	71 12	−0 10	+0 04	−0.4	0.0	3.1	3.9	1.6
1149	Tiverton (between bridges)	41 38	71 13	+0 21	+0 21	+0.3	0.0	3.8	4.7	1.9
1151	Beavertail Point	41 27	71 24	−0 02	−0 05	0.0	0.0	3.5	4.4	1.8
1153	NEWPORT	41 30	71 20	Daily predictions				3.5	4.4	1.8
1155	Prudence Island, Sandy Point	41 36	71 18	+0 10	+0 09	+0.4	0.0	3.9	4.0	
1157	Bristol Point	41 39	71 16	+0 21	+0 12	+0.5	0.0			
	RHODE ISLAND and MASSACHUSETTS Narragansett Bay—Co									
1159	Fall River, Massa									
1161	Taunt									

Fig. 11.21 Table of tidal differences on Newport, Rhode Island, from the *American Tide Tables.*

Examples by British ATT

The examples worked out by ATT are pretty well explained by *Fig. 11.12* and *11.18*, the first of which shows Example 1, giving a height of water at St Helier one tenth of a metre lower than when done by the Reed's method — this could be regarded as a safety margin. The Admiralty Tidal Prediction Form makes a potentially tiresome and complicated method exceedingly simple. Sample

NEWPORT, R.I., 1980
TIMES AND HEIGHTS OF HIGH AND LOW WATERS

JULY

DAY	TIME h.m.	HEIGHT ft.	HEIGHT m.	DAY	TIME h.m.	HEIGHT ft.	HEIGHT m.
1 TU	0306	-0.4	-0.1	16 W	0343	0.1	0.0
	0952	3.7	1.1		1028	3.5	1.1
	1515	-0.2	-0.1		1551	0.4	0.1
	2211	4.2	1.3		2243	3.5	1.1
2 W	0353	-0.4	-0.1	17 TH	0414	0.3	0.1
	1043	3.8	1.2		1115	3.4	1.0
	1605	-0.1	0.0		1630	0.6	0.2
	2303	4.0	1.2		2331	3.3	1.0
3 TH	0441	-0.3	-0.1	18 F	0449	0.4	0.1
	1139	3.8	1.2		1203	3.3	1.0
	1705	0.0	0.0		1713	0.8	0.2
	2359	3.8	1.2				
4 F	0534	-0.2	-0.1	19 SA	0019	3.1	0.9
	1236	3.9	1.2		0531	0.5	0.2
	1810	0.2	0.1		1254	3.2	1.0
					1802	0.9	0.3
5 SA	0058	3.6	1.1	20 SU	0111	2.9	0.9
	0632	-0.1	0.0		0615	0.6	0.2
	1336	4.0	1.2		1347	3.3	1.0
	1922	0.2	0.1		1858	0.9	0.3
6 SU	0200	3.5	1.1	21 M	0204	2.8	0.9
	0735	0.0	0.0		0707	0.6	0.2
	1437	4.1	1.2		1440	3.3	1.0
	2038	0.2	0.1		2002	0.9	0.3
7 M	0301	3.5	1.1	22 TU	0259	2.8	0.9
	0841	0.0	0.0		0802	0.6	0.2
	1534	4.3	1.3		1531	3.5	1.1
	2154	0.1	0.0		2107	0.8	0.2
8 TU	0401	3.5	1.1	23 W	0354	2.9	0.9
	0944	-0.1	0.0		0902	0.5	0.2
	1631	4.4	1.3		1621	3.7	1.1
	2258	0.0	0.0		2207	0.5	0.2
9 W	0456	3.6	1.1	24 TH	0445	3.1	0.9
	1044	-0.1	0.0		0959	0.3	0.1
	1724	4.5	1.4		1709	4.0	1.2
	2353	-0.1	0.0		2300	0.3	0.1
10 TH	0549	3.7	1.1	25 F	0533	3.3	1.0
	1138	-0.2	-0.1		1053	0.1	0.0
	1814	4.6	1.4		1756	4.2	1.3
					2349	0.0	0.0
11 F	0041	-0.2	-0.1	26 SA	0622	3.6	1.1
	0638	3.8	1.2		1145	-0.1	0.0
	1228	-0.2	-0.1		1841	4.4	1.3
	1901	4.6	1.4				
12 SA	0123	-0.2	-0.1	27 SU	0035	-0.2	-0.1
	0727	3.8	1.2		0708	3.8	1.2
	1315	-0.2	-0.1		1236	-0.3	-0.1
	1948	4.5	1.4		1928	4.6	1.4
13 SU	0201	-0.2	-0.1	28 M	0118	-0.4	-0.1
	0813	3.8	1.2		0754	4.0	1.2
	1356	-0.1	0.0		1325	-0.4	-0.1
	2033	4.3	1.3		2015	4.6	1.4
14 M	0238	0.0	0.0	29 TU	0204	-0.6	-0.2
	0857	3.8	1.2		0841	4.1	1.2
	1436	0.0	0.0		1414	-0.5	-0.2
	2116	4.1	1.2		2103	4.5	1.4
15 TU	0310	0.0	0.0	30 W	0249	-0.6	-0.2
	0943	3.7	1.1		0931	4.1	1.2
	1513	0.2	0.1		1505	-0.4	-0.1
	2201	3.8	1.2		2151	4.3	1.3
				31 TH	0335	-0.5	-0.2
					1022	4.2	1.3
					1558	-0.3	-0.1
					2243	4.2	1.3

AUGUST

DAY	TIME h.m.	HEIGHT ft.	HEIGHT m.	DAY	TIME h.m.	HEIGHT ft.	HEIGHT m.
1 F	0422	-0.4	-0.1	16 SA	0409	0.3	0.1
	1115	4.2	1.3		1123	3.4	1.0
	1654	-0.1	0.0		1633	0.6	0.2
	2339	3.9	1.2		2338	3.1	0.9
2 SA	0515	-0.3	-0.1	17 SU	0446	0.4	0.1
	1213	4.2	1.3		1210	3.3	1.0
	1757	0.1	0.0		1718	0.7	0.2
3 SU	0037	3.6	1.1	18 M	0027	2.9	0.9
	0611	-0.1	0.0		0528	0.5	0.2
	1313	4.1	1.2		1301	3.2	1.0
	1908	0.3	0.1		1810	0.8	0.2
4 M	0139	3.4	1.0	19 TU	0124	2.7	0.8
	0712	0.1	0.0		0619	0.6	0.2
	1415	4.1	1.2		1357	3.3	1.0
	2029	0.4	0.1		1911	0.9	0.3
5 TU	0243	3.3	1.0	20 W	0221	2.7	0.8
	0822	0.2	0.1		0718	0.6	0.2
	1515	4.1	1.2		1453	3.4	1.0
	2150	0.3	0.1		2019	0.8	0.2
6 W	0342	3.4	1.0	21 TH	0320	2.9	0.9
	0936	0.2	0.1		0823	0.5	0.2
	1613	4.2	1.3		1547	3.6	1.1
	2300	0.2	0.1		2125	0.6	0.2
7 TH	0439	3.5	1.1	22 F	0415	3.1	0.9
	1040	0.1	0.0		0928	0.3	0.1
	1708	4.3	1.3		1639	3.9	1.2
	2346	0.1	0.0		2229	0.3	0.1
8 F	0532	3.6	1.1	23 SA	0506	3.4	1.0
	1135	0.0	0.0		1029	0.1	0.0
	1756	4.3	1.3		1729	4.2	1.3
					2320	-0.1	0.0
9 SA	0030	0.0	0.0	24 SU	0556	3.8	1.2
	0620	3.7	1.1		1127	-0.2	-0.1
	1220	0.0	0.0		1817	4.5	1.4
	1841	4.3	1.3				
10 SU	0108	0.0	0.0	25 M	0010	-0.4	-0.1
	0704	3.8	1.2		0644	4.1	1.2
	1259	0.0	0.0		1220	-0.5	-0.2
	1926	4.3	1.3		1906	4.6	1.4
11 M	0139	-0.1	0.0	26 TU	0054	-0.6	-0.2
	0749	3.9	1.2		0730	4.4	1.3
	1336	0.0	0.0		1311	-0.7	-0.2
	2008	4.2	1.3		1953	4.7	1.4
12 TU	0207	0.0	0.0	27 W	0141	-0.8	-0.2
	0831	3.9	1.2		0818	4.6	1.4
	1412	0.1	0.0		1402	-0.7	-0.2
	2050	4.0	1.2		2041	4.6	1.4
13 W	0236	0.0	0.0	28 TH	0226	-0.8	-0.2
	0913	3.8	1.2		0908	4.6	1.4
	1444	0.2	0.1		1452	-0.7	-0.2
	2129	3.8	1.2		2131	4.5	1.4
14 TH	0303	0.1	0.0	29 F	0313	-0.7	-0.2
	0955	3.7	1.1		0958	4.6	1.4
	1519	0.3	0.1		1545	-0.5	-0.2
	2209	3.6	1.1		2222	4.2	1.3
15 F	0335	0.2	0.1	30 SA	0400	-0.5	-0.2
	1036	3.6	1.1		1053	4.5	1.4
	1555	0.5	0.2		1641	-0.2	-0.1
	2251	3.3	1.0		2318	3.9	1.2
				31 SU	0451	-0.3	-0.1
					1150	4.3	1.3
					1742	0.1	0.0

SEPTEMBER

DAY	TIME h.m.	HEIGHT ft.	HEIGHT m.	DAY	TIME h.m.	HEIGHT ft.	HEIGHT m.
1 M	0016	3.6	1.1	16 TU	0449	0.4	0.1
	0547	0.0	0.0		1219	3.2	1.0
	1251	4.1	1.2		1731	0.7	0.2
	1856	0.3	0.1				
2 TU	0120	3.3	1.0	17 W	0045	2.7	0.8
	0652	0.3	0.1		0541	0.5	0.2
	1353	4.0	1.2		1317	3.2	1.0
	2022	0.5	0.2		1831	0.7	0.2
3 W	0224	3.2	1.0	18 TH	0147	2.7	0.8
	0811	0.4	0.1		0640	0.6	0.2
	1456	3.9	1.2		1417	3.3	1.0
	2147	0.4	0.1		1940	0.7	0.2
4 TH	0325	3.2	1.0	19 F	0250	2.9	0.9
	0934	0.4	0.1		0748	0.5	0.2
	1554	3.9	1.2		1515	3.5	1.1
	2247	0.3	0.1		2051	0.5	0.2
5 F	0421	3.4	1.0	20 SA	0346	3.2	1.0
	1039	0.3	0.1		0902	0.3	0.1
	1647	4.0	1.2		1610	3.8	1.2
	2335	0.2	0.1		2155	0.2	0.1
6 SA	0511	3.5	1.1	21 SU	0439	3.6	1.1
	1132	0.2	0.1		1010	0.0	0.0
	1737	4.0	1.2		1704	4.1	1.2
					2252	-0.2	-0.1
7 SU	0012	0.1	0.0	22 M	0529	4.0	1.2
	0558	3.7	1.1		1109	-0.4	-0.1
	1211	0.1	0.0		1753	4.4	1.3
	1820	4.1	1.2		2343	-0.5	-0.2
8 M	0044	0.1	0.0	23 TU	0618	4.4	1.3
	0642	3.9	1.2		1204	-0.7	-0.2
	1247	0.0	0.0		1842	4.6	1.4
	1902	4.1	1.2				
9 TU	0107	0.0	0.0	24 W	0030	-0.8	-0.2
	0723	4.0	1.2		0707	4.7	1.4
	1316	0.0	0.0		1257	-0.9	-0.3
	1941	4.0	1.2		1930	4.6	1.4
10 W	0133	0.0	0.0	25 TH	0117	-0.9	-0.3
	0802	4.0	1.2		0756	4.9	1.5
	1347	0.0	0.0		1347	-0.9	-0.3
	2021	3.9	1.2		2019	4.6	1.4
11 TH	0158	0.0	0.0	26 F	0204	-0.9	-0.3
	0841	3.9	1.2		0845	4.9	1.5
	1418	0.1	0.0		1438	-0.8	-0.2
	2058	3.7	1.1		2109	4.4	1.3
12 F	0226	0.0	0.0	27 SA	0250	-0.8	-0.2
	0920	3.8	1.2		0935	4.8	1.5
	1449	0.2	0.1		1529	-0.6	-0.2
	2137	3.5	1.1		2201	4.1	1.2
13 SA	0257	0.1	0.0	28 SU	0339	-0.6	-0.2
	1001	3.7	1.1		1028	4.6	1.4
	1523	0.3	0.1		1625	-0.3	-0.1
	2217	3.3	1.0		2257	3.8	1.2
14 SU	0330	0.2	0.1	29 M	0428	-0.3	-0.1
	1043	3.5	1.1		1126	4.3	1.3
	1558	0.4	0.1		1723	0.0	0.0
	2302	3.0	0.9		2355	3.5	1.1
15 M	0407	0.3	0.1	30 TU	0526	0.1	0.0
	1128	3.3	1.0		1227	4.0	1.2
	1641	0.6	0.2		1835	0.3	0.1
	2349	2.8	0.9				

TIME MERIDIAN 75° W. 0000 IS MIDNIGHT. 1200 IS NOON.
HEIGHTS ARE REFERRED TO MEAN LOW WATER WHICH IS THE CHART DATUM OF SOUNDINGS.

Fig. 11.22   A page from the *American Tide Tables* for Newport, Rhode Island.

TABLE 3.—HEIGHT OF TIDE AT ANY TIME

Duration of rise or fall, see footnote (h. m.)	Time from the nearest high water or low water														
	h. m.	h. m.	h. m.	h. m.	h. m.	h. m.	h. m.	h. m.	h. m.	h. m.	h. m.	h. m.	h. m.	h. m.	h. m.
4 00	0 08	0 16	0 24	0 32	0 40	0 48	0 56	1 04	1 12	1 20	1 28	1 36	1 44	1 52	2 00
4 20	0 09	0 17	0 26	0 35	0 43	0 52	1 01	1 09	1 18	1 27	1 35	1 44	1 53	2 01	2 10
4 40	0 09	0 19	0 28	0 37	0 47	0 56	1 05	1 15	1 24	1 33	1 43	1 52	2 01	2 11	2 20
5 00	0 10	0 20	0 30	0 40	0 50	1 00	1 10	1 20	1 30	1 40	1 50	2 00	2 10	2 20	2 30
5 20	0 11	0 21	0 32	0 43	0 53	1 04	1 15	1 25	1 36	1 47	1 57	2 08	2 19	2 29	2 40
5 40	0 11	0 23	0 34	0 45	0 57	1 08	1 19	1 31	1 42	1 53	2 05	2 16	2 27	2 39	2 50
6 00	0 12	0 24	0 36	0 48	1 00	1 12	1 24	1 36	1 48	2 00	2 12	2 24	2 36	2 48	3 00
6 20	0 13	0 25	0 38	0 51	1 03	1 16	1 29	1 41	1 54	2 07	2 19	2 32	2 45	2 57	3 10
6 40	0 13	0 27	0 40	0 53	1 07	1 20	1 33	1 47	2 00	2 13	2 27	2 40	2 53	3 07	3 20
7 00	0 14	0 28	0 42	0 56	1 10	1 24	1 38	1 52	2 06	2 20	2 34	2 48	3 02	3 16	3 30
7 20	0 15	0 29	0 44	0 59	1 13	1 28	1 43	1 57	2 12	2 27	2 41	2 56	3 11	3 25	3 40
7 40	0 15	0 31	0 46	1 01	1 17	1 32	1 47	2 03	2 18	2 33	2 49	3 04	3 19	3 35	3 50
8 00	0 16	0 32	0 48	1 04	1 20	1 36	1 52	2 08	2 24	2 40	2 56	3 12	3 28	3 44	4 00
8 20	0 17	0 33	0 50	1 07	1 23	1 40	1 57	2 13	2 30	2 47	3 03	3 20	3 37	3 53	4 10
8 40	0 17	0 35	0 52	1 09	1 27	1 44	2 01	2 19	2 36	2 53	3 11	3 28	3 45	4 03	4 20
9 00	0 18	0 36	0 54	1 12	1 30	1 48	2 06	2 24	2 42	3 00	3 18	3 36	3 54	4 12	4 30
9 20	0 19	0 37	0 56	1 15	1 33	1 52	2 11	2 29	2 48	3 07	3 25	3 44	4 03	4 21	4 40
9 40	0 19	0 39	0 58	1 17	1 37	1 56	2 15	2 35	2 54	3 13	3 33	3 52	4 11	4 31	4 50
10 00	0 20	0 40	1 00	1 20	1 40	2 00	2 20	2 40	3 00	3 20	3 40	4 00	4 20	4 40	5 00
10 20	0 21	0 41	1 02	1 23	1 43	2 04	2 25	2 45	3 06	3 27	3 47	4 08	4 29	4 49	5 10
10 40	0 21	0 43	1 04	1 25	1 47	2 08	2 29	2 51	3 12	3 33	3 55	4 16	4 37	4 59	5 20

Range of tide, see footnote (Ft.)	Correction to height														
	Ft.	Ft.	Ft.	Ft.	Ft.	Ft.	Ft.	Ft.	Ft.	Ft.	Ft.	Ft.	Ft.	Ft.	Ft.
0.5	0.0	0.0	0.0	0.0	0.0	0.0	0.1	0.1	0.1	0.1	0.1	0.2	0.2	0.2	0.2
1.0	0.0	0.0	0.0	0.0	0.1	0.1	0.1	0.2	0.2	0.2	0.3	0.3	0.4	0.4	0.5
1.5	0.0	0.0	0.0	0.0	0.1	0.1	0.2	0.2	0.3	0.4	0.4	0.5	0.6	0.7	0.8
2.0	0.0	0.0	0.0	0.1	0.1	0.2	0.3	0.3	0.4	0.5	0.6	0.7	0.8	0.9	1.0
2.5	0.0	0.0	0.1	0.1	0.2	0.2	0.3	0.4	0.5	0.6	0.7	0.9	1.0	1.1	1.2
3.0	0.0	0.0	0.1	0.1	0.2	0.3	0.4	0.5	0.6	0.8	0.9	1.0	1.2	1.3	1.5
3.5	0.0	0.0	0.1	0.2	0.2	0.3	0.4	0.6	0.7	0.9	1.0	1.2	1.4	1.6	1.8
4.0	0.0	0.0	0.1	0.2	0.3	0.4	0.5	0.7	0.8	1.0	1.2	1.4	1.6	1.8	2.0
4.5	0.0	0.0	0.1	0.2	0.3	0.4	0.6	0.7	0.9	1.1	1.3	1.6	1.8	2.0	2.2
5.0	0.0	0.1	0.1	0.2	0.3	0.5	0.6	0.8	1.0	1.2	1.5	1.7	2.0	2.2	2.5
5.5	0.0	0.1	0.1	0.2	0.4	0.5	0.7	0.9	1.1	1.4	1.6	1.9	2.2	2.5	2.8
6.0	0.0	0.1	0.1	0.3	0.4	0.6	0.8	1.0	1.2	1.5	1.8	2.1	2.4	2.7	3.0
6.5	0.0	0.1	0.2	0.3	0.4	0.6	0.8	1.1	1.3	1.6	1.9	2.2	2.6	2.9	3.2
7.0	0.0	0.1	0.2	0.3	0.5	0.7	0.9	1.2	1.4	1.8	2.1	2.4	2.8	3.1	3.5
7.5	0.0	0.1	0.2	0.3	0.5	0.7	1.0	1.2	1.5	1.9	2.2	2.6	3.0	3.4	3.8
8.0	0.0	0.1	0.2	0.3	0.5	0.8	1.0	1.3	1.6	2.0	2.4	2.8	3.2	3.6	4.0
8.5	0.0	0.1	0.2	0.4	0.6	0.8	1.1	1.4	1.8	2.1	2.5	2.9	3.4	3.8	4.2
9.0	0.0	0.1	0.2	0.4	0.6	0.9	1.2	1.5	1.9	2.2	2.7	3.1	3.6	4.0	4.5
9.5	0.0	0.1	0.2	0.4	0.6	0.9	1.2	1.6	2.0	2.4	2.8	3.3	3.8	4.3	4.8
10.0	0.0	0.1	0.2	0.4	0.7	1.0	1.3	1.7	2.1	2.5	3.0	3.5	4.0	4.5	5.0
10.5	0.0	0.1	0.3	0.5	0.7	1.0	1.3	1.7	2.2	2.6	3.1	3.6	4.2	4.7	5.2
11.0	0.0	0.1	0.3	0.5	0.7	1.1	1.4	1.8	2.3	2.8	3.3	3.8	4.4	4.9	5.5
11.5	0.0	0.1	0.3	0.5	0.8	1.1	1.5	1.9	2.4	2.9	3.4	4.0	4.6	5.1	5.8
12.0	0.0	0.1	0.3	0.5	0.8	1.1	1.5	2.0	2.5	3.0	3.6	4.1	4.8	5.4	6.0
12.5	0.0	0.1	0.3	0.5	0.8	1.2	1.6	2.1	2.6	3.1	3.7	4.3	5.0	5.6	6.2
13.0	0.0	0.1	0.3	0.6	0.9	1.2	1.7	2.2	2.7	3.2	3.9	4.5	5.1	5.8	6.5
13.5	0.0	0.1	0.3	0.6	0.9	1.3	1.7	2.2	2.8	3.4	4.0	4.7	5.3	6.0	6.8
14.0	0.0	0.2	0.3	0.6	0.9	1.3	1.8	2.3	2.9	3.5	4.2	4.8	5.5	6.3	7.0
14.5	0.0	0.2	0.4	0.6	1.0	1.4	1.9	2.4	3.0	3.6	4.3	5.0	5.7	6.5	7.2
15.0	0.0	0.2	0.4	0.6	1.0	1.4	1.9	2.5	3.1	3.8	4.4	5.2	5.9	6.7	7.5
15.5	0.0	0.2	0.4	0.7	1.0	1.5	2.0	2.6	3.2	3.9	4.6	5.4	6.1	6.9	7.8
16.0	0.0	0.2	0.4	0.7	1.1	1.5	2.1	2.6	3.3	4.0	4.7	5.5	6.3	7.2	8.0
16.5	0.0	0.2	0.4	0.7	1.1	1.6	2.1	2.7	3.4	4.1	4.9	5.7	6.5	7.4	8.2
17.0	0.0	0.2	0.4	0.7	1.1	1.6	2.2	2.8	3.5	4.2	5.0	5.9	6.7	7.6	8.5
17.5	0.0	0.2	0.4	0.8	1.2	1.7	2.2	2.9	3.6	4.4	5.2	6.0	6.9	7.8	8.8
18.0	0.0	0.2	0.4	0.8	1.2	1.7	2.3	3.0	3.7	4.5	5.3	6.2	7.1	8.1	9.0
18.5	0.1	0.2	0.5	0.8	1.2	1.8	2.4	3.1	3.8	4.6	5.5	6.4	7.3	8.3	9.2
19.0	0.1	0.2	0.5	0.8	1.3	1.8	2.4	3.1	3.9	4.8	5.6	6.6	7.5	8.5	9.5
19.5	0.1	0.2	0.5	0.8	1.3	1.9	2.5	3.2	4.0	4.9	5.8	6.7	7.7	8.7	9.8
20.0	0.1	0.2	0.5	0.9	1.3	1.9	2.6	3.3	4.1	5.0	5.9	6.9	7.9	9.0	10.0

Fig. 11.23　The *American Tide Table* form with instructions for finding the height of tide at any time. The instructions are self-explanatory.

forms are in ATT, and pads of them can be bought. The only thing that has to be watched is that you select the right high and low water that you need, and watch out if you are changing time zone going to the secondary port. It might seem at first glance that multiplying the range by the factor would be complicated (unless you use a calculator) because a lot of people have forgotten how to do arithmetic in small decimals. But in the front part of ATT is a simple multiplication table, Table 2, from which the result can be read straight off.

The reproduced examples show how simple the tidal prediction forms are. They can also be used with *American Tide Tables* to keep a record of all the data used, and applying the correction for times between high and low water from the table in the US book, reproduced as *Fig. 11.23*.

12
Navigation instruments

Whenever you go into a yacht chandler or chart agent you will find stacks of navigational goodies on show, because salesmen know they have great appeal for the would-be navigator, especially when he is shorebound during the off-season. You may even be tempted to buy one of these parallel rules which are supposed to 'walk' across the lurching chart to a compass rose.

If you feel this urge coming on, I repeat my advice from Chapter 1: don't buy. The walking type of parallel ruler is useless in a small boat, and has few advantages even in a big one with a large steady chart table. The only effective type of parallel ruler is the rolling kind, most of which are too big and heavy for a small boat, though there is one rolling type, the American-made Parallel (originally the Paraline) Plotter, which I recommend highly and give details of below.

BASIC REQUIREMENTS

Perhaps it is time to emphasize again how little you can get by with to navigate safely in coastal waters. This basic minimum is:

1. The right charts.
2. A yachtsman's pilot book.
3. A properly adjusted compass.
4. An almanac with tide tables, tidal atlases and a light list.
5. A reliable clock or watch, and a radio to get weather forecasts.
6. Lead and line or echo-sounder.
7. A logbook to record courses, times and distances.
8. Dividers, pencil, eraser and ruler — at a pinch you can do without the dividers, measuring distances on the ruler and then taking them to the latitude scale.
9. Binoculars, of the type known as 7×50s.
10. A protractor or plotter.

That's all, indeed, some people might say that the almanac is not necessary, a booklet giving high water at your local standard port would do, lights being obtained from your charts. So, though the above list can obviously be improved, keep a tight hand on your cheque book when tempted, because all those flashy devices you see have one snag, which looms bigger the smaller the boat: they clutter up stowage space so you cannot find the things you really need.

In case the spending bug overcomes you round Boat Show time, I am going to discuss some of the things that I have found by practical test to be worth their cost and stowage space. I don't claim to have tried every device, but I have tried a great many. Failure to mention something that you find is your favourite aid does not mean that I don't think it works: it means that it is more complicated to work, or bulkier to stow, or more expensive than the help it can give will justify. Simplicity is the thing to go for in a small boat.

Charts

We have already discussed charts elsewhere, so there is only a little to add about buying and using them. Charts of all nations are tending more and more to use the same or similar symbols for buoys, lights, shoals and rocks, as part of the slow move towards internationally agreed symbols, and some of the more important ones are shown in *Figs. 2.1–2.4*. French charts are, I think, unique in having a small tee-shaped mark to indicate rocks that never cover.

You will need a relatively small-scale chart for passage making, so both ends of the passage can be included, and any obstructions round which you must go. You must also have large-scale charts for the approach to whatever port you are making for, any hazardous areas en route, and possible ports of refuge if weather keeps you from your planned destination. Never skimp on charts, it is false economy.

British Admiralty charts cover most areas of the world, and private firms do excellent charts for yachtsmen which sometimes give more useful details looked at from the point of view of the small boat man. Australia and the Pacific are covered by the Hydrographic Service of the Royal Australian Navy, much of it based on British and American surveys. In the USA, the National Ocean Survey is the agency which charts the sea coast, coastal rivers, the Great Lakes and connecting water. Waters foreign to the USA are charted by the Naval Oceanographic Office.

I must mention again my warning about United States charts, already given in Chapter 11; it is of sufficient importance to need repeating. You must be particularly cautious when using American charts because:

1. They are not corrected up to date when you buy them, like British

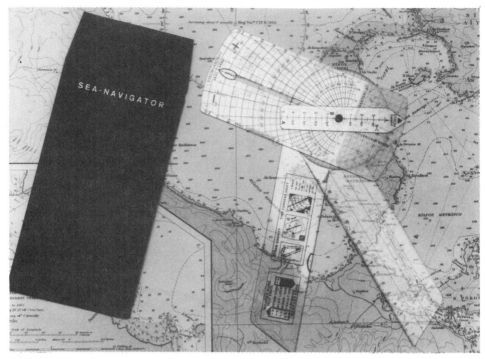

Plate 20. The German-made Sea Navigator is a brilliantly compact device for the pocket cruiser. It will do almost everything the navigator wants except make coffee and it is not expensive.

Admiralty charts, and it is quite difficult to get the notices to mariners that apply to any particular chart. Even a recent date stamped at the bottom of the chart does not mean that it has all corrections to that date.

2. They operate to a chart datum below which water level often falls. This is because East Coast American charts use Mean Low Water, the average of all low tides, as datum, so even an ordinary spring tide can go quite a lot below datum. To confuse the issue further, West Coast charts have a datum of Mean Lower Low Water, which is approximately the equivalent of the British Mean Low Water Springs. But American charts based on a foreign chart can easily use a datum of Lowest Astronomical Tide. It should declare this prominently, but some of them are very shy about it, and tuck the vital information away in small letters.

The effect of all this is that a new British metric chart, a French chart and most other European charts will be much more pessimistic about soundings than the equivalent American one, and consequently less likely to lead you into error. Donald Street, the well known American sailor and author, has said in print that he advises people to have French or British charts for the Caribbean in addition to their American ones.

The same warning about datum also applies to American Tide Tables. But provided the warning is remembered, there are advantages to American charts. Many people prefer soundings in feet and fathoms. There is a useful American series for small craft provided by the National Ocean Survey. There are also yachtsmen's charts put out by state authorities. The book of charts of the upper half of Chesapeake Bay put out by the Maryland Government is a model of what the yachtsman needs to know, but it is a pity that it stops so abruptly at the Potomac. Most American charts now have Loran or Omega graticules.

French charts are excellent, but agents do not always correct them up to date. Large numbers of alterations to buoyage have been made in recent years as the IALA system goes into force. Most French and Italian charts do not have compass roses.

Scandinavian charts, both the 'official' ones and privately produced yachtsmen's charts, are excellent in design and detail, but you may have a problem if you do not know the language.

Always check the date of any chart you are using, particularly when going to a charter boat, and also the date of corrections since publication. Good charter agencies will ensure that charts are at least updated from Notices to Mariners for the current year, usually done by chart agents in waterproof violet ink. Up to date corrections are particularly important in West Europe, now so many buoys have recently changed to the IALA system.

Pilot Books

No chart can tell you *everything* you would like to know, or it would be so densely printed it would be indecipherable. This is where pilot books come in useful; carefully chosen, the right one can often save you its cost by reducing the number of large-scale charts needed for final approaches. A good pilot book for yachts gives details of dangers, suitable refuelling points, facilities, lock times, height of bridges or cables, and generally builds up a picture of the port or creek you are aiming for so you can enter as a stranger without difficulty. They are invaluable at the planning stage of a cruise. Pilot books also draw attention to off-lying dangers that might be overlooked on a chart.

Waters round the USA are covered by eight volumes of the *Coast Pilot*, and American pilots for foreign waters are called *Sailing Directions*; Britain publishes *Admiralty Pilots* for most areas of the world. You will find these publications are written with big ships in mind, and many of the best places for pleasure craft are brushed off with a phrase like 'Good anchorage for small craft in lee of Deathshead Point, but should only be approached with local pilot.' A good yachtsman's pilot book will give all the leading marks and dangers for such an anchorage, and a chart too. When buying a pilot book give preference to one designed for and by yachtsmen, and check you have the most up-to-date edition available. Be wary of books called pilot's 'guides'. They often give only photographs without chartlets, or worse, charts without soundings.

Compass

I have already stressed the importance of eliminating all possible deviation from the compass, and having a card with the residual deviation always handy. Treat your compass well, and if it is a good one it will serve you faithfully. Don't forget the occasional check on a familiar transit near your home port so you quickly discover when error has crept in — junior has hung his transistor radio on the bulkhead behind the compass again . . .

Almanac

You can't do better than the appropriate volume of *Reed's Nautical Almanac*, for which editions cover most of western Europe and the eastern United States. If sailing in an area not covered by *Reed's* take the advice of the local chandler or bookstore. For the English Channel *Channel West and Solent* is most useful.

Timepiece

Radio time signals are available all over the world on even the simplest radios. Coupled with a quartz watch or clock with a seconds reading, you have timekeeping accurate enough for navigation by the stars. For coastal work reliability is more important than the utmost accuracy, so a timepiece that does not have to be wound every 24 hours is an advantage.

Depthfinder

Echo-sounders are described under electronics. It is always a good thing to have aboard a lead and line in case the echo-sounder fails. Very few people can use a lead and line effectively under way in more than about 20 feet of water, so a line about 30 feet long is enough, and often a heavy fishing weight will do.

Logbook

Fancy logbooks waste space. A hardcover school exercise book ruled in columns to suit does very well.

Dividers, Pencils etc

DIVIDERS.   Don't make the mistake of getting expensive draughtsmen's dividers, because extreme accuracy is not necessary. What is needed is quickness and handiness in use, and the 'one-handed' pattern shown in Plate 18 is best. They are available in several sizes, and for a small boat the smaller sizes are better. Be sure that the ones you get have stainless, not plated, points, because points which rust are tiresome. This pattern is not cheap, but the ability to set them to a given distance with one hand is valuable.

PENCILS.   People who deal in their working life with drawings tend to bring hard pencils with them to do chart work. This is a mistake, because firmness of line is less important than ease of visibility. A softish lead (about 2B grade) is best, and shows up well in dim lights. The most important thing with the navigator's pencils is that they belong to him. Always make a terrible scene if one of yours is taken for making shopping lists, though writing down the weather forecast might be allowed. Thump the table and shout:
'Our lives may depend on being able to find that one day.'
While only an approximation of the truth, there is enough in it for the crew to need to absorb it. By the same token a proper rack for pencils and dividers is valuable, as it stops them sculling about and getting lost.

ERASERS.   With india rubbers, the rule is to have plenty, of good quality, soft, and fairly large in size.

RULERS.   A transparent ruler is worth its storage space. It is best to have one which combines inches and centimetres. If you can get one 18 inches long it is handier than a 12 inch one.

Binoculars

Binoculars are described by their magnification multiplied by the size of their objective lens. A glass of 7×50 would magnify seven times and have an objective lens of 50 mm, and these are a good size for general marine use. Any greater magnification means that you will not be able to hold the binoculars steady at sea. The large 50 millimetre object glass does not, as many people

Plate 21. Three calculators well worth having afloat. On the left is the CBM N 60, designed for aircraft use, but valuable in a boat if used intelligently. In the centre is the state-of-the-art Tamaya NC 77, which is expensive, but far the best for the navigator. On the right is the Casio FX 502 P, which is excellent in a boat, having useful facilities like automatic switch-off and retention of programmes when turned off. Sadly the instruction book is not too good.

think give a wider angle of view, it allows more light in. The object glass diameter divided by the magnification gives a figure known as the exit pupil, and if it is over seven, the glass will utilise the whole of the eye pupil. The effect of looking for something around dusk with a 7×50 is dramatic, and in almost total darkness it shows up things that are otherwise quite invisible.

Turning to things that are useful but not essential, let me repeat; if your boat is small, you must be strongwilled. The most superlative navigational calculator, for instance, is unlikely to give of its best if its only stowage is among the galley gear. Those handy spaces for charts inside the flap of a chart table tend to get choked up with unwanted goodies, and then one day you cannot get at the chart that you very urgently need. For the navigator the word stowage must mean, not the housewife's stuffing of unsightly objects at the back of an overfilled drawer, but quick accessibility in the dark in a boat lying on its ear and bouncing up and down.

Protractors and Plotters

Any protractor will do for finding the direction of a line on the chart, but one with 360° coverage is better than 180°, and the square type is best of all, with or without a plotting arm. The US Navy air navigation plotter, a protractor and ruler combined, is very good. Here is a list of devices that I have tried and found excellent. You do not of course need all of them – more than one plotter will drive you mad. But this is a guide when shopping. And when you have thrown away that enormous walking parallel rule that some fool gave you for Christmas, you will gain quite a lot of stowage space . . .

THE DOUGLAS PROTRACTOR.   Evolved by Admiral Douglas, this is square and comes in two sizes, 5 inches or 10: a similar instrument is available in Britain called the *Portland Navigational Protractor*. The advantages of the Douglas type, illustrated in *Fig. 6.3*, lie in the square grid engraved on it, all lines being parallel to the sides thus providing a convenient scale, and the anti-clockwise degree measurement in addition to the regular marking, which make it convenient for plotting reciprocal bearings. The straight sides enable tracks to be drawn and, if the boat has no chart table, the smaller of the two sizes can be used on a folded chart on your knee with reasonable effectiveness. Where it is necessary to transfer parallel lines, this can easily be done by drawing one or two lines along the edge or sliding it along a ruler. The lines engraved at right angles enable you to transfer any line due to the human eye's instinct for parallelism.

US NAVY AIR PLOTTER.   This is compact, handy and cheap. *Fig. 6.2* shows it better than any description.

HURST PLOTTER.   This is the best of the plotters that have a straight edge rotating as an arm from the centre of the protractor. For those who prefer the outdated method of working in magnetic, it has the benefit that variation may be set, the locking screw tightened, and then it transfers directly to true or vice versa. It is well made (in Britain), but somewhat expensive and bulky. Weems and Plath stock a similar American plotter.

PARALLEL PLOTTER.   This is an American device from Weems and Plath of Annapolis, but also obtainable in Britain from Warsash Nautical Bookshop, Newtown Road, Warsash, Hampshire. It is not desperately expensive and the 12 inch size, which is ideal for most boats up to 40 feet or so, still costs less than

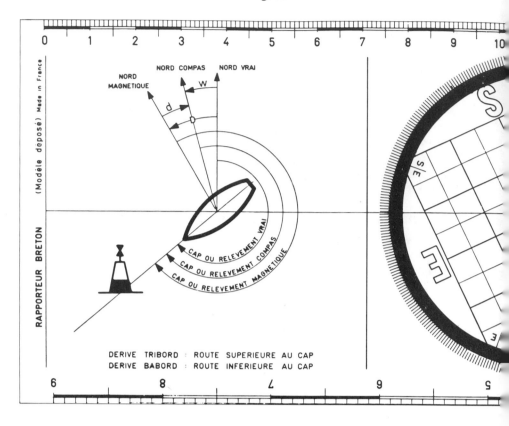

Fig. 12.1   The centre disc of the plastic Rapporteur Breton rotates so that the direction of a course can be quickly determined. The instrument is also particularly useful for plotting bearings.

a good lunch for two. It looks like a fairly normal rolling parallel ruler, but has a number of advantages.

1. The rollers bite much better than many, so the tendency to deviate is reduced almost to nothing, even on a slightly uneven surface.

2. You never have to roll it far because it works, not off a compass rose (which some charts in any case do not have), but off the nearest meridian or parallel. For courses which are more or less north and south, lay the edge of the plotter along the line, then roll it the short distance until the point of origin of the central protractor is on a meridian, when the course and its reciprocal may be read off. Courses or bearings tending more to east and west are applied in the same way, but read off a parallel using one of the quarter-protractors at either end of the instrument.

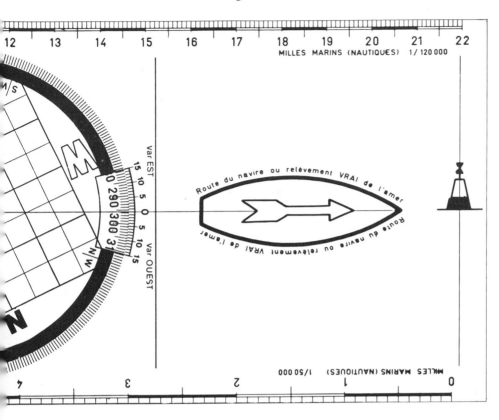

3. It has a number of useful scales, which can be used for measuring distance on large scale charts.

4. The Parallel Plotter is particularly handy for laying off bearings. The bearing is aligned with either the middle or end protractor most convenient, on either a parallel or meridian, and then rolled to the landmark used and the bearing plotted directly.

5. The flat part of the plotter can be removed from the roller and used as a scale or ordinary ruler.

6. The whole thing is small, light, compact and easily stowed.

RAPPORTEUR BRETON.   This is a French plotter, now also made in Britain, consisting of a flat piece of transparent plastic with a rotating protractor

Plate 22. A home-made wooden box like this, made so that a calculator, in a plastic bag (not shown here) for water resistance, can be used inside it, will lengthen the life of your calculator. It must be foam padded, and have a strong metal eye to which a lanyard can be attached, so if it is knocked, or slips, off the chart table the lanyard stops it hitting the cabin sole.

carrying grid squares built into the middle. To measure the direction of a course, you lay the edge of the plotter on the course and rotate the protractor until the grid lines are parallel to any convenient meridian or parallel. Plotting bearings is particularly convenient. You set the bearing (corrected to true) on the protractor, put a pencil on the position of the landmark and, using the pencil as a pivot, swing the plotter until the rotating grid is parallel to a meridian or latitude line, then draw in the bearing. The device measures 14 inches by 5 inches, and stows absolutely flat; it costs about the same as the Parallel Plotter.

SEA NAVIGATOR.   This comprehensive name makes one expect some kind of computer that would occupy the whole of one deck of the bridge structure on a cruiser, but it is in fact the most compact, efficient and useful combined plotter, nautical slide rule and course computer you can get, and it costs a lot less than lunch for two (see Plate 20.) It is German-made, but the instructions are given in English too. Its only fault is that you cannot pick it up and use it instantly, you must learn how to work it and use its multiple functions. It packs into a neat, flat plastic case only 10 inches by 3. Once you have mastered the device, you will find it invaluable — it will even act as a rough and ready, but adequately effective, pair of dividers. One or two people, borrowing mine, have said the main plotting arm is too short, but this is what gives the device its compactness. The things it will do or act as are:

1. Protractor and plotter.
2. Speed, time and distance calculator.
3. Course calculator in tideway.
4. Distance off by vertical sextant angle.
5. True wind calculator.
6. Dividers and distance scale.
7. Speed made good to windward calculator.
8. Fuel consumption calculator.
9. Foreign currency converter.

This is a formidable list of attainments, and I am surprised you do not see the device about more frequently. It is coy about its source, declaring only that it comes from D. Butterweck, Box 641, D 5800 Hagen 1, Hagen being in the North Rhine-Westphalia province of West Germany. It can be bought at J. D. Potter, the British Admiralty chart agent in the Minories, London.

I strongly recommend the Sea Navigator for those who cruise in dinghies and small open keel boats — it comes to no harm stuffed in an oilskin pocket, and is quite effective working on a folded chart held on a thwart. Make sure you have learned really well how to use it before putting it into service in these conditions.

MECHANICAL SPEED, TIME AND DISTANCE CALCULATORS. There are many of these made, in either circular or straight slide rule form, and the important thing in a small boat is that they should be compact, and you must be familiar with how to use the one you have. I have a stately object eight inches square and a quarter of an inch thick called a Nautical Slide Rule, which I was given as a souvenir of a wonderful cruise on Chesapeake Bay. It converts speed and time into distance, and the other normal conversions, excellently, though I have to confess to never using it except as a status symbol. But I frequently carry, and use, a handy little thing like a six-inch ruler with a sliding piece inside, called a *Portland Speed-Time-Distance Calculator*, (Plate 16), which does all the same things more easily and a lot more cheaply. *Fig. 6.7*, which can easily be drawn up roughly on any squared paper, is an effective and free-of-cost way of working out speed, time and distance problems if you dislike doing things the mathematical way.

YOUNG'S TIDAL DEPTH ESTIMATOR. This is an excellent and compact device, available at a reasonable price, which will give present rise of tide accurately enough for areas where tides are regular (Plate 1). For those who find that they let errors creep in when working out tidal levels, its relatively loose accuracy is better than a totally wrong worked out figure. To work the thing you obtain the range for the day from tables, set the arm to this range and read off the height for the hour. It is quite easy to interpolate by eye for intervening periods such as a quarter of an hour. The device stows flat, and it also has the instructions engraved on it, so they do not get lost. I strongly recommend this to people who may frequently have a canal lock to catch at a certain level of tide, or perhaps a sandbar at the mouth of a river to cross before the water is too low. It is, however, no good in areas of irregular tides such as the Solent.

STATION POINTER. Americans usually call this a three-arm plotter. Intended for quick fixes when using horizontal sextant angles, you can find impressive metal examples made for big ships that will cost you more than a new genoa — there is even a kind that incorporates mirrors and can be used for measuring the angles, and then taken to the chart and the plot transferred directly. But this is not for small boats. Excellent plastic ones are available which are quite accurate enough.

TIDAL DRIFT CALCULATORS. There are many plastic devices that will work out the tidal drift triangle for you mechanically or graphically, or with a combination of both means. I have tried more than a dozen. Almost all did the job adequately, but they nearly all had the snag that learning, and remembering, how to operate them was more tedious than drawing a quick triangle on the back of a chart or piece of squared paper. The mechanical devices are often fragile and awkward to stow, and in any case are being overtaken by electronic calculators. These are dealt with separately under electronics.

CHART MAGNIFIERS.   These are invaluable for people without perfect eyesight. The best ones incorporate a battery operated light, and for a quick check they have the advantage that, carefully used, they impair night vision adaptation less than turning on a chart table light. There are dozens of models made as motorists' map-readers, so pick one to suit your eyesight and the stowage space available. Some may need the bulb to be dimmed: nail varnish does it quite well — if you can get it, a brown or orange tint.

NAUTICAL TABLES.   Most of the tables you will need are adequately covered by *Reed's*, but when your cruising becomes more extended you may find a book of nautical tables valuable; they include traverse tables, which tell you, given the latitude and longitude of the starting point and the required destination, what course to steer and the distance to sail. If given a starting point and the course and distance steered, they will also give the latitude and longitude you reach. *Reed's* has only abbreviated traverse tables. The best buys are those you best understand, so spend time choosing.

13
More about the compass

The time has come to look a bit more closely at compass problems — choosing one (which is closely allied to where it is going to be mounted), making out a deviation card to find out its error, and finally, how to adjust it, that is cut down its error to the minimum possible with corrector magnets.

CHOICE OF COMPASS

It is remarkable how designers and builders, most of whom go to sea themselves, build boats with compasses stuck on in a hopeless position, a kind of undesirable afterthought. As with nearly everything else in boats, compass position has to be a compromise, and the larger the boat the easier it is to reach the compromise. The one fatal thing to do, on signing a cheque for a boat, is to go and buy a large and splendid compass, take it out to the boat as soon as she is delivered and start thinking 'where on earth shall I put this?'

Marine compasses should always be liquid damped, with a means of topping up, and there are certain principles to remember when considering mounting one for steering.

1. It must be reasonably clear of magnetic interference such as an engine, iron keel or electronic instruments. Distances involved are 6 feet from one ton of iron in a keel, four feet from an average engine with an alternator, between two and three feet from any electronic instrument or loudspeaker, or any wires through which current of more than one amp flows.

2. It must be easily visible to the helmsman, on either tack, and from any position the helmsman is likely to take up, and well (not brightly) illuminated by a system with a dimmer control. Positioning problems are greater with a tiller than with a wheel.

These two points are of equal importance, and neither should be sacrificed to the other. Two further points of great desirability, but less important than those above, are:

3. By sighting along a centre pin in the compass, it should be possible to take a bearing reasonably accurately.

4. The compass should have a system of corrector magnets so that it can be properly adjusted to reduce deviation, or a corrector box adjustable with a key or non-magnetic screwdriver.

Problem 3 can always be solved by carrying a separate handbearing compass, and using that for taking bearings. But a large dome-top steering compass with a centre pin is most useful for the kind of quick check bearing, that probably will not be taken if someone has to dive below to get out the proper handbearing compass.

Correctors

Problem 4 is almost always overlooked by people who buy compasses at boat shows, but it should one of the first questions asked of a salesman. A professional compass adjuster will charge much more if he has to make or supply little brass or alloy holders for the tiny corrector magnets he may want to fit, and lash-up jobs are liable to be removed by ignorant tidiers-up. Another point is that corrector boxes designed for a brass screwdriver should always have proper covers for the adjusting screws, or some clot will be bound one day to come along 'tightening up', and can increase your compass deviation from one degree to 27° in a moment. The kind that come with a special brass key are probably safest, provided you never lose the key. A pressed steel key from a wind-up toy, if you happen to have one around, even if it fits, simply will *not do* because it is magnetic. If you lose your key you must buy square-section brass stock of suitable size, drill out a centre hole and, using the tiny files called warding files, square the circular hole until it is the right size. Then fit it in a wooden handle, *using a brass fastening*. A brass screwdriver is easily shaped out of a piece of flat stock.

If your corrector magnets are hidden in a plastic container, you may want to know if they are in the neutral position. This the manufacturer's instructions should tell you. Most correctors are in the neutral position when set in the centre of their travel, but some are neutral at one end or the other. Normally they have four adjustment points, but some have only two. They all work on the same principle, they apply a magnetic correction force to the compass down the centre line of each quadrant — 360°, 090°, 180° and 270°. When you adjust the control you either cause a magnet to approach nearer to the compass, or apply a scissors action that increases its effect. With compasses that have little boxes or slots for correctors, you either vary the number in the box, or put in one of greater or lesser power as required. This last system is best left to professionals who are thoroughly familiar with it, because different makers have different methods of indicating the force of corrector magnets.

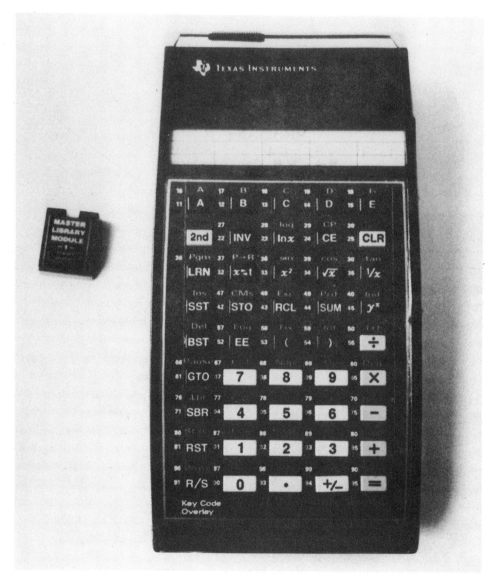

Plate 23. The Texas 59 has the ability to record and read programmes on magnetic cards, as well as take a complete navigation programme on a tiny module the size of the one shown. The small numbers shown on the key face here are from a plastic overlay to help in checking programmes.

Types Available

If you own a splendid 48-footer with wheel steering, you will have an equally splendid dome-top compass with a centre pin enabling you to take bearings,

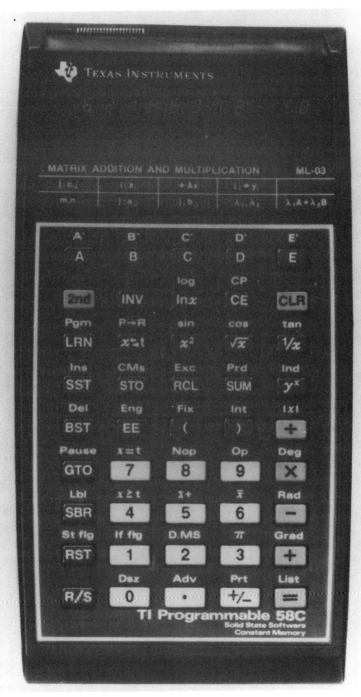

Plate 24. The Texas 58C will also take the internal navigation module, and has the useful ability of retaining programmes and memory when turned off. Avoid buying the only slightly cheaper model 58 (without the C) which does not have this useful facility.

and a corrector box in the binnacle that has been carefully set up by an elderly gentleman of vast experience. Unless someone loops a transistor radio over the binnacle, you have no worries except an occasional check to see that it is still doing its stuff correctly. This can be done running down a transit or range that is not affected by tidal streams.

This book, however, is intended for those a little less fortunate. They want an effective, accurate, easy-to-read compass, but they do not want to pay more than they must. The very hard-up sailor may look hopefully at some of the ex-service compasses that are still to be found. These, particularly the RAF grid pattern and some US tank compasses, used to be excellent, and the fact that they corroded away almost to dust in three years due to the mixture of brass and light alloy in them did not matter because in those days you would easily

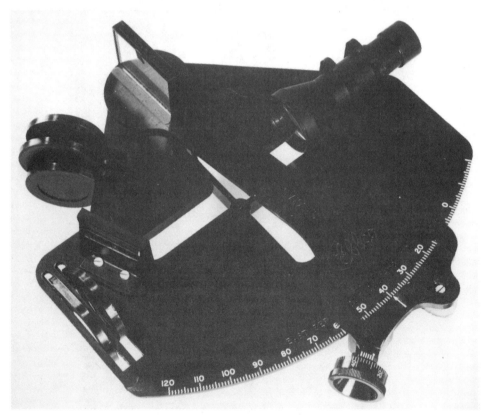

Plate 25. The Ebbco plastic sextant is quite adequate for coastal work, though the optics are not very convenient for real astro. However, since it costs about a tenth of the price of a high-grade metal sextant, it is a valuable standby even where a metal sextant is available; it is especially useful for the knockabout work of angles for coastal navigation. *(Photo: East Berks Boat Company)*

find another cheaply. But now the supply has dried up, so it is better to forget military compasses from surplus stores.

One of the most useful things to have is a dome effect that magnifies the card. Not many people have perfect sight these days, and the better the compass can be seen, the easier for the helmsman to hold a good course, even though his eyes should not be glued to it. He should be glancing at it at frequent intervals, and if he can read it easily the glance can be shorter and the time spent looking at the sails and the boat's way in the water longer, which is the aim of good sailing.

SITING

Even bulkhead compasses have a dome magnifier. But here we come to the chief snag of this pattern — they can seldom be centrally sited, and a compass sited on the centre line is always more satisfactory. If it has deviation, at least it is unlikely to be very much more on one tack than the other.

This is one reason why bulkhead compasses are usually fitted in pairs, one each side of the companionway. If you remain to windward when you tack there should be no change in deviation from, say, an iron keel (the other reason for pairs is a clearer view straight on, when steering with a tiller). Whatever compass is fitted it must be really adequately gimballed, either internally or externally, so it stays level; and adequate means at least 45 degrees. Quite a lot of bulkhead compasses fall down on this, open-top dome models are usually better. A compass that is only gimballed to 30 degrees is going to make you look foolish one day on a brisk beat to windward when it keeps binding up because of the heel.

Many people say a steering compass must be *in front of* the helmsman, which often sets a great problem for a tiller-steered boat. It is certainly convenient, when watching the luff of a jib, not having to shift the angle of vision much. But I have sailed many hundreds of miles in boats that had aft-mounted compasses with *four lubber lines*. When helming from the side of the cockpit with a tiller you check you are on course and then find what the reading is on the more convenient side lubber line, and you are away. It is a better system than a bridgedeck-mounted compass six inches from the engine. Some compasses have six lubber lines, and all should have at least two unless they can be very clearly seen from above and slightly aft.

So when looking for a compass site in a boat, don't immediately spurn a position above or just abaft the tiller. I have also used good compasses let into cockpit seats below the tiller (these may need a guard) and high up above the hatch, with a special aft-reading ring card. The last kind is excellent except sometimes clarity is poor, and also sheets and halyards can snarl in it. In the dark watches of a cold night, I have occasionally dreamed of a compass with a card as big as a dinner plate, somewhere in the deckhead of the cabin, with the lubber line and relevant section of card reflected aft by a system of prisms. The cost, of course, would be higher than an electronic repeater compass, which is the answer to everyone's dream, but they are expensive.

Card Notation

The card of any compass should be marked in degrees up to 360, at every 10, with a mark halfway between each 10 degree figure. The actual figure need only appear every 30 degrees. Compasses with points only are for interior decorators and museums. Many compass cards are now marked round the edge, as well as on top, and have a separate lubber line. Notation can be larger if the final zero is dropped.

COMPASS ERRORS

Before you can do anything with a compass you must have absolutely at your fingertips the way to get a corrected reading from it — allowing for variation and deviation as briefly touched on in Chapter 5. Going over again points made there, no compass needle points to true north, where the geographic north pole lies; if it is not affected by electronic or metallic influences which would sway its reading, it points to the magnetic pole, which lies somewhere in northern Canada.

Variation

The extent to which a compass reading is away from true north is called **variation**, and this is a characteristic of the geographical area in which the compass is being used. In certain places, like the eastern and south eastern American seaboard, it is very slight, sometimes not even one degree. In parts of Canada and Greenland it can exceed 40 degrees. Variation changes very, very slowly over the years, at the rate of about one degree every ten years, so at any particular spot it can be taken as remaining constant. The amount of variation for any particular part of the world is found from the chart for the locality in which you are operating, or from a chart of variation, or from a diagram printed in *Reed's*. There are other minute changes that we can ignore.

Depending on where you are in the world, the north-seeking end of the compass needle — in magnetic and compass diagrams, this end is always the red end, the south-seeking end being blue — will be diverted according to whether the magnetic pole is to the east or west of the true pole from the position where the needle lies. If the magnetic pole lies to the west the deviation is called **westerly**, if it lies to the east, variation is **easterly. It remains the same whatever the boat's heading.**

Any true course (one plotted in relation to true north) must be adjusted for variation before it can be applied to a compass. Any bearing taken on a compass must be corrected for variation before a true bearing line can be plotted on the chart. A heading altered from true by the amount of variation is a **magnetic** heading.

Deviation

The other error of the compass, called **deviation**, is trickier because it is highly changeable, varying with the direction the boat is pointing, with what gear is aboard, what iron or steel and electronics are around, and where they are sited in relation to the compass; it is personal to each compass and remains the same regardless of geographic area. In steel ships, if not fixed by complicated witch-doctory with correctors, it can be as large as 90 degrees, and it can change in amount during use of a boat, or because she is laid up for the winter on a particular heading, or perhaps alongside a building or another vessel with a strong magnetic influence. Deviation is the navigator's bugbear. He must always watch for it, and allow for it if it becomes too large. Anything over two degrees is too large in a small boat. Luckily for the small boat owner, it is not difficult to correct in the average fibreglass or wooden boat, and the problem is not insoluble even in steel vessels.

Deviation, though caused by a multitude of small, or large, pieces of iron in the boat making up her magnetic field, can be thought of as originating in a single magnetic lump in the boat, shown in *Fig. 13.1* as a shaded box forward of the compass, on the centreline. If it moves away from the centreline it becomes even more tiresome to correct for, which is why stowage of large steel objects like anchors in cockpit side lockers near the compass is so undesirable, and why the compass should always be on the centreline if possible.

The drawing shows why the deviation changes according to the boat's heading. Sometimes, according to heading, the box is between the compass and magnetic north, sometimes it is to one side, sometimes the other. Since it is made up of a number of smaller magnetic components, the force it exerts can also vary according to the direction the boat is heading in relation to these components.

Preliminary Compass Check

Before going to sea for the first time with a new compass, perhaps in a new boat, you should check immediately how much error there is in the instrument.

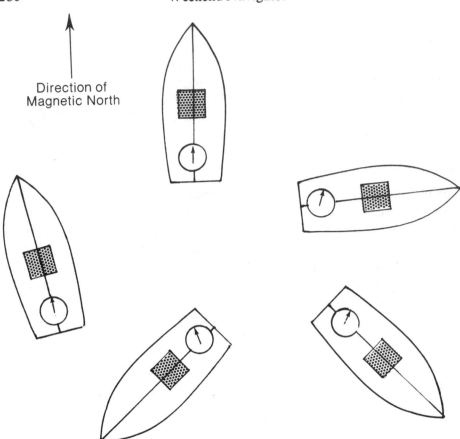

Direction of
Magnetic North

Fig. 13.1   Why deviation changes according to where the boat is heading. If you think
of the shaded box·as being the total component of all the magnetic forces in the boat, its
effect on the compass will change according to its position relative to the compass and
magnetic north as the boat points this way or that. In this simplified instance, when the
boat's head is anywhere on a westerly course, the magnetic component draws the
compass needle away to the west; when the boat is heading anywhere to the east, the
effect can be reversed and the needle is drawn away to the east.

You can do this roughly with a handbearing compass standing on the dock or
marina pontoon and sighting the backstay in line with the mast. Get someone
aboard to call out what the steering compass says immediately, in case the boat
is a bit restless on her lines and moving. What you get from the steering
compass is of course a *compass* heading, and the handbearing compass, used
intelligently, away from steel, should give a correct *magnetic* heading. Any
difference between the two is *deviation*. If it is under five degrees, it will be OK
to take your new boat out in fine visibility and do a swing on at least eight
different headings.

SWINGING THE COMPASS

Far the most accurate way of doing a quick swing is to pick out four ranges or transits from a large scale chart, that you can sail gently or motor down at a time when there is little or no tidal stream. They should be picked out carefully so they give you a heading on the *magnetic* course you want. Two of the main yachting centres of the world, Annapolis on Chesapeake Bay and the Hamble River on the Solent, are well equipped with multiple charted landmarks like radio towers and refinery chimneys, Annapolis being slightly better because the tidal streams are gentler; I once did an effective swing at Annapolis in 20 minutes. Nearly every sailing centre has masses of suitable transits.

The key thing when using transits is to make sure the boat will point straight down the line. If she won't, she is being set off by tidal stream, and you must either find somewhere else or wait for slack water.

Unless you are very expert already with variation and deviation, you would do well to refresh your memory now on the points made in Chapter 5, particularly the distinction between *correcting*, going from compass to true, and *converting*, going from true to compass, with magnetic the intermediate stage in each.

CONVERTING

TRUE — apply VARIATION — MAGNETIC — apply DEVIATION — COMPASS
TIMID   —   VIRGINS   —   MAKE   —   DULL   —   COMPANY

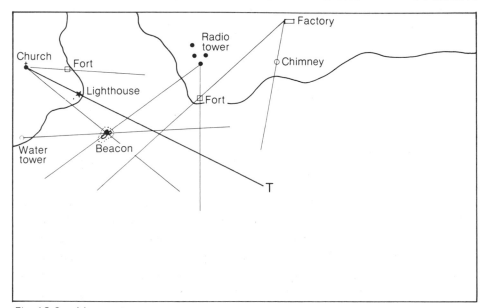

Fig. 13.2   Most sailing areas have plenty of ranges, or transits of objects marked on a large-scale chart, that can conveniently be used to help swing the compass.

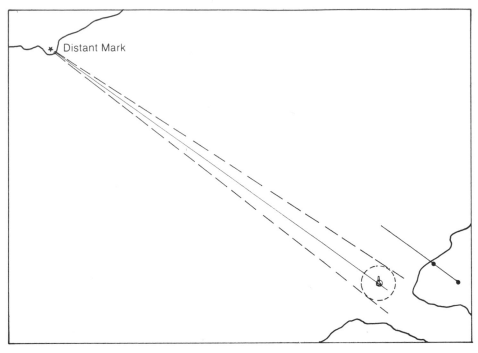

Fig. 13.3   Compass swingers are fond of going to a handy buoy, and using bearings of distant marks to check the deviation. This is only entirely accurate when the buoy is in shallow water and swings round a very small circle. Here, where the buoy is in deep water and can vary its position by as much as 250 yards, it would be better to use the nearby transit or range.

CORRECTING
COMPASS — apply DEVIATION — MAGNETIC — apply VARIATION — TRUE
CAN   —   DEAD   —   MEN   —   VOTE   —   TWICE?
Also:
ANYTHING WEST, COMPASS BEST: ANYTHING EAST, COMPASS LEAST

This of course means that with either westerly deviation or variation, compass will be highest, reading round the compass clockwise 005° counts as higher than 355°. For this reason it is handiest to think of any westerly error, either variation or deviation, as a *plus* quantity, and easterly error as a *minus*. This is the normal situation when *converting*, and must be reversed when *correcting*. But converting is what you do most with your steering compass, you take a true course off the chart, apply variation, then deviation, and end up with a compass course. So:

WHEN CONVERTING WEST IS PLUS, WHEN CORRECTING WEST IS MINUS

Except when taking a bearing, the first part is the most important. Try to keep clear of the US Navy-favoured phrase *uncorrecting* instead of converting. It not only gobbledegooks the tongue of Shakespeare and Milton, it is confusing.

The benefit of giving + and − signs to westerly and easterly deviation and variation is that it makes things simpler when you have a considerable quantity of each. Suppose you want to sail 270° True, in an area where variation is 11° East, and your deviation on a heading of about 270° is 4° West:

Totalled the correction is:

$$
\begin{array}{r}
-11° \\
+\ 4° \\
\hline
-\ 7°
\end{array}
\qquad
\begin{array}{r}
270° \\
-\ 7° \\
\hline
\end{array}
$$

Course to steer 263°

Reverting to our trip out in a new boat in which we are going to swing the compass and obtain a preliminary deviation card. Let us assume that we are in an area of 8°W variation, and we have picked out four transits that will give us the following lines (magnetic)

008°	053°	098°	143°
188°	233°	278°	323°

These are perfect, and will give us a correct swing, provided there is no tidal set on any of them, but if any of the lines that offered were just a few degrees out from the exact eight main points of the compass, it would not matter, provided you recorded all the figures correctly. The difference of deviation between, say, 098°M and 101°M would not be enough to notice. On these headings you obtain the following compass readings, which give you the deviation shown in the righthand column:

Heading M	Compass	Deviation
008°	011°	3°W
053	054	1°W
098	097	1°E
143	140	3°E
188	184	4°E
233	231	2°E
278	278	0°
323	326	3°W

If you draw these results out in a graph as in *Fig 13.4* it probably gives you a

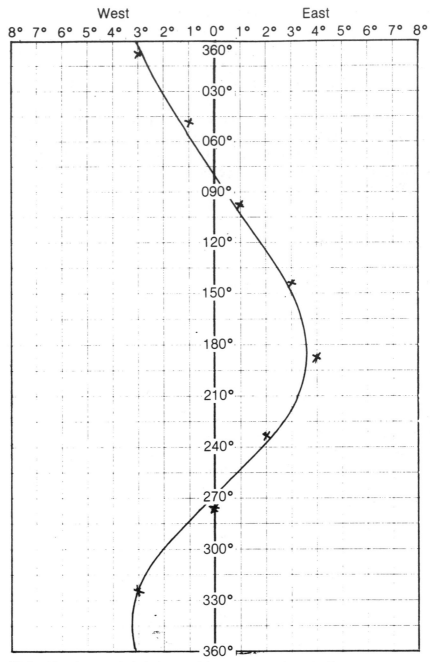

Fig. 13.4   Here is a rough deviation card drawn as a graph on the figures found in the swing described on page 283. Note that great exactitude with the graph cannot be achieved because of human error in trying to read a compass. The deviation is just about four degrees, so adjustment is necessary.

clearer picture, and if you have drawn a smooth and accurate curve, you also have intermediate points for when you are not steering exactly on one of the headings you have swung on. Note that between 323° and 008° the line of the graph has extended out to 4°W deviation, because the curve of a graph is always a curve, it cannot suddenly develop flat spots.

Making Adjustments

As soon as you look at the graph in *Fig. 13.4* it tells you that the greatest deviation is when heading roughly north and south; when travelling east and west it is less than one degree. The main adjustment will need to be done when the boat is heading north and south. If loose magnets were being used they would be placed transversely, almost certainly in front of the compass. Using a corrector with four screw adjustments or screw slots, you must first find out which adjustment is the one to use — if the manufacturer does not tell you, trial and error will. Align the boat on the 008° transit and, with your brass key or screwdriver, take out *half* the error. Turn the boat 180°, align her on the transit again, and again take out *half* the error with the opposite adjustment.

Now turn the boat onto the easterly and westerly courses and make the adjustments, again taking out only half the error each time. The reason for taking out half the error is that the various adjusting magnets can affect other headings. If you take it all out at once, you can induce new errors on other headings. Working very carefully, and trying to estimate half degrees on the compass, you might end up with a graph like *Fig. 13.5*. You have reduced the deviation to just over 2° maximum. But it is immediately apparent that the error is now asymetrical. This can be due to the boat having a lopsided magnetic field because of auxiliaries like alternators being to one side of the centre line, or the way gear is stored — maybe all those drink cans which were handled in the factory with electro-magnets are on one side of the boat? But it is more likely to be that the compass is not mounted correctly with its lubberline force and aft. Careful adjustment of this, and quite a lot of compasses are supplied with gauging marks to adjust their mountings, will reduce the error to only just over one degree all round, which is pretty good. Now make out a proper deviation graph in waterproof ink and keep it where it can be referred to easily. In the early life of a new boat it is a very good thing to make frequent checks of the compass as extra gear is put aboard.

Other Heading Systems

It is not always necessary to find four individual transits for your compass swinging, and there are places that are not so generous with their transits. You

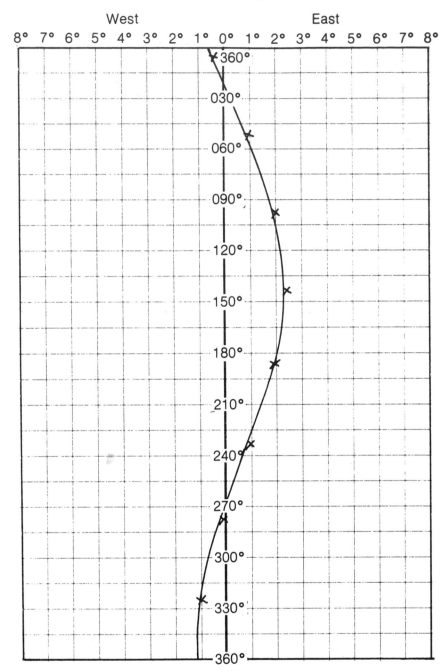

Fig. 13.5   After adjustment, and using the same ranges or transits, the error is now little more than two degrees. It is, however, asymetrical, probably because the compass is not absolutely aligned on the centre line. Careful adjustment of this will bring the error to less than two degrees on any heading, when it may be ignored.

may even want to check the compass when you are in open water out of sight of land. What you need is a single reference mark, whose magnetic direction can then be obtained. Common ways in which this is done are:

1. The bearing of the sun. Nautical tables give what they call amplitudes, which is the bearing of the sun for various latitudes at sunset and sunrise. For this system to work you need a pelorus, or means of taking the bearing of the sun with the steering compass, not usually easy in a small boat. You also need the declination of the sun. This is more a system for big ships than small sailing craft.

2. Anchoring on a single transit, checking the bearing of the compass on each heading to obtain the deviation. If you can take precise bearings with your steering compass, and those with a sighting pin do it very well, this is probably the most satisfactory way of swinging. You will need a piece of paper or card drawn up with four columns, and space underneath for eight headings, or more if you feel like it:

Heading	Magnetic bearing of transit by chart	Compass bearing	Deviation
360°C	282°M	284°C	2°W
045°C	282°M	285°C	3°W

The only thing to watch with this system is that the objects forming the transit are well apart, and far enough away so that as you motor or tow your boat round her anchors (two, forming a mooring, are usually essential) you remain on the transit.

3. Bearing of a distant object. If you place your boat close to a buoy or beacon, whose position is charted relative to an object such as a television tower at least six miles distant, you can obtain a line sufficiently accurate to swing your compass, by motoring and sailing around on the different headings, all the time *remaining close to the buoy or beacon*. The snag to this system is that buoys move with the tide around their charted positions, and bearings of objects six miles distant are not too reliable. But it is a way that is commonly used, mainly because it is quick and easy for the compass adjuster. Where a good single transit is available, sailing or motoring around on the transit would be more reliable.

4. If you are in open but relatively calm water, out of sight of any useful landmarks or even the sun, a rough check on deviation can be made the fisherman's way. Throw overboard a piece of wood, plastic foam, floating cushion, even a cardboard box — any object that can be seen easily and returned to from 200 yards off, and will not get much blown through the water

by the wind. Head directly away from it for about 100 yards, noting what the compass reads — say 190°. Turn as quickly as you can onto your still visible wake line and head down the reciprocal of 190°–010°. If you have no deviation on the south heading your bow should be pointing straight to whatever you threw overboard. If it lies to your starboard, you have westerly deviation on this heading, if it lies to port you have easterly. The degrees of deviation cannot be measured by this method, and it is most imprecise.

5. If in open water and you lack the ability to take sun amplitude bearings, by far the easiest way of checking on the steering compass is from a handbearing compass carefully used in a position where it will have the minimum of deviation. One of the best places is standing in a stainless steel pushpit sighting against the mast, with a couple of bits of bright tape stuck six inches apart on the bow pulpit to make sure you are looking down the centreline of the boat. You must also make sure that things like horseshoe lifebelts that have lights attached, which often live on pushpits, are removed, and that the compass is well away from any kind of power adjuster for the backstay. If the water is calm, you can even take the handbearing compass away in a dinghy, but make sure you do not have steel rowlocks. Check not only where you are sighting from, but also yourself — pockets and all gear. Harnesses and lifejackets can have magnet-attracting pieces in them, as do certain watches. Finally draw up your headings on a card.

Heading by compass	Handbearing reading	Deviation
360°C	004°M	4°W
045°C	047°M	2°W
090°C	090°M	0°
135°C	134°M	1°E
	etc etc	

The person steering must be very exact on headings and must control wishful thinking. The best technique is to declare the heading he is going to steady on and then say 'Mark' to show he is on. If you have a third person to write down immediately what the handbearing compass reads it saves a lot of time.

When swinging a compass it is important to distinguish between a casual check and a properly carried out swing. A good idea is to keep a special notebook aboard in which details of all compass swings are entered, making a separate card to keep near the compass. Sometimes having a compass history like this can reveal a growth of magnetic influence in your boat which can be avoided by quite a small measure. Perhaps there is a power pump on the dock where you usually lie that is making your deviation swing towards one side of the centreline on your graph. Perhaps sometimes docking your boat facing the other way, will reverse the trend, or moving to another berth stops it altogether. One of the most sinister causes of changing deviation is a huge floating gin-palace with hundreds of horsepower tied up beside you, that is always plugged into a shore power line pushing in thousands of watts to run colour TV, sauna, washing machine, radio telephones to the office . . . the only thing to do is find another berth.

14
The sextant

For all the work in this book an expensive, high-precision sextant is unnecessary, and may be a liability on board, since they are easily damaged. Even if you can afford, and have the stowage space for, an expensive sextant, learn how to use the instrument by means of a cheap one, a plastic one will do. It is pointless fiddling with a device costing hundreds of dollars or pounds as a fumbling learner's plaything. When you have learned the basic idea, then you can get value from the real thing.

USING THE SEXTANT

The principle of the sextant is shown in *Fig. 14.1* and a plastic model that I recommend, the Ebbco Special, is shown in *Plate 25*. It is apparent that it is vital to accuracy that the mirrors are absolutely at right angles to the frame and the arm, yet many people constantly lift up sextants by the mirrors — perhaps because, as they are stowed in the box, the handle is underneath. So here are some basic rules before you take a sextant out of its case:

1. Never pick a sextant up by its mirrors or telescope; if the handle does not fall easily to hand, pick it up by the frame.

2. Before using it at sea make a lanyard of stout light line, large enough to go over your head and so that it hangs round your neck. Attach this to the handle. Now if a lurch of the boat makes you grab something for your life, there is a good chance the sextant will not be over the side or smashed on the deck. The moment you take the sextant out of its box, loop the lanyard round your neck.

3. Every time you use a sextant, check its index error. This involves looking at the horizon (if you are ashore, you must choose a horizontal line at least 2 miles away) and adjusting the arm until the horizon is one straight line (*Fig. 7.5*). At this point the reading should be zero. In practice it never is. There will be an error, the **index error**, which may be as much as 15'. Careful adjustment of the mirrors should reduce this to less than 3', but a hot day,

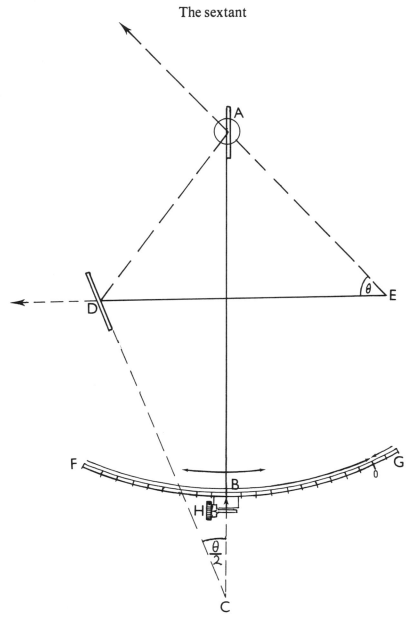

Fig. 14.1   Theory of the sextant. The object of the sextant is to measure the angle Θ at your eye E. It does this with great accuracy using two mirrors: one at A attached to a pivoted arm; the second at D fixed, and silvered only on its right side, so that you can look through the clear part and compare something looked at directly with something reflected through the two mirrors. The lower part of the arm swings against a scale of degrees; it has another scale, for minutes, on a drum which moves the arm one degree for each complete turn. The worm gear can be disengaged for quick adjustment of degrees, and then re-engaged to get the fine adjustment. The angle at C, the angle between the mirrors, is exactly half the angle at E, and the scale FG is compressed.

jolting in the box by the sea, can all change the index error. So check it every time, it only takes a moment. The way to apply index error is described below.

4. Never put a sextant loose on a table or chart table in a boat. The box should have a firm stowage, and unless you are using it, the sextant should be in its box. Otherwise you will soon be the ex-owner of a sextant.

APPLYING INDEX ERROR.   Index error is described as 'on the arc' when the key line is on the main part of the arc, and 'off the arc' when the line lies against the little short bit of scale below zero. It is apparent that on the arc error will make the reading too high, so it must be subtracted to correct for it. When it is off the arc the reading will be too low, so the error must be added. It is not a bad idea to write in large letters on a piece of card that you can stick inside the lid of the sextant box: OFF THE ARC — ADD: ON THE ARC — SUBTRACT.

CORRECTION.   Any worthwhile sextant will have a means of adjusting the mirrors should they come slightly out of true — not the haggled 27° bend you get from dropping the instrument, but about 3 minutes of arc due to the frame or arm expanding or contracting with temperature or humidity. The actual adjusting screw system varies with the make of sextant, but the principle is simple. The first mirror to correct is the one at the pivot, so this is the **first correction**. Hold the sextant horizontally, with the arm set at about 45°, and with the mirror at the pivot nearest to you. Look into this mirror until you can see the reflection of the highest part of the arc. Follow this curve with your eyes until you are looking at the point where the reflected arc lies against the actual arc at its lower end. The two arcs should match. The eye will detect even a tiny amount out. Carefully and gently operate the adjusting screw, first freeing any locking device there may be, until the arcs appear continuous.

The **second correction** is to the horizon mirror. Look at any distant vertical object that is stationary — a lamp-post or radio mast is better than the nodding mast of a boat. Have the sextant set just a tiny bit above zero so that you can distinguish a reflected and a direct view. The reflected image should be immediately below the image you see directly. If it is displaced to one side, adjust the horizon mirror.

Having made the second correction, go back and check the first correction again, the adjustment for second may have affected it. Make any further correction very cautiously — checking first one correction, then the other. Finally you should, even on a cheap sextant, be left with less than 2' of index error, which must be applied to every reading.

CHOICE OF SEXTANT

This book being aimed mainly at the man who goes to sea on a shoestring, a powerful consideration when choosing a sextant is price. It is an unfortunate fact that good sextants seldom come on the market secondhand, and when they do the price is only a little below a new one. If you are lucky enough to be offered a good secondhand sextant the things to look out for are:

1. Check it all over for the tiniest signs of violence. One fall can ruin a good sextant for ever. Check that when the tangent screw is disengaged the arm swings smoothly without binding or loose spots — a tendency to bind is a sure sign it has been subjected to stress. Study it to see if it shows much signs of spray: a man who will leave salt spray on his sextant is a man who is likely to drop it. Corrosion round mirror edges need not be disastrous, these can be resilvered economically. Home-made alterations or repairs should be viewed with suspicion, so should bodged-over screw heads. If there are covers for adjusting screws, they should all be there. Mildew or fungus is a discouragement. Check that there is no undue wear between worm wheel and teeth — some people do not disengage the spring properly and scrape away the teeth, leading to backlash, which is fatal. This applies particularly to plastic sextants.

2. Get it in the open, out of the shop, and look at a distant horizontal line to check the index error. If this is reasonable, say less than 2′, it is a hopeful sign that the previous owner took good care of the instrument. Check the certificate which should be inside the lid of the box.

3. Check the optics as you would a pair of binoculars. The ring holding the telescope should show no sign of bending. If it is adjustable, it should move smoothly, and should centre on the horizon mirror without difficulty. Check for mildew or fungus inside the optics by turning to a bright light and looking in from the wrong end.

4. Don't buy a sextant that has not got a box; it will have deteriorated into an antique.

5. Don't, except as a decoration for your den, buy a Vernier sextant — they are too difficult to read. The main reading of minutes should be off a micrometer drum, with a Vernier only for parts of a minute.

Most marine sextants have a radius of around six to seven inches, but the compact ones with a radius of about three and a half inches have a lot of advantages for small craft in weight and ease of stowage. They are usually only a little cheaper, the saving often being made on the optics, but a good one is often as accurate as a full-size one.

BUBBLE SEXTANTS. Thousands of artificial horizon sextants using a bubble, and usually an averaging device, have been made for air use in the wars of the past 40 years. Many are superlative precision instruments, available at giveaway prices in surplus stores. Sadly, the majority are little use to the sailor, except perhaps for practising star sights at home where he can get no horizon. The reason is that the very slightest movement of a boat makes it impossible to keep the bubble steady enough even for a sun sight. They are no use in any case for vertical sextant angles and horizontal sextant angles.

If you want a bubble sextant the type to look for is the US Navy Mark V Air Sextant, which has a prism which can be clicked in to give a regular horizon. Some similar models of a different Mark number lack this facility, so check you are getting a Mark V, and that it has a little button marked 'horizon in'. Check also that some enthusiastic aviator has not removed the horizon prisms. The horizon prism gives a very limited angle of view.

The Royal Air Force bubble sextants, at one time much touted in yachting magazines, are virtually useless for marine use, and the clockwork averaging device used on the most frequently seen model reduces its value even for practice.

The United States Air Corps A 12 bubble sextant is no use to sailors for anything at all except perhaps its box, which is quite a handy small tool box. I would hate to find myself in an aircraft depending on an A 12 to find its way across the Pacific — or indeed from anywhere to anywhere.

There are artificial horizon attachments made for marine sextants, but it is doubtful whether they are worth their high cost, except to someone who wants to use the sextant in the air, or for practice or instruction. The Plath artificial horizon has a much steadier bubble than any air sextant, but costs a lot of money.

Sextants have a great appeal for grounded boat-owners in midwinter — indeed some well-heeled wives have been known to buy models that have been tossed around by hundreds of people at boat shows as a surprise present for the spouse. This may be why some people don't think much of sextants in small craft. So here are some virtues for a sextant in a small boat to keep in mind when you go near a boat shop:

A Lightness and compactness.

B Easy to read.

C Cheap, so it doesn't break your heart if smashed.

D Strong, but not over-bulky box.

E Accuracy to half a minute is quite good enough.

Plate 26. This handy pelorus, for measuring angles off the bow when swinging a compass or calibrating a D/F set, is made at a very economic price by the Danish Linex drawing instrument company.

IT'S AS EASY AS THAT

You are somewhere in the Mediterranean between Cannes and the Balearics, lazing along on a placid sea, when the owner of the boat you are in says: 'Why don't you take a noon sight?'

For a purely coastal navigator, this can be a moment of truth. Do you admit you don't know how or do you, knowing there is a copy of *Reed's*, a Quartz clock set to GMT, a good sextant you have used and know is free of error, have a go?

It is really very simple, and *Reed's* will tell you what you need to know, and even what to do. The things you need to know are:

1. The date at Greenwich. It is September 3, 1980.

2. Your approximate longitude. From your DR plot it is between 6° and 7°
East. You only need to know this so you can tell at what time to look for the
sun at its highest. A table in *Reed's* indexed as 'Arc into Time' relates the
passage of time to longitude, and tells you that the sun will pass over 7°E at
28 minutes before noon at Greenwich, and over 6°E at 24 minutes before.
The sun does not always pass over Greenwich at noon, since it travels at an
uneven rate, but the first September page of the sun tables in *Reed's* tells you
that, on the third, it crosses the Greenwich meridian only one minute early,
so you do not need to worry much about this. You just allow a margin of a
few minutes, and are all ready with the sextant about 32 minutes before noon
GMT. You have already checked you have the right shades set on the
sextant, as the sun is dazzling. You are to bring the lower 'limb' of the sun —
its bottom in plain language — down until it just touches the horizon. You
note that the sun is south of you. When you have obtained the greatest
altitude the sun reaches, you will subtract it from 90° to give you what is
called *zenith distance*, which carries the 'name' North if you faced south to
take the sun sight. If you had faced north to take the sight, as is usual in the
southern hemisphere, or in the northern hemisphere in summer when you are
close to the equator, zenith distance is named South.

3. The declination of the sun when it is at its highest. You do not need to be
very exact about time. Declination, often shortened to dec. or even d., is the
amount the sun is north or south of the equator as the year advances. In the
spring it is on the equator, moving north of it during the northern summer,
back to the equator in September, and then on south for the southern
hemisphere's summer. It is named just like latitude, North or South, and is
given in a table in *Reed's* for every two hours on every day of the year. At
1000 GMT on September 3 it is 7° 25·5N and at 1200 it is 7° 23·6. The
letter beside it says N. You can safely interpolate by eye for about 1130 to
give a declination of 7° 24N.

4. The last things you need are various corrections to apply to the sextant
reading. These allow for such factors as the height of your eye above sea
level (let's say 3 metres), the fact that you are sighting the bottom of the sun
not its middle, and the effect of the earth's atmosphere called *refraction*.
These you will find all combined in one figure in a table of *Reed's* headed
'Sun's Altitude Total Correction Table'. You enter the table from the left
with the altitude you read off the sextant, and take out the figure under your
height of eye at the top of the table.

   Right. At 1132 you have been watching for several minutes as the altitude
steadily increased. *Never* bring the altitude down, wait for the sun to reach it
if it is still increasing. Suddenly there is a gap between the disc of the sun and

the horizon. After checking again to make sure it's on the way down, you read the sextant — it says 54° 31·2, but let's not be pedantic about the ·2 because even in calm water few people can take a sight that accurately.

Write in the log: 1133 Sept 3, sun lower limb south, 54° 31·0.

Now you start a small table:

Observed altitude	54°	31·0
Sextant error	nil	
Height of eye 3m, sun total correction		+12·1
True altitude	54°	43·1
Subtract from 90°	90°	00
Zenith distance	35°	16·9N
Declination	7°	24·0N
THIS IS YOUR LATITUDE!	42°	40·9N

(There is a rule which says if zenith distance and declination are same name add, if they are different subtract, and give the name of the greater.)

It's really that easy. You have taken a first step in astro-navigation. You can't stop now.

Appendix

Appendix

ANSWERS TO EXERCISES

Do not worry if you have got minor variations from these answers in cases other than when converting or correcting between true and magnetic, or in applying variation. But a large error means that you have done something wrong, so go over the problem again to see what you have missed.

2.1. From Les Hanois you are **276°T 19·4 miles.**
2.2. (a) Barnouic buoy is **49° 0·5'N 2° 52.8'W.**
   (b) From La Corbière the buoy is **248°T 26·4 miles.**
2.3. (a) The track, or true course, from Fowey Rocks to Great Isaac Light is **064°T.**
   (b) The distance is **59·5 miles.**

3.1. The present height above datum is **2·8 metres.**
3.2. (a) **15·1 feet** over the bar now.
   (b) Latest time it is safe is **3¾ hours after HW.**
3.3. **2·3 knots.** It is half way between springs and neaps, so it is half way between 1·2 and 3·4 knots.

5.1. $225 + 8 - 3 = $ **230°C.**
5.2. With the steering compass, using 3°E deviation, you plot $227 - 8 + 3 = $ **222°T.** With the handbearing compass, which is used in an area free of deviation, you have only to apply variation of 8°W, so the bearings are $162 - 8 = $ **154°T** and $265 - 8 = $ **257°T.**
5.3. (a) Anything west, compass best; and all the error is westerly. So your True course is $048° - 6° - 6° = $ **036°.**
   (b) On port tack the corrections are $138° - 3° - 6° = $ **129° True.**

6.1. You need a **Class A triangle.**
6.2. The **port tack** is far better to start on because not only do you point closer

301

to your destination, but the tide will be setting you to windward as you go.

6.3. **Go onto starboard tack** (in order to be set to windward once again), and **draw a Class B triangle** to discover your course for the track to the destination.

6.4. (a) Your track is **246°T.**

(b) Your groundspeed is **4·1 knots.**

(c) You have drawn a **Class A triangle.** Notice the very large angle between course and track.

6.5. Your speed is **5·1 knots.**

6.6. You have travelled **2·6 miles.**

6.7. (a) It takes you **1 hr 52 mins.**

(b) **2 hrs 26 mins.**

7.1. (a) **Lat 49° 15·5′N**

Long 02° 24·2′W

(b) The sides of the cocked hat are about 1·5 to **2 miles.**

7.2. The light is **0·99 of a nautical mile** away.

7.3. **2° 49′** for the inner danger angle and **1° 39′** for the outer will give a safety margin of 0·2 of a mile.

7.4. A compass bearing and distance off by vertical sextant angle is the best you can do, unless a charted object on shore can be brought into line with the light to give you a transit or range.

7.5. This question has several parts to it, which have not been separated so that you have to work out for yourself how to proceed. You will need to draw two diagrams, a Class A vector triangle to find your track and then a diagram for a running fix. First you need your true course after deviation, variation and leeway — it works out at 073°T. Using this you find that your track is 087°T and ground speed is 4·7 knots. Distance covered between the two bearings in 20 minutes is 1·99 miles. On your running fix diagram you find the lighthouse and draw in two bearings, not forgetting to allow the 1° deviation on the bearing taken with the steering compass, and also correcting for variation. The transferred position line crosses the second bearing at a point **2·85 miles** from the light. It should be remembered that this is far from a good fix because:

1. The angle of cut of the bearings is too fine for accuracy.
2. If the tide is not doing exactly what you have allowed, there may be an error in your track.

If you had had time to snatch up a sextant and obtain a vertical angle at the time of the second bearing, the fix would have been much improved.

8.1. (a) In this tide, your track is **138°T.**

(b) Ground speed is **5·2 knots,** which would in fact put you a little east of the target buoy.

8.2. On discovering your position, a Class C triangle tells you that the tide has been setting **125°T at 1·5 knots.**

8.3. (a) For the first hour you steet **247°T** and make **6·2 miles.**

(b) For the second hour you steer **248°T** and make **6·7 miles.**

(c) For the third hour you steer **236°T.** In a complete hour you would make 8·5 miles, but you reach your destination before then.

(d) In fact, you reach it at **1145 hrs.**

Index

Index